CONTEMPORARY ITALY
POLITICS, ECONOMY AND
SOCIETY SINCE 1945

Donald Sassoon

LONGMAN
London and New York

61351

Longman Group UK Limited
Longman House, Burnt Mill, Harlow
Essex CM20 2JE, England
and Associated Companies throughout the world

Published in the United States of America
by Longman Publishing Group, New York

First published 1986
Sixth impression 1991

British Library Cataloguing in Publication Data
Sassoon, Donald
    Contemporary Italy: politics, economy and
    society since 1945.
    1. Italy—History—1945-
    I. Title
    945.092   DG576.8

ISBN 0-582-29551-3

Library of Congress Cataloging in Publication Data
Sassoon, Donald.
    Contemporary Italy.
    Bibliography: p.
    Includes index.
    1. Italy—Politics and government—1945–1976.
2. Italy—Politics and government—1976–
3. Italy—Economic conditions—1945–1976.   4. Italy—
Economic conditions—1976–   5. Italy—Social
conditions—1945–1976.   6. Italy—Social conditions—
1976–   . I. Title.
DG577.5.S28   1986   945.092   85–18044
ISBN 0-582-29551-3

Produced by Longman Group (FE) Ltd
Printed in Hong Kong

CONTEMPORARY ITALY

Editorial adviser Bernard Crick

CONTENTS

Contents

LIST OF TABLES

List of Tables

PREFACE AND
ACKNOWLEDGEMENTS

This book is an introduction to one of the largest European democracies: Italy.

It is a country which has been united relatively recently. It became a nation-state in 1861, but was able to obtain its capital, Rome, only ten years later. Its history is, of course, much more ancient and rich. Italy has given the world the poetry of Dante and the art of the Renaissance, the political theory of Machiavelli and the science of Galileo. It has produced the first international banking system, great explorers, famous composers.

After 1861 Italy has been a constitutional monarchy before becoming the first instance of a modern authoritarian state, the Fascist State. Since the war it has been a parliamentary republic. Those who follow the daily press will know that Italy has had many governments, terrorism and a large Communist Party. Italian film-makers have become famous all over the world and so have her designers, car manufacturers and footballers. But the overall picture is chaotic and confusing. This book seeks to provide the interested reader as well as students of Italian society with a text which would give not just a general picture, but also an idea of the changes which have affected the country.

Italians are their own worst critics. They complain of the political leaders and of the *immobilismo* which seems to them to be the main feature of their country. In a sense these critics are right: alone of all European democracies Italy has been ruled by the same political party since the end of the war: the Christian Democratic Party (DC). This, however, cannot be the whole story. I have tried to explain and map out the changes which have affected the country in its economic structure, in its people, in its political system. A nation cannot be judged solely by those that rule it.

The result of this endeavour has been a book which is neither political science, nor sociology, history nor economics. It straddles these fields yet it cannot claim to give an image of the whole of Italian society, not even in the sense in which such a task can be contemplated. Space and my own limitations have prevented me from examining Italian culture, the changes which have occurred in its language and everyday life. Even when it comes to topics which are usually covered by books such as these I am only too aware of what I have left out, and rather than bore the reader with explanation and justification of what is not there, let me explain what is in it and why.

The book is divided into three parts: 'Economy', 'Society' and 'Politics'. Part I amounts to an economic history of Italy since 1945 and has a dual purpose: first of all it seeks to explain the transformation of the Italian economy from the point of view of the activities of the political system. I have tried to examine the economic effects of government policies and the way in which economics has been shaped by politics. In so doing I have tried to examine the constraints which have limited the terrain of successive Italian governments. The second purpose is simpler: to tell the history of Italy since 1945. I have chosen to do so 'through' economic history because I felt the narrative would somewhat alleviate the dryness of much economics and because it gave me the opportunity of emphasizing the extent to which political actors are not free to do as they choose. In the very first pages I explain how the most important political choices made by the first Italian governments, namely free trade within the American sphere of influence, were extremely compelling and virtually unavoidable. This, of course, does not mean that all political and economic choices are predetermined and that no criticism can ever be made of Italy's principal political party, the DC. It means, however, that the leading opposition, the Italian Communist Party (PCI), has had gradually to face the issue that it is extremely difficult to envisage major changes occurring in Italy or anywhere else on the basis of the nation-state and that, in the modern era, the requirements of the international market and of the international division of labour seriously limits the freedom of action of any national force. Thus any national force must become 'international', that is, it must seek to bear in mind constantly the international impact of national actions and the domestic impact of world events. This does not mean that I subscribe to the view that the international economy determines everything, because the international economy is also politically determined. It means, simply, that in the second half of the twentieth century it is no longer possible (assuming it has ever been possible) to consider separately economics and politics. Hence one-third of the book consists of four rather dense economic history chapters.

Part II ('Society') describes Italian society first in terms of social stratification: classes, income groups, occupation, etc. the changes which have taken place and the reasons behind the changes as well as the consequences. Then I examine Italian society in terms of social groups which cannot be reduced to classes. I have chosen women and youth (as opposed to, say, the old) for two reasons: the first is that both groups (but especially the former) have given rise to a social presence with political effects and to groups of political activists which have had effects not only on the social group from which they come but also on the political system as a whole. Thus women are important because *as women* their entry into the labour market, their role as citizens and consumers, their position in the family, etc. have accelerated many of the changes which have occurred in Italian society. They are also important because as feminists (i.e. those women who are feminists) they have also challenged the existing conception of politics and have forced other political forces to react – and this holds true of communists and Christian Democrats as well as the Church and the trade unions. Also in Part II I examine institutions which are not overtly political, but which do have political effects: trade unions, firms, the Church and the media. These very different 'institutions' are not strictly speaking political in the sense that their main business is something else; in the case of the trade union this is the defence of the working conditions of their members and of their standard of living, in the case of enterprise this can be profits, or product range, or size, etc.; in the case of the Church the maintenance and diffusion of its beliefs and values; in the case of the media, information and entertainment. All four, however, are in the business of organizing people: trade unionists, workers and managers, the audience and the faithful and all have important political effects. For this reason I would not claim to have given an account of the complexities of trade-union negotiations, or of the production problem of modern firms, or of theology or of mass communications. In all cases I have tried to relate these institutions to what have been and still are the principal forms of organization of the Italian political system: parties.

Part III ('Politics') is the more conventional one: it explains the Italian Constitution, the role of Parliament, elections and governments, the regional system and the political parties. This part comes last because I wanted to establish the general setting – historical, economic and social – within which the political system must operate. It does not mean that politics comes last because I have tried to let politics have a high profile throughout the book whether what is being discussed is Italy's export trade or the expansion of its universities.

The real protagonists of this book are in fact the political parties whose presence pervades the whole of Italian society in a way which is inconceivable in the UK or in the USA.

The post-war period begins with the political parties clearly in charge. They constituted the commanding forces of the Italian Resistance: the Committee of National Liberation was made up of a coalition of six parties. The partisan bands were organized on the basis of party affiliations. The trade-union movement was reorganized in 1944 on the basis of equal representation for the three leading parties: Christian Democrats, Communists and Socialists. Pressure groups, civic organizations, the professions, etc. were directly connected to specific parties. The main competition was between the PCI and the DC. The latter could rely on the formidable organization of the Roman Catholic Church and, through this, establish a presence in virtually all sectors of society. This forced the PCI to compete at the same level. It was not possible to conceive of communist militancy in the traditional way: a tightly led group of reliable and committed members. The PCI had to be a mass party able to create and develop a whole range of organizations from sporting associations to cultural clubs so as to penetrate into civil society at all levels and challenge the DC.

It has been said that Italian political parties have 'colonized' Italian society. To some extent that is true. The mere act of joining a trade union is necessarily also a political act because the prospective member must also decide whether to join the communist–socialist trade union, the Confederazione Generale Italiana del Lavoro (CGIL) or the Catholic union, Confederazione Italiana dei Sindacati dei Lavoratori (CISL) or the social-democrat/republican union, Unione Italiana del Lavoro (UIL). The mere act of joining a sporting club is similarly 'political': which sporting club? The one run by the mainly communist Associazione Ricreativa Culturale Italiana (ARCI) or the Catholic one or the less well-established 'third force' club?

This politicization of facets of civil life which in most countries would be totally outside politics has also led to the politicization of economic life, particularly in the public sector: state enterprises, banks, credit institutions, newspapers, have been systematically colonized by the government parties and in particular by the DC.

It is then *also* because of the extent of interpenetration between the political level and the social–economic level that it would have been difficult to write a book on the Italian political system which would not give a great emphasis on economic and social factors.

This book has been written assuming no knowledge of Italy or of Italian politics and history. Of course the reader who has some acquaintance with the history of fascism or the development of Europe since the war will be at an advantage, as will the reader who has some grounding in economics.

A general book such as this has had to rely massively on other people's research. In many cases I have tried to give an idea of the kind of debates which surround a particular issue by examining different interpretations. The result is that there is a considerable number of notes and bibliographical acknowledgements which impinge on the size of the book. Most of these sources are not available in English, but it is my hope that younger scholars will be encouraged to study this or that aspect of modern Italy and to contribute to the expansion of the field.

My own acknowledgements and thanks must include first of all the scholars who have enabled me, through their writings, to come to some understanding of at least some of the issues concerning post-war Italy. Then I would like to thank Bernard Crick who had the idea for this book and encouraged me to write it. I would also like to thank those friends who have read some of the chapters and given me valuable advice, in particular Leslie Cauldwell for the section on women, Philip Schlesinger for the section on the media and Bill Brierley for that on the economy. Special thanks must go to Paul Auerbach who went through all the economic history chapters with a remarkable degree of fortitude and spared me some embarrassing mistakes. I am also grateful to Alice Lawson of the inter-library loan service of Westfield College for her unfailing help and to Miss Theresa Tennent of Westfield College Library for her invaluable help and, more specifically for having organized with the University of London Library a key-word computer search. I also thank Jill Tilden for helping me with the index.

My frequent trips to Italy have enabled me to acquire a 'feel' for the country, the kind of thing one cannot find in books. In particular I wish to thank my old friend Beppe Vacca whose discussions on Italian politics and society have always been an immense reservoir of stimulating insights. I cannot thank all my other Italian friends, but must mention Peppino Cotturri, Renato Mannheimer, Cesare Luporini, Carlo Donolo, Leonardo Paggi, Mario Telò and Ferdinando Targetti.

Finally a special word of thanks to Anne Showstack Sassoon who shares not only my life but also my enthusiasm for Italy and whose moral and intellectual support has never failed. She has read through the manuscript and helped to improve it considerably. I, however, did all the typing.

Donald Sassoon

We are indebted to the following for permission to reproduce copyright material:

Financial Times Ltd for Table 12.1 from *The Financial Times* 13.7.81; International Labour Office for Table 3.1 from *ILO Yearbook of Labour Statistics* 1965; Organisation for Economic Co-operation and Development for Table 14.1 from *OECD National Account Statistics 1950–1968*; Oxford University Press for Table 3.4 from p127 *Development and Crisis in the Postwar Economy* by G. Podbielski, 1974; the Editor *Rinascita* for figs 5.4, 5.5 from *Rinascita* No 22, 2.6.84; Societa Editrice il Milano and the author, Prof. C. Trigilia for Table 5.3 from 'aviluppo, sottosviluppo e classi sociali in Italia' p263 *Rassegna Italien di Sociologia* Vol 17, No 2, 1976.

We have unfortunately, been unable to trace the copyright holders of figs 2.2, 2.3, 3.3, 6.3 and Tables 12.2, 12.4 and would appreciate any information which would enable us to do so.

LIST OF ABBREVIATIONS

AC	Azione Cattolica
ACLI	(Associazione Cristiana dei Lavoratori Italiani) Association of Italian Christian Workers
AIMC	Catholic organization of primary-school teachers
ARCI	Associazione Ricreativa Culturale Italiana
CAP	Common Agricultural Policy
CA	Constituent Assembly
CGIL	Confederazione Generale Italiana del Lavoro
CISL	Confederazione Italiana dei Sindacati dei Lavoratori
CISNAL	Confederazione Italiana Sindacati Nazionale dei Lavoratori
DC	(Democrazia Cristiana) Christian Democratic Party
EGAM	Italian State Mining Company
ENEL	Ente Nazionale per l'Energia Electrica
ENI	Ente Nazionale Idrocarburi
ERP	European Recovery Programme
IRI	Istituto per la Ricostruzione Industriale
ISTAT	(Istituto Centrale di Statistica) Italian State Statistical Office
MSI	(Movimento Sociale Italiano) Italian Social Movement (neo-fascist)
NAP	Nuclei Armati Proletari
OECD	Organization for Economic Cooperation and Development
OPEC	Organization of Petroleum Exporting Countries
PCI	(Partito Comunista Italiano) Italian Communist Party
PLI	(Partito Liberale Italiano) Italian Liberal Party
PR	(Partito Radicale) Italian Radical Party
PRI	(Partito Repubblicano Italiano) Italian Republican Party
PDUP	(Partito di Unità Proletaria) Party of Proletarian Unity
PSI	(Partito Socialista Italiano) Italian Socialist Party

PSDI	(Partito Social Democratico Italiano) Italian Social Democratic Party
PSIUP	(Partito Socialista di Unità Proletaria) Socialist Party of Proletarian Unity
PSU	(Partito Socialista Unificato) Unified Socialist Party
RAI	Radiotelevisione Italiana
STVP	(Südtiroler Volkspartei) South Tyrol People's Party
SVIMEZ	(Associazione per lo Sviluppo Industriale del Mezzogiorno) Association for Development of Industry in the South
UNRRA	United Nations Relief and Rehabilitation Administration
UIL	Unione Italiana del Lavoro

INTRODUCTION

The country which emerged as Italy out of the process of political unification known as the Risorgimento was united only in name. Regional and economic divisions were only one aspect of the lack of unity of the country. Most Italians did not speak Italian but their local dialect. Most of them were in fact 'outside' the political system altogether: they had not participated in the Risorgimento and remained barred from participation in political affairs even after the achievement of unity. The Italian Liberal State, a constitutional monarchy, had in 1861 a very narrow electoral basis. Only 2 per cent of the adult population had the right to vote and, of these, less than 60 per cent did vote.

In the years that followed the suffrage was extended, but even by the 1909 elections only 8.3 per cent of the population was entitled to vote. The social bloc which constituted the Italian ruling class was internally as divided as the rest of the country. Northern industrialists and southern landlords did establish a compromise akin to the German alliance between landed and industrial interests (the 'rye and iron' alliance), but the terms of this compromise had to be constantly negotiated by the political representatives of these interests in the Italian Parliament. By the beginning of the century the Prime Minister – Giovanni Giolitti – had, at least formally, a large parliamentary majority. The existing political parties, however, were loose coalitions with no strong membership and no definite programme. Italian governments had to construct their majorities on a day-to-day basis. Through patronage, corruption and wheeling and dealing, majorities were cobbled together in order to approve specific pieces of legislation. Each law required separate negotiations to achieve a majority. This system was known as *trasformismo*. Giolitti tried, sometimes successfully, to open up the parliamentary system to other groups, in particular to the socialists and the Catholics, but, on the whole, the basis of consent for the Liberal State remained narrow.

Until the First World War, then, Parliament had an essential task: to provide the political terrain on which the different interests which constituted the Italian ruling class could negotiate and find their unity. This was possible because Parliament, by and large, was relatively homogeneous: its members represented only a small fraction of the Italian population, but it was a homogeneous one. This was due to the fact that the electorate was small, the socialists unwilling to bargain with the Liberal establishment and the Catholics barred from taking an active part in politics by the Pope against whose wishes Italian unity had been achieved.

By 1913 quasi-universal manhood suffrage was introduced and the electorate grew to 23.2 per cent of the adult population. But the most important changes in Italian politics occurred as a result of the war. As in other countries the war brought together masses of people, strengthened industrial concentrations, increased the numbers of wage workers, expanded urban centres (particularly Turin, Milan and Genoa) and gave the State wider economic functions and a more authoritarian political role. The war mobilized 5.5 million people, killed 600,000 and wounded 700,000. An entire region, the North-east (where most of the fighting occurred) was devastated. Inflation hit those on fixed incomes but enabled many sharecroppers to pay their debts and buy some land. Mass parties emerged: in 1914 the Socialist Party had 50,000 members, by 1921 it had 216,000. In 1919 for the first time in Italian history a Catholic party was created, the Partito Popolare, with 100,000 members. By 1920 it had 255,000 members. The trade unions had, before the war, less than 1 million members. After the war they had 4 million.

The elections of 1919 were fought under proportional representation. The Catholics of the Partito Popolare obtained 20.5 per cent of the vote, the Socialist Party 32.4 per cent. Half of Parliament was now in the hands of mass parties who were outside the traditional system of negotiations (*trasformismo*). Parliament could no longer provide the terrain for the unification of the ruling class. Popolari and Socialists could not form a coalition: the former were anti-socialists, the latter anti-clerical. Workers occupied the large industrial plants of the North, revolutionary slogans backing the new Soviet republic appeared. Landless labourers voiced their discontent. The Liberal State was crumbling. It was no longer able to impose law and order. Its Parliament could no longer be used as it had been in the pre-war period.

Fascism represented the extra-parliamentary solution to the Italian crisis. The old Liberal establishment, which acted as a sort of political representative of bourgeois and landed interests, could no longer utilize the instrument of Parliament. Extra-parliamentary violence was increasingly used, particularly by groups of the Right. Mussolini, the leader of the National Fascist Party (the largest of these right-wing groups with around thirty deputies in the Chamber) seemed to be willing to strike a bargain with the old establishment. It was at this stage, in

October 1922, that the old Liberal establishment ceded power to Mussolini. It assumed that he would be a mere puppet, but it was wrong. Liberal Italy had played its last card, it would never rise again but the 'system' based on the systematic exclusion of the popular masses from politics had been saved by changing the rules of the game: from now on Italy would be run by an authoritarian regime of a new type.

Having been given political power (there was no real 'fascist revolution' despite what the fascists themselves claimed at the time), Mussolini proceeded to strengthen the authoritarian features of the Liberal State by destroying its instruments – Parliament and civil liberties – which had allowed the popular parties (Socialists and Catholics) to emerge.

In allowing fascism to emerge and consolidate itself as a regime, the Italian bourgeoisie had demonstrated that it was not able, or not willing, to develop its own mass party. The National Fascist Party was not a bourgeois party, but it performed many of its functions: it kept wages down by destroying the trade unions and so enabled Italian entrepreneurs to compete in foreign markets, it facilitated the rationalization of Italian capitalism through industrial concentration; in the 1930s it developed powerful instruments of economic intervention, such as the IRI (Istituto per la Ricostruzione Industriale) and saved the banking system from bankruptcy. The rise of fascism showed how weak the Italian Liberal State had been and how it had been unable to achieve the kind of popular consensus capitalism succeeded in obtaining in other countries.

Fascism, on the other hand, had been able to obtain at least the passive consent of large sections of the Italian people. To do so it used a mixture of repression, indoctrination and bribery. At least until 1938 it had also been able to achieve a remarkable popularity among the intellectuals. Fascism organized consent and used a veritable army of opinion-makers (teachers and broadcasters, clergy – after the Conciliation with the Church of Rome – and journalists, technocrats and philosophers, artists and writers) to transform what was a fairly ghettoized intelligentsia into a force committed to fascism, the nation and the people. This commitment was not linked to the upholding of capitalist values. On the contrary, fascist propaganda always insisted that it was trying to develop a social system which would be 'neither capitalist nor communist'. By 1938, as the alliance with Nazi Germany had been established and Italy was being mercilessly dragged into a second world war it was not equipped to fight, let alone win, the younger members of this intelligentsia turned against fascism. They did not, however, return to the ivory tower within which the Liberal State had confined them. They did not uphold the old liberal view that culture is above parties. They did not accept the view of the most distinguished of the anti-fascist philosophers, Benedetto Croce, who had written in his *Answer to the Manifesto of the Fascist Intellectuals*:

> Intellectuals as citizens exercise their rights and perform their duty when they join a party and serve it loyally. But as intellectuals they have one duty: by critical analysis and artistic creation, to raise all men and all parties to a higher spiritual sphere .... . To mix up literature and politics, science and politics is an error .... .

The intellectuals who had grown up with fascism and had accepted it before turning against it, remained committed to the fascist slogan of 'going to the people'. During the Second World War, many of them even took up arms against fascism and joined in the Resistance. Even when this was over they did not return to the old liberal position: they remained politically committed.

They fought with workers and peasants, with communists and Catholics. This heterogeneous coalition of anti-fascists was not held together – as in France or Yugoslavia – by charismatic figures such as De Gaulle or Tito. From its very inception the Resistance was organized by political parties: the Communist Party, the Socialist Party and the Christian Democratic Party. Much of the intelligentsia found its own niche in the Action Party. This had played a key role during the Resistance, but it disappeared soon after the war: intellectuals could not have their own political party.

When the war was over the only political structures which had survived were the political parties. The monarchy, discredited, was abolished by a popular referendum in 1946. The Fascist Party was banned. Yet no single party was strong enough to capture political power. This had to be jointly managed by the same coalition of parties which had organized the Resistance and fought against fascism: the Christian Democratic Party (DC), the Italian Communist Party (PCI) and the Italian Socialist Party (PSI). The PSI was the oldest of the three leading anti-fascist parties. It soon revealed itself unable to obtain the mass following necessary for an independent role in the Italian political system. In the elections to the Constituent Assembly, in 1946, it had 20 per cent of the electorate. Its vote then fell drastically and has been oscillating ever since between 10 and 14 per cent. It could never call the tune but only choose which piper to follow: the DC or the PCI. At first it chose to ally with the PCI. After 1956 it began to disengage itself from it. By the early 1960s it had joined the DC in coalition. With some interruptions it has been a subordinate ally of the DC in central government while continuing to rule in most 'red areas' with the PCI as the senior partner. Its electoral size may not have changed much and its alliance strategy may have oscillated between the twin pillars of communism and the DC, but it has not stood still. Its great strength has been its intermediary position between the DC and the PCI. Its long-term project has been to supplant the PCI as the party of the Italian Left. So far, alone of all socialist parties in Western Europe, it has failed to do so perhaps because it has never wanted to face the fact that the communist party it is in competition with is, as we shall see later, unique in the West.

When the PSI was a close ally of the PCI, that is, from the Second World War to about 1956, it modelled itself as closely as possible on the PCI. In foreign policy it was virtually indistinguishable from the PCI, upholding the USSR, opposing the North Atlantic Treaty Organization (NATO) and Marshall aid. Even its own distancing from the PCI, after 1956, was not only due to domestic reasons such as the defeat suffered by the communist–socialist trade union confederation (CGIL) at the Fiat works in 1955 but mainly to the general crisis of the international communist movement: the de-Stalinization begun by the Communist Party of the Soviet Union (and never taken to its logical conclusions) at its Twentieth Congress (1956) and the invasion of Hungary by Soviet troops. The PSI assumed that international communism had entered a phase of decline and that the PCI too would be part of this decline. The PSI began its *rapprochement* with the DC and, by 1963, had become part of the DC-led governing coalition.

Thereafter the PSI became more and more a junior version of the Italian Christian Democratic Party. It sought to compensate for the gradual loss of its working-class base by the uninhibited acquisition of a clientele system. This had become possible by its partnership in central government with the DC and in local government with either the DC or the PCI.

Yet the role of the PSI, though subordinate to the two larger parties has been far from negative in post-war Italy. The mere fact of being the PCI's sole ally in the difficult years of the first 'Cold War', helped the leadership of the PCI to follow a relatively moderate course and to resist the temptation of sectarian and bitter opposition. When the PSI became the DC's main ally it enabled the more progressive factions of the DC to ensure that their party would not come under the control of right-wing factions which would transform it into a clerical party. The pendulum movements of the PSI were an important contributing factor to the maintenance of reasonable relations between governing party and opposition and the avoidance of extreme polarization.

The PCI had originated as a split from the PSI in Leghorn in 1921. There the Bordiga faction of the Socialist Party, unable to impose on the rest of the party the 'Twenty-one Conditions' which the Comintern had set for affiliation to the communist movement, seceded and formed the Communist Party of Italy, Section of the Third International. By the time it had emerged from the Second World War the party had undergone at least two transformations. In the first, the sectarian Bordiga leadership was removed in 1924 by Antonio Gramsci and Palmiro Togliatti with the decisive support of the Comintern. Soon afterwards the party was banned, Gramsci was jailed and Togliatti remained abroad in exile. During this period of clandestinity the party followed the vicissitudes of Comintern policies. In his prison cell

Gramsci was laying the theoretical foundations for a new communist tradition sharply demarcated from the doctrine of Marxism-Leninism which Stalin's leadership was imposing on the rest of the communist movement. Togliatti, who had become the *de facto* leader of the PCI, had at first attempted to oppose Comintern policies, but in 1929 the Tenth Plenum of the Comintern imposed on all parties the new 'class against class' line which considered the proletarian revolution to be imminent and all socialist and social-democratic parties to be the 'left-wing' of fascism. Togliatti obeyed adding, in reference to the intermediate political objectives he had been forced to drop, 'If the Comintern says that this is not correct, we shall refrain from posing these objectives. We shall think these things, but we shall not say them. We shall only say that the anti-fascist revolution shall be the proletarian revolution.'

During the 1930s the PCI was a small, marginal clandestine group of agitators and conspirators numbering a few thousands. Its messianic Stalinism enabled it to tolerate political persecutions and defeat. Sooner or later the day of the insurrection would come and, in Italy too, as in Russia, a socialist revolution would destroy capitalism. When the insurrection came, on 25 April 1945, it was a quite different affair from what had been imagined by the old generation of militants.

The insurrection had been made possible by a number of factors: the successes of the Allied troops who had landed in Italy two years before, the collapse of the German war machine in the East and the Anglo-American landing in the West and the broad basis of the Resistance itself which succeeded in uniting monarchists and republicans, socialists and communists, Catholics and anti-clericals. The PCI itself had undergone, in the course of the struggle, a further transformation: it had begun to shed the mentality and attitudes of a small sect of conspirators and to acquire the size and politics of a large mass party. By the end of 1945 the PCI had nearly 2 million members. Togliatti had played the key role in this transformation. His authority among communist cadres was immense. He was helped in this by the fact that, as leader of the party, he could enjoy a share of that personality cult which had become established in the communist movement. Undoubtedly the prestige of the USSR played a crucial part in this, but so did the fact that the PCI had been the leading force of the Resistance.

Togliatti took advantage of these factors to devise an alternative to the insurrectionist model which was still the framework within which much of the party was operating. Party membership was opened to all those who accepted its political programme: it was not necessary to accept the party's Marxist doctrine. The tripartite coalition with the PSI and the DC was assumed to provide an adequate form of government to oversee the transformation of Italy into a 'progressive democracy', a stage in the eventual transition to socialism. Gradualism and compromise were the order of the day. Togliatti and the PCI participated fully in the drafting of Italy's new Constitution. This based itself on the principles of liberalism but also recognized new 'social rights'; freedom of private enterprise was guaranteed but only 'as long as it did not conflict with social utility'.

The Cold War brought this compromise to an end. In 1947 the PCI and its socialist allies were expelled from the government. Italy was now clearly in the US sphere of influence. Togliatti had to follow the Soviet line once again, at least in foreign policy. At home the PCI continued to develop, with difficulty, the 'Italian road to socialism'. It sought to implant itself throughout Italian society using not only the traditional instruments of party and trade union, but also cultural, recreational and sporting associations it had sponsored with the PSI. It organized its own intellectual cadres, its own press network, party schools, research institutes – in a word: its own 'society'. This allowed the PCI to survive the worst years of the Cold War and – after the post-1956 de-Stalinization which occurred in the Soviet Communist Party – to develop further its own independent strategy.

The process was gradual and slow. At every turning-point in the history of the post-war international communist movement – China, Vietnam, Prague 1968, Afghanistan and Poland – the PCI increased its distance from Moscow.

The DC was the newest party of the young Italian Republic, but from the very beginning it was the strongest. It enjoyed some unique advantages. In the first place it was heir to the tradition of the Popular Party, the largely peasant-based Catholic party which had been created in 1919. In the second place it could use the vast machine of Catholic societies and organizations which had been allowed to operate under fascism thanks to the Concordat Mussolini had signed with the Pope in 1929. These provided the DC with a useful network of leading cadres. Thirdly the DC was able to rely on the support of the Church, from the Pope and the bishops to the village priests and including the mass lay organizations of the Church itself such as Azione Cattolica (AC). Fourthly the weakness of the old Liberal Party, the nearest equivalent to a clearly pro-capitalist party, meant that the DC soon became the obvious choice of industrialists. Once again the political weakness of Italian capitalism was evident: in the age of democracy it needed a party able to obtain the consent of the electorate, but it was not able to create its own conservative party. It thus had to rely on a composite party: a coalition of traditional Catholics, young technocrats, populists and other disparate groups all united under the banner of catholicism.

Finally the DC was very soon able to become the only party on which the United States could rely to take Italy into the North Atlantic Alliance and to anchor it definitively in the Western camp.

These five factors were the base of the DC's success in becoming Italy's dominant party throughout the post-war period. The DC, however, realized early on that it could not depend on the Church for ever:

it needed to develop its own political machine. This was done in a variety of ways. In the first place the DC became the mirror-image of the PCI in the sense that it too developed a policy of 'presence' in all sectors of society through the creation of a variety of 'non-party' organizations linked more or less informally to the DC. Soon much of what is called 'civil society' was divided along party lines. Sport, culture, leisure time, pressure groups, etc. became extensions of the main political parties.

In the second place the DC could use its control over the state machinery and over public money to support specific social groups and interests. A network of clienteles was developed, particularly in the South. While the DC facilitated the growth of private industry, it was also able to alleviate some of the negative effects of economic growth by intervening directly to protect specific social and interest groups which were thus, in turn, dependent on the continuation of the DC in power.

Finally the DC, because it was always in government and because it tended to be a party which actively encouraged the expansion of the public sector, had also at its disposal a vast array of jobs which it could offer to those who were politically reliable. Thus through professional and trade associations and a clientelistic system of patronage, the DC developed a formidable machine thanks to which it could withstand the PCI and maintain its hold on the country.

However, all this was not enough to achieve a permanent electoral majority. Only in 1948 was the DC able to obtain more than half the parliamentary seats, but even then it decided to rule with other parties. It follows that the DC has always had to rely on coalition partners. These tended to be the smaller parties of the Centre: the Liberal Party, the Republican Party and the Social Democratic Party. After 1962 the DC extended the coalition to include the PSI.

The strength of the DC in Italy has been sufficient to ensure a remarkable continuity of governments: since 1945 all governments had the DC at their centre. But this was not sufficient to guarantee government stability. The DC is itself a coalition of tendencies, factions and ideas. Negotiations and bargaining within the party must be continuous. The politics of patronage and clientele means that there must be a proper share-out of political power according to the strength of the various factions. This constant process of bargaining can give rise to considerable internal dissent and, at times, this dissent is manifested by the withdrawal of support by some factions of the ruling government. There follows further bargaining for a new government with a new division of offices and power. This bargaining is far from being the prerogative of the DC. It must also involve the other coalition partners. Thus each government is the result of a specific set of bargains struck within the coalition parties and among them. It follows that, though there is considerable agreement on the sort of coalition which must emerge, there is constant strife over specific policies and appointments. Thus Italian governments have been extremely short-lived.

The internal strife at the government level has increased the power of the communist opposition. While it is true that this opposition cannot become a government (at least as long as it is not able to fracture the DC-led coalition system and obtain the support of some of the other parties), the opposition has ample room for manoeuvre, because it can intervene in the bargaining process by throwing its weight on one side or the other. Thus bargaining and compromise are the hallmark of the Italian system of government. Unlike the UK there is no 'adversary system' whereby two more or less stable and disciplined parties face each other and alternate in government. On the surface of things the Italian system may appear to be markedly polarized, divided as it is between the DC and the PCI. In practice all parties accept the need for compromise.

Nevertheless there is a strong element of potential instability: should the PCI ever succeed in ousting the DC from power it would have to rule with a machinery of government which has largely been created by the DC and would face a system of clienteles (which includes powerful interest groups, such as the banking system) unlikely to be supportive. Furthermore, agencies such as the secret services and the armed forces have grown accustomed to consider themselves 'at war' with communism and would probably attempt to destabilize a regularly elected communist-led coalition government. Finally the United States government would also play a destabilizing role unless it were convinced that the presence of a non-DC government in Italy would not cause an international shift in the balance of power in favour of the USSR. It was partly in order to prevent such a crisis situation that the PCI came to accept that Italy needed to remain within the North Atlantic Alliance and, at least until the early 1980s, envisaged that it could come to power only on the basis of an agreement with the DC: the so-called 'historic compromise'.

The PCI, however, was never entirely excluded from political power. In the first place, as I have already mentioned, the weakness of coalition governments and their internal dissension often meant that the government has needed PCI support to pass legislation. Secondly the PCI has always been in power in some key areas of central Italy where it could apply some of its ideas at the local level. After 1970 the legislation which provided for regional devolution of power increased the extent to which the PCI could exercise some form of direct political control. Thirdly the alliance with the PSI has survived even the most bitter divisions within the Left in at least two distinct settings: in local government and in the largest of the three trade-union confederations: the CGIL. As the PSI has been in government most of the time since 1963, the PCI has had in the PSI a local government partner through which it could make its voice felt at executive level. Fourthly, in the 1970s PCI members have been accepted in various state institutions, such as the board of Italian television or the national institute in charge of social security and pensions (the INPS). This has enabled the party to develop some of the skills of political management which a permanent opposition would normally find it difficult to achieve. Fifthly, because of the dominant position of communists in the CGIL the PCI has been able to negotiate directly with government and employers. Thus the PCI has not existed in an opposition ghetto in the years since its expulsion from government. Finally, its large size and the fact that it has always been able to attract intellectuals and professionals meant that there are very few institutions in which it would be difficult to find communist supporters or sympathizers. Even the top echelons of the armed forces had at least one communist sympathizer: General Nino Pasti who, after his retirement, was elected to Parliament in 1976 in the communist list!

The existence of a permanent government party (the DC) and a permanent opposition (the PCI) suggests a considerable degree of *immobilismo*. It does not follow from this, however, that there has been little change in the forty years of history of the Italian republic. On the contrary the transformations have been considerable, as we shall see in more detail in Parts I and II.

The Italian economy has been transformed beyond recognition and has, by and large, caught up with the rest of Europe. In terms of purchasing power and standard of living, the Italian working class has narrowed the gap with Germany and France and is, probably, at the same level as the UK. The 'necessities' of the consumer society, such as remote-control colour television, multi-programme dishwashers, freezers, push-button telephones, etc. are as available in Italy as they are in most other Western countries. Its agricultural population has decreased constantly and so has the birth-rate (in line with European countries). Fewer people go to church, more use contraceptives and live together without being married. Italians can now get a divorce, have abortions and purchase pornographic material. The dominance of the DC, the strong presence of the Church and the puritanical tradition of the communist movement (now virtually evaporated except in some working-class strongholds) has not stopped the development of a life-style which is, by and large, an adaptation of many positive and negative aspects of the 'American way of life'.

The market and the free enterprise system have played the major role in the diffusion of consumer goods in Italian society. But this has been only one aspect of its social transformation. As in the rest of Europe, the State has had to intervene to keep costs of production lower than they would otherwise have been by taking into public ownership some basic production inputs such as energy, and some basic segments of the infrastructure of the nation, such as transportation, and subsidizing them out of the public purse. Furthermore, the State has also had to ensure that minimum standards of health, housing, education and old-age care and welfare are maintained. In other words, Italy too has had to become a Welfare State. As in other European countries this form of state was achieved and maintained on the assumption that there would be constant economic growth. This was the case in Italy for most of the 1950s and for well into the 1960s. Economic growth and the Welfare State have been the basis for that unwritten compromise between the dominant economic groups and the working classes which ensured a remarkable degree of social peace in most of Europe in the post-war period.

Problems began to appear in the 1960s and developed in the 1970s when economic growth slowed down, when the expansion of the tertiary sector associated with the Welfare State was supported by a decreasing manufacturing sector, when the financial basis of public spending became narrower, causing inflationary tendencies. The public sector was less and less able to maintain a high level of employment and large areas of the private sector succumbed and had to be rescued by the State. In the 1980s attempts were made to control inflation by controlling public spending, by containing wages and by loosening the controls exercised on the private sector.

The pattern I have just described (development of the Welfare State, State intervention, crisis of the Welfare State) occurred not just in Italy but virtually everywhere else in the developed West. Two points must then be made: in the first place Italian socio-economic development has followed that of the rest of Europe in spite of the 'anomalous' nature of its political development, namely, the lack of an alternance of political parties in power and the dominance in Italy of two cultures, communist and political catholicism, which are not dominant in the rest of the West. In the second place it is increasingly obvious that it is no longer possible in the second half of the twentieth century to talk of 'national' development: the extent of international integration is such that similar problems and similar solutions are the norm rather than the exception. All countries must face the same questions, but face them on the basis of their particular national political tradition. The Italian anomaly has not had the effect of increasing the distance between Italy and the rest of Europe, but on the contrary that of integrating the two.

International integration has not occurred by accident. There are two fundamental ways in which Italy has actively sought to be part of this process. In the first place it became party to a supranational defence organization, NATO, which has closely tied its foreign policy to that of the dominant superpower in the Western sphere of influence: the USA. In the second place Italy was one of the original signatories of the Treaty of Rome which established the European Economic Community (EEC) and thus took a clear stand in favour of the creation of a specific European economic (and perhaps, eventually, political) entity. In both cases the treaties were signed after the *de facto* recognition that Italy was part of the West both politically and economically. This recognition was achieved in the immediate post-war period by the DC and their partners in government and was bitterly opposed by communists and socialists. Later the socialists accepted both NATO and the EEC. By the 1960s the

PCI too had come to accept that participation in the institutions of the EEC had some potentially positive aspects. By the 1970s the PCI had become a supporter of the need for further economic integration and had accepted the fact that this was an objective process which would have occurred even without the EEC. By 1976 the PCI had also come to accept NATO. Thus thirty years after the end of the war all the main forces of the Italian political system shared the view that Italy's role in the world had two fundamental parameters: the NATO alliance and the EEC.

The chapters that follow will take the reader through Italian economic, social and political development. Due emphasis will be given to those aspects which are specific to Italy. What must not be forgotten is the international perspective. In our age the nation-state is fast becoming a hollow shell. Those who forget this, in politics as in political research, run the risk of dealing with the terminal stages of the twentieth century with the language and concepts of the nineteenth. These dangers are particularly present in what is, after all, a 'national' study. The temptation to remain enclosed in the narrow confines of national boundaries is particularly strong when dealing, as I do, with a country which, on the surface of things, has such marked peculiarities. I have tried to scratch this surface and in so doing bear in mind what an old German Jewish thinker (who has still a thing or two to teach us) wrote: 'If there were no difference between reality and appearance, there would be no need for science.'

Part One

THE ECONOMY

The decision to 'choose' to open up the Italian economy to the international market is of importance for the following reasons: to 'open' an economy means that one has to find appropriate trading partners, that is, eventual customers. Thus one has to gear one's production to their demands; production must be geared towards export. Thus certain priorities must be established, certain industries must be favoured and hence certain economic interests will prevail at the expense of others. These choices will determine a particular class structure and the eventual incidence of a certain kind of labour, i.e. skilled or unskilled, male or female, southern or northern, etc. Besides, the choice of partners (again in the specific circumstances of the post-war period) was also, to a certain extent, forced on Italy by the international situation.[1] The partners could not be the states of Eastern Europe because of obvious political circumstances, nor could they be in those countries we now call of the Third World because their markets were then tiny and dominated either by the USA (Latin America), or by the UK and France (Asia and Africa) or by all three (the Middle East). Hence Italy's customers could only be West Europeans and North Americans. It is thus not surprising that the decision to enter the world market entailed membership of the Atlantic Alliance and, later, of all the European economic organizations including the EEC.

None of the political forces in government at the time (and that includes, until 1947, the Left) were opposed to an opening up of the Italian economy. The real dispute was on the priorities to be given in the context of this policy. To give top priority to exports, as was done, meant that economic development would be essentially determined by outside circumstances (i.e. the demand for imports of Western Europe and North America), but it also meant that certain sectors of the Italian economy would have to be sacrificed. The most important of these would be agriculture. To put it crudely instead of making Fiat cars for the European market (or eventually, washing machines or clothing) some of the resources available could have been directed towards making tractors for the agricultural sector. This could have expanded Italian food production which would have reduced Italy's need to import food. However, there were only two ways to revitalize the agricultural sector.[2] The first would have been to encourage the concentration of agricultural lands and their modernization along capitalist lines. This, however, would have caused the expulsion of considerable numbers of agricultural labourers from the countryside. In the conditions of 1945–50 this would have entailed a dramatic increase in unemployment and would have been politically dangerous for the DC which relied on the consistent support of the peasant masses. The other way, favoured by the Left, would have been to ensure the creation of agricultural cooperatives helped by the State. This, however, would have considerably weakened the historical alliance between northern industrial entrepreneurs and southern landlord interests, and this too would have been politically dangerous for the DC. Thus the Italian economy was opened up and exports were given top priority.

It must be added that at no time did the Left present a concrete alternative plan for the reconstruction of the Italian economy. This too must be seen as a contributing factor to their eventual defeats, i.e. their expulsion from the ruling coalition in 1947 and their electoral defeat in 1948.

As we shall see later, Italy derived considerable benefit from export-led growth: both production and productivity eventually increased, leading to the period of sustained growth known popularly as the 'economic miracle' of 1958–62. However, there were also serious negative factors. The examination of these leads us directly to a consideration of the so-called dualism of the Italian economy.

The concept of 'dualism' is used in different ways by various specialists of economic development. We shall use it in the sense in which it is normally understood in Italy, i.e. as synonymous for 'imbalance' or 'disequilibrium'. Historically, there are three kinds of dualism in Italy[3]:

1. *Territorial dualism,* i.e. dualism between economically prosperous regions and those which are economically backward. In the Italian context this can be seen in terms of the gap between the industrial North and the agricultural South.
2. *Industrial dualism,* i.e. dualism between advanced, modern and highly productive sectors of industry and those which are not.
3. *Dualism in the labour market,* i.e. dualism between the labour force employed in relatively well-paid, stable jobs and that employed in badly paid, marginal and precarious occupations.

The evidence indicates that the opening up of the Italian economy increased rather than reduced all three kinds of dualism at lease up until 1961 and probably (though here there is less agreement) until today. In other words exporting firms were essentially located in the North and eventually used southern labour at the expense of agriculture (territorial dualism); they grew at a faster rate and had to adopt modern methods because they were competing in the international market (industrial dualism) and their workers were better paid and their jobs were more secure (dualism in the labour market).

Of course there are many countries which exhibit 'dualistic' features in their economic system. These features are difficult to quantify and comparative data in this field are notoriously unreliable. A study by Williamson attempted to quantify territorial dualism for a group of twenty-four countries in the period 1949–61.[4] Of the countries examined the one with the biggest regional variation was Brazil with an index of 0.700, while at the other end there was New Zealand with 0.063. The average was 0.299. Italy ranked sixth with 0.360, thus exhibiting a more marked dualism than India, Ireland and virtually all industrialized countries.

It is worth pointing out the gravity of Italian dualism compared to that of a country such as the UK which has always regarded its regional problem (the gap between the depressed areas of Scotland and the North and the relatively prosperous South-east) to be sufficiently serious as to warrant government intervention since the 1930s.

As we stated at the beginning of Part I the question of opening up the Italian economy was not the only major problem facing the Italian political system. There was also the question of the relation between the State and the economy. In its crudest form the choice was perceived as being between a planned economy and a *laissez-faire* regime. In practice it was not so clear-cut. The PCI, for instance, was not in favour of a planned economy. That party and its leader, Palmiro Togliatti, were developing a political strategy which did not take Soviet communism as its principal reference point. They took it for granted that Italy was not ripe for a socialist transformation partly because, as they were committed to the principle of a democratic transformation, they realized that there was not the necessary consensus, and partly because Italy's presence in the US sphere of influence made it impossible. Thus Togliatti not only declared in August 1945 that even if the PCI were in power on their own they would call on private enterprise for the task of reconstruction but also that central planning was Utopian and what was needed were 'elements of planning', i.e. limited state intervention in key sectors.[5] Only the left-wing faction of the PSI called for a national plan, but it encountered no support.

The true debate thus could not have been between 'central planners' and neo-liberals but rather between the latter and the supporters of Keynesian intervention. It is true that Keynes was virtually unknown in Italy at the time and that all the leading economists were neo-liberals whose belief in the necessity to allow a spontaneous development of market forces was deeply rooted. Historically the neo-liberals had been an important force in Italian economic culture, but the Italian State had always been interventionist. What were the reasons for their eventual success? In part it was a reaction against the *dirigisme* of the Fascist State which had set up a state-holding system and nationalized the banks. In the post-fascist climate the equation liberty = liberalism had strong currency even among left-wing intellectuals. The reason for the neo-liberal success must also be traced to the fact that they were in virtual control of the economy. It is true that the Communists and the Socialists controlled (until 1947) the Ministries of Finance, Trade, Labour and Agriculture, but the neo-liberals controlled the Treasury and, even more importantly, the Bank of Italy which, since the 1936 reform of the banking system, had become the key institution of the entire financial system.[6] In July 1947, after the expulsion of the Left from the government, Luigi Einaudi, the foremost Italian economist and the champion of economic liberalism, moved from the Bank of Italy to the Ministry of the Budget and was able to push his deflationary line very quickly. It is remarkable that the strongest Italian political party, the DC, kept out of economic affairs preferring to allow the small Liberal Party and its political representatives, such as Luigi Einaudi, to dominate economic affairs. As De Gasperi explained to a communist minister who was urging him to adopt more radical policies:

> It is not our millions of voters who can give the State the thousands of millions and the economic power necessary for tackling the situation. Apart from our parties, there is in Italy a fourth party which may not have many supporters but which is capable of paralysing all our efforts by organizing the sabotaging of loans, the flight of capital and price rises. Experience has convinced me that it is not possible to govern Italy today without inviting into the new Government the representatives of this fourth party, the party of those who have money and economic power.[7]

Luigi Einaudi was an obvious political representive of the 'fourth party' (the other three being the DC, the PCI and the PSI), and he had a key role in government. But other representatives of this party could make their voice heard without the need for the mediating force of an officially constituted political party. The leading Italian industrialists were very clearly committed against state intervention. Thus Angelo Costa, President of the Italian Employers' Confederation (the Confindustria), in the course of an investigation conducted by the government explained that he thought that the adoption of policies for the localization of industry along the UK model would be detrimental to the Italian economy. He asserted that it would be preferable to 'move people' rather than things.[8] In other words Costa was in favour of internal immigration rather than the localization of industry in the South. This clearly envisaged that the role of the South in post-war reconstruction would have to be that of providing the northern industries with the necessary supply of cheap labour. Costa, however, accepted the need for public works programmes in the South, but specified the conditions of acceptability of these policies: wages in southern public-sector programmes would have to be inferior to wages in the industrial northern sector in order not to compete for labour with private industry. As we can see, the tenets of liberalism are here not adhered to so closely. There is a clear vision of the specific role of the state: to intervene where private industry is reluctant to intervene and to do so on the basis of a low-wages policy. A high-wage policy would have made Italian industry less competitive on the world markets and would have entailed a different approach to the problem of post-war reconstruction. Thus a low-wage policy is not something which is determined only by market forces but is, to use the word in its literal sense, a *policy*, i.e. a conscious political decision which, in turn, determines a particular range of political alliances which would exclude the Left.

It is true that there were technical obstacles to the adoption of a public works programme directly conducted by the State (as opposed, say, to subsidies for industry): the inefficiency of administration and the lack of coordination between the various state organs. Yet, when all the political forces as well as the private sectors were united in a particular kind of public works programme, all obstacles were removed easily as was the case when the Italian motorway system was developed towards the end of the 1950s.

That low wages were a 'good thing' was also asserted, not surprisingly, by industrialists like Vittorio Valletta, the chairman of the largest private firm in Italy, Fiat. In his declarations to a government investigative commission Valletta explained that there was a main obstacle to the development of the Italian automobile industry: the scarcity of raw materials. There were, however, three favourable conditions: low wages, the possibility of importing American technology and the possibility of withstanding foreign competition by concentrating on small cars. The overall reduction of costs could be achieved by an expansion of the industrial scale of production. Here we have in a nutshell a global understanding of the political determinants of a specific pattern of economic growth: a government decision not to engage in any activity which would push wages upward, the need to remain in the American sphere of influence in order to have access to American know-how, the necessity to develop as trading partners markets which would be interested in small cars (i.e. Western Europe).[9]

The debate on state intervention had also an important role to play when the USA launched its European Recovery Programme (ERP), better known as the Marshall Plan. This programme presented Italian decision-makers with a new set of variables. The options were essentially two: to use American money to increase state intervention in the economy by setting up infrastructures or to increase Bank of Italy reserves in order to maintain the stability of the currency and the equilibrium in the balance of payments. Here the Left was in particular difficulty because both Communists and Socialists had rejected the principle of Marshall aid and hence could not at the same time fight for a particular use of the programme. The neo-liberals in control of economic decision-making had already decided that the ERP money had to have a currency-stabilizing function. In so doing they did not have the support of ERP itself. Paradoxically enough the Marshall aid administrators had a conception of the relation between the State and the economy which was not so different from that of some of the leaders of the PCI. The Americans who were working in the Marshall aid programme were in fact deeply imbued with the spirit of the New Deal and had accepted much of Keynes' analysis. Their position and that of the United Nations Relief and Rehabilitation Administration (UNRRA) – the predecessor of ERP – was that Italy should adopt elements of planning to integrate the activities of the entrepreneurial classes with that of the State. Marshall aid was supposed to be used for a rapid development of investments to ensure industrial growth, not, as the Italians by and large did, in order to increase reserves.

The PCI (and to some extent the small Republican Party led by Ugo La Malfa) wanted to direct the flow of public expenditure towards real investments. But Marshall aid money was tied in with a set of political preconditions (to integrate Western Europe and North America in a web of political and economic relations of interdependence) which, for obvious international reasons, such as the start of the Cold War, could not be accepted by the Italian Left. But if the connection with Moscow prevented the Italian communists from any clear-cut attempt to intervene in a constructive manner, such problems could not affect the ERP administrator for Italy, Paul Hoffman. In his report to the US Congress he maintained that there was no need for deflation and that there was no need for the Italians to worry about the balance of payments problem that a Keynesian use of ERP might cause: this would be taken into account by an increase in aid. What the Italian government should do, suggested Hoffman, was to set up a plan in order to coordinate public intervention and the financing of public works programmes.[10] In fact the US authorities thought it strange that the Italian government which, through its state holding agency, Istituto per la Ricostruzione Industriale (IRI), virtually controlled the banking system and massive means of production would not attempt some sort of planning and a policy of reducing unemployment then at very high levels (19%). The fact that there were differences between the US and the Italian governments on such an important question is significant. What it does is to weaken the long-held view of many commentators particularly on the Left, that American–Italian relations were relations of master and servant and that the Italian government and particularly the DC were totally subservient to the diktats from Washington. It also invalidates the arguments of the Centre-Right that once Italy found itself in the Western sphere of influence she had no choice but to act as she did. The tendency to use the USA as a justification for a whole range of internal political decisions can be explained by the fact that this instrumental use of the special link with Washington was a strong factor in the legitimation of DC rule (to put it bluntly: 'we do what we do because otherwise there would be no American help'). American–Italian relations were in fact more complex than they appeared at the time.

It should also be stated that 'Keynesian planning' and other forms of state intervention had been adopted in a number of European countries who were all as committed to an anti-Soviet position as Italy. A strongly interventionist programme was adopted in July 1945 by the Labour government in Britain based on vast nationalization plans and implementation of the Beveridge Report on the Welfare State. Similar programmes were adopted in the Scandinavian countries as well as in Belgium and in the Netherlands. In January 1946 the French government under De Gaulle created the *Commissariat Général au Plan* and, in 1947, launched the Monnet Plan. France, Belgium and Holland also adopted a range of special taxes on private wealth and war profits.[11] But Italy seemed to have become the bastion of *laissez-faire* ideology. The cost of this *laissez-faire* strategy had an effect on the amount of aid obtained. There was no planning structure within which an accurate estimate could be made of what Italy needed. Thus when it came to put in a bid for qualitative aid (i.e. in kind rather than in cash) Italy put forward its requests in a disorganized manner while the French had a special *plan de modernisation et d'équipement*.[12]

On the side of indicative planning along the French model one could find only the left wing of the DC (Ezio Vanoni and Amintore Fanfani) and the Republican Party. Against these were ranged the bulk of the DC and also the Confindustria, Fiat and industrialists like Gaetano Marzotto, a leading wool producer, who, in 1946 to the question, 'Do you think that the State should establish what quantity and kind of goods should be produced?' answered 'This would be Russian Bolshevism!'[13]

But were the interventionists totally defeated? Did the Italian economy recover only on the basis of *laissez-faire*? We have already hinted at the fact that, in its strict sense, *laissez-faire* does not really exist. In the conditions of the second half of the twentieth century, the State's decision not to intervene so as, for example, to maintain wages low, is already a form of intervention. In the period 1945–50 as well as later, Italian economic decision-makers intervened to the extent of favouring a particular kind of economic growth based on low wages and sustained exports.

But were there also more direct forms of economic intervention? An accurate examination of government policy shows, for instance, that the combined efforts of the Left and of other centrist forces such as the left wing of the DC were able to obtain something substantial. First and foremost there is the fact that the fundamental mechanisms of state intervention set up by the fascists were not eliminated. The important national stateholding company IRI was preserved. The holdings under the control of IRI were very diversified: engineering, steel, electricity, telephones, the arms industry, etc. This had come about as a result of the crisis of the post-First World War period and the crisis of 1929. During each crisis the State had been forced to acquire greater control over the banking system until, in 1933 IRI was created to administer the industrial holdings of three major banks. The Italian banks had followed the German model, that is, they were banks which owned a considerable portion of the shares of those firms they were financing. Thus when the banks were taken over, the State also took over a diversified portion of Italian industry. By 1938 IRI controlled 77 per cent of cast-iron production, 45 per cent of steel, 12 per cent of electricity and 82 per cent of shipyards. By 1942 it had 210,000 employees. Established as an emergency measure by the fascist authorities, IRI became the main industrial group in Italy. In the post-war period it accomplished little with one exception: the modernization of the steel industry. Suffice it to say that at this stage the very survival of IRI was the major achievement of the interventionist 'party' which had been faced with the onslaught of the neo-liberal forces. In the 1950s IRI played a central role in the public works programme which would be one of the preconditions of the Italian economic miracle, but in the late 1940s its single, though important success was the steel industry.

The situation in 1945 was that one-third of the much-disrupted steel industry was still owned by the State through Finsider (an IRI company). In 1937 Oscar Sinigaglia on behalf of Finsider had prepared a steel plan aimed at expanding steel production in Italy and lowering steel prices by adopting a method of production based on the system of integral cycle (i.e. beginning from the raw material and not from scraps as had been the case hitherto in Italy). The plan had not been implemented because of the war and the opposition of private steel-makers. After the war a modified version of the plan was put forward by Finsider. This encountered the strong opposition of Confindustria and in particular of Giorgio Falck, then the leading private producer of steel in Italy.[14]

However, after the expulsion of the Left from government and their electoral defeat in 1948, there were sufficient political guarantees for the private sector to tone down their opposition which was essentially a political one: not against state intervention as such but against an intervention in which the forces of the Left would have had an important say. The Sinigaglia Plan was carried out partly thanks to ERP aid. Italian steel became internationally competitive. Even though production was at a standstill in 1945, by 1950 Finsider had reached pre-war levels (1 million tons) and when the Sinigaglia Plan was fulfilled in 1955 nearly 3 million tons were produced.[15] Steel production constituted one of the most important preconditions for the development of private engineering and private building programmes in the course of the 1950s. The adoption of the Sinigaglia Plan showed that IRI was able to carry out what no private steel company would or could have done: the introduction in Italy of modern methods of steel production. This modernized Italian industry enormously. This was done because, for the first time, steel was conceived of as an infrastructure which was to the immediate advantage of steel consumers and in particular to Fiat.[16] This also illustrates the general conception of the public sector held by the dominant political parties: that of supporting the development of the private sector. Before 1947 the Left conceived of the public sector as having a leading role in development. With the defeat of the Left a conception of the public sector as a subordinate prevailed. A compromise had been reached between the interventionists and the neo-liberals: the former would look after the provision of adequate infrastructures, while the latter would look after the implementation of orthodox finances, the balance of payments and the currency.

The position of the neo-liberals was consolidated not because they fought against state intervention, but because they were able to impose their own conception of the 'correct' way of approaching the issue of inflation and of the balance of payments in the post-war period. It was probably on this terrain that the interconnection between the defeat of the Left and economic policies can be best established.

The starting-point for this discussion must be, once again, the decision to 'open up' the Italian economy because this poses the question of the control of foreign exchange. Given that foreign currency was scarce and yet vital for the importation of raw material the government could have imposed strict exchange controls as, for instance, the British government did. To do so would have meant that entrepreneurs, in order to import raw material would have had to ask the government for foreign currency. The government would then have been in a position to use its control over foreign exchange in order to establish some priorities. If it decided to give priority to a particular sector it could have done this by providing the necessary foreign currency. If this path had been chosen the government would have had, from *the very beginning* the direction of the reconstruction of the Italian economy.

Again the interventionist position was not supported just by the Left. Guido Carli, who would eventually become Governor of the Bank of Italy and who is generally considered an 'orthodox' economist, advocated the imposition of exchange control precisely because the government could then use foreign currency to buy those foreign goods which it considered necessary to the national economy.[17] Obviously the decision *not* to intervene would also have favoured some sectors at the expense of others. For instance it would have favoured exporters. They would be able to sell abroad and then enjoy freely the foreign currency gained. They could, for example, use it to speculate against the lira in what was called the 'parallel market', the *de facto* black market in currency. In March 1946 the government decided that exporters could keep for themselves 50 per cent of the foreign currency they had obtained and would have to exchange the rest in Italian currency at a rate fixed by the Central Bank. This compromise in economic policy reflected to some extent the political compromise between the DC and the left in government. After the expulsion of the Left from government the liberalization of the foreign exchange received a further boost: while the 50 per cent deposit system was maintained it was decided that the government would adapt its own rate of exchange to the 'parallel' or black market every month. In practice this meant that the 'political' rate of exchange (i.e. that decided by the government) would follow the market – a clear indication of the subordination of the State to private initiative. This caused a constant devaluation of the lira because the lira dropped in the black market as people preferred to hold dollars. (see Table 1.1).

By 1949 the general situation had improved much in economic and in political terms for the DC, now solidly in control, and the general direction of Italian economic development was clear. At this stage, and at this stage only, controls were imposed. The lira was anchored at 625 lire per dollar and remained there until August 1971 when the entire post-war system of fixed exchange rates collapsed with the American devaluation of the dollar.

TABLE 1.1 Devaluation of the lira, 1945–49

1945	1 dollar = 100 lire
1946 (March)	1 dollar = 225 lire
1947	1 dollar = 350 lire
1949	1 dollar = 625 lire

But why did the lira fall continuously? The chief, but not the sole, reason was that there was a strong inflationary tendency characteristic of the post-war years. What one could have bought for 100 lire in 1938 would have required 858 lire in 1944, 2,060 lire in 1945, 2,884 in 1946 and, 5,159 lire in 1947. Clearly, inflation was approaching the 'runaway' stage and was jeopardizing the Italian economy. Different strategies were expressed within the ruling coalition. One of the most contentious ones was the proposal to 'change the currency'. The motivation behind this proposal was that one of the liabilities inherited from the fascist administration was the considerable amount of paper currency in circulation.[18] Much of this had been accrued in the hands of individuals through black market dealings. This quantity of uncontrolled cash added considerable fuel to the inflationary process. The proposal coming from the Left was that a new currency should be adopted (i.e. new banknotes) and the operation could be connected to a wealth tax. This would give the State a considerable amount of cash at its disposal which it could use for the financing of reconstruction.[19] Furthermore, this policy would have had the effect of a tax on war profits.[20] Far from being a revolutionary proposal a change of currency had already been implemented in many European countries such as France, Belgium and the Netherlands.[21] However this measure not only would have weakened the middle classes but would have also strengthened the interventionist position of the State and was thus opposed by the neo-liberals whose delaying tactics were fairly successful, and the project was abandoned. Another anti-inflationary policy advocated by the Left and in particular by the communist Finance Minister, Mauro Scoccimarro, was the use of rationing and direct controls (as was being done in the UK under a Labour government). The Treasury Minister, Epicarmo

Corbino, who was a Liberal, advocated instead cuts in public spending. Unable to obtain what he wanted Corbino resigned and this was heralded as a victory for the Left. But the Left too was soon forced to abandon its ministerial positions and this permitted the government to resort to the policies advocated by the new Budget Minister, Luigi Einaudi (who had been until August 1947 Governor of the Bank of Italy). These consisted essentially in a drastic deflation achieved by a harsh credit squeeze. It did stop inflation, although some economists maintain that inflation was on the decrease anyway,[22] but this was achieved at a great cost. A credit squeeze works by having a negative effect on investments, thus Italy was deprived of investments in those very years when top political priority should have been given to the task of post-war reconstruction. The Italian economy was substantially stagnant in the years 1947–50. It began to pick up only after 1950 and this was due essentially to external conditions: the Korean War had given rise to a general expansion of international demand and Italian exporters were able to benefit from this.

Of course the stagnation of 1947–50 was also due, in the final analysis, to international conditions. Priority had been given to the struggle against inflation because inflation was causing the constant depreciation of the Italian currency. The West, ever since the Bretton Woods Conference of 1944, had decided to opt for a system of fixed exchange rates. If Italy, which had been admitted to the International Monetary Fund in 1942, wanted to partake of the benefits of the international economy (i.e. the Western economy) it would have had to play by the rules and maintain the stability of its currency against the dollar.[23] It was thus necessary to deal with inflation in order to stabilize the lira and thus join, although in a subordinate capacity, the international economy.

The victory over inflation and the stabilization of the lira had also important political effects.[24] In the first place it undoubtedly helped the DC to obtain a major victory in the elections of 1948 because the decrease in inflation ensured its growing popularity among the middle classes. The DC was able to obtain this result without endangering the vast support it had among the rural classes, many of whom were still connected to a subsistence agriculture and were not directly affected by the credit squeeze. Finally the credit squeeze hit the bargaining strength of the trade unions. It was thus on the terrain of economic policy that the DC fought, in the post-war period, one of its major victorious battles: it emerged as the party of the middle classes without losing its rural connection. By incorporating the neo-liberal strategy in matters of economic policy it avoided the birth of a rival bourgeois party of the Centre. Furthermore, it defeated the Left not only by expelling it from government and clinching this expulsion with an astounding electoral victory in 1948, but also by working successfully towards the break-up of the hitherto united trade-union movement in the same year. In so doing it established one of the conditions for the remarkable economic development in the 1950s: a low-wage economy.

REFERENCES AND NOTES

1. Graziani, A. (1971) pp.22–3
2. Silva, Francesco and Targetti, Ferdinando (1972), p. 18.
3. Valli, Vittorio (1979), p. 10.
4. Williamson, J. G. (1968), p. 112. See also Valli (1979), pp.11–12.
5. Palmiro Togliatti, speech to the Economic Conference of the PCI, Rome, 21–23 Aug 1945, extracts in Graziani (1971), pp. 111–13.
6. Castronovo, V. (1975), p. 371.
7. This is reported by Emilio Sereni, the communist minister, in his *Il Mezzogiorno all'opposizione,* Turin 1948, pp. 20–1.
8. In Villari, L. (1975), vol. II, pp. 486–7.
9. In Graziani (1971), pp. 126–30.
10. Castronovo (1975), p. 384.
11. Ibid., p. 362.
12. Daneo, C. (1975), p. 248.
13. In Villari (1975), p. 519.
14. Ibid., p. 531
15. Amoroso, B. and Olsen, O. J. (1978), p. 66.
16. Colajanni, N. (1976), p. 15.
17. Carli, G. (1946); now reprinted in Graziani (1971), pp. 113–15.
18. De Cecco, M. (1972), pp. 162–3.
19. Gambino, A. (1975), p. 111.
20. Silva and Targetti (1972), p. 17.
21. Castronovo (1975), p. 362.
22. Silva and Targetti (1972), pp. 18–19.
23. Graziani (1971), p. 30.
24. Castronovo (1975), p. 382.

Chapter 2:

THE POLITICS OF DEVELOPMENT, 1950–1963

During this period the Italian economy grew at a faster rate than it had ever achieved. The growth-rate was such, particularly in the years 1958–63, that this phase became known as 'the economic miracle'. The economic and social transformation this development brought about are of the utmost importance for an understanding of the Italian political system. On the one hand Italy was transformed into a modern industrial state, on the other there was an exacerbation of the duality characteristic of the economy. This phase of growth began with a Christian Democratic Party (DC) solidly entrenched in a position of domination at the centre of political power and ended with that party having to renegotiate and recast its system of alliances by shifting towards the Socialist Party (PSI). It opened with the ideological supremacy of neo-liberal economists and terminated when Italy was about to embark on one of the biggest expansions of the public sector in its history. It opened with the trade unions at the nadir of their power and influence and ended with the unions ready to become one of the central forces of Italian society. It opened with the socialist and communist Left united but excluded from power and ended with a government with a socialist presence but a divided Left.

The years of the 'economic miracle' did not resolve Italy's problems. What they did was to change the country sufficiently to force the political system to reconstitute itself on a new basis of consensus. To understand how this was done and the new range of problems this gave rise to, it will be necessary to examine in this chapter the kind of economic development which occurred and its fundamental features.

It should be stated at the outset that the essential characteristics of this period, namely the growth of the manufacturing sector, the integration of the country in the international economy and the development of rapid urbanization, were general features of all industrialized countries. Italy, in fact, took her part in the post-war expansion which had begun with the Korean War and ended in the first half of the 1960s. What was specific to Italy was the continuation of the duality we have already described in Chapter 1 and the appearance of yet another duality: a profound distortion in consumption patterns. The massive development in private consumption (e.g. household goods) was not matched by a similar growth in collective consumption goods and services such as education, housing, transport and health.

It would, of course, be interesting to speculate what sort of policies could have promoted industrial growth, international integration and urbanization without increasing industrial and territorial dualism. At the time no single political force presented a concrete economic programme which was an authentic alternative to the pattern which prevailed. This does not mean that this programme could not have existed, or that the kind of economic growth Italy did undergo was somehow historically inevitable, or even that no policies were presented which sought to modify this or that aspect of government policies. If we take the example of Japan, a country with which it could be reasonable to compare the Italian economic system as it emerged after the war, it could be possible to point out that Japan did not adopt, in spite of American pressures, free trade. Japan chose economic development on the basis of a strong direction by the State, on the basis of protectionism and of a deliberate compression of private consumption.[1] Japan devoted itself to the production of investment goods and prepared the ground for a staggering growth and its development into a force which could invade the world markets from a position of strength. In so doing Japan built on its previous tradition: the war was for Japan the interruption of an ongoing process. Its old project, the conquest of Asian markets, was fulfilled with a vengeance: not only were the old imperial powers (France and the UK) virtually expelled from these markets, but Japan was also able to challenge in their home territory the great industrial enterprises of Europe and North America.

If we were thus to analyse Italian economic development in terms of economic decisions separate from politics we could construct an alternative scenario for the way in which the Italian economy could have developed. But economic decisions are never taken in isolation from political factors. It was not only the position of Italy in the US sphere of influence which 'forced' the internationalization of the Italian economy. Japan too was in the Western sphere, albeit in a different way. The Italian decision was also determined by a specific geographical position which reduced the availability of export markets to either the Mediterranean or Western Europe. Here again political factors intervened: Italy could not hope to enter the Middle Eastern markets which anyway could not then provide a terrain for expansion. Furthermore, its northern-oriented industries had always considered the northern European sector as their natural outlet. Its history was interconnected with the development of Western capitalism in a way Japanese history was not. The presence of a strong Left in Italy made it difficult to resort to a systematic squeeze on living standards. The work

Contemporary Italy

ethics characteristic of Japanese development were not applicable in Italy. Finally the Europeanization of the Italian economy was seen by Alcide De Gasperi – who was Prime Minister until 1954 and who, with Robert Schuman and Konrad Adenauer, is generally considered as one of the founding fathers of European integration – as a factor guaranteeing the political reliability of Italy within the Western camp.

Italy, however, shared with West Germany and Japan some specific advantages which might explain why the three countries which lost the war were able to overtake all the others in growth-rates in this period: all three countries had a huge reserve of labour.[2] In Japan and Italy this was present in the countryside, in the case of West Germany this was constituted first by East German labour and then by foreign labour. All three countries were able to repress or control their trade-union movements. In the Italian case this repression was done through the division of the trade-union movement along political and religious lines, the use of anti-communism as a weapon in industrial relations (e.g. sacking communist shop stewards) and the use of internal migration as a mechanism militating in favour of low wages. Countries like France and the UK which did not have a huge reserve of labour and which were faced with a stronger trade-union movement did not have the possibilities open to Italian, West German and Japanese decision-makers. In the British case in order to follow a policy of full employment necessary to maintain social peace a low-growth-rate policy was pursued as a means of avoiding inflation and an adverse balance of payments. France did not try to stop growth as much as the UK and paid a heavy price in terms of inflation and a balance of payments crisis which led to the devaluation of the French franc in 1958–59 and which was a contributory factor to the change of regime from the Fourth to the Fifth Republic. The differences in growth-rate can be illustrated with the statistics given in Table 2.1. In the first period (1950–58) the Italian growth-rate is high, but not exceptional, particularly when compared with the second phase where it overtakes West Germany (which is out of phase with the general trend).

Thus we could divide the period into two. The phase which goes from 1950 to 1957 is one of preparation for economic expansion, while the years 1958–63 are the years of fastest economic growth. Until 1958–59 the Italian economy follows the American cycle: when the US rate of growth of the national income goes up (1955, 1959) the Italian rate of growth follows the trend (and so does that of Japan, West Germany and Western Europe in general); when the US rate goes down so do all the others. After 1958–59 there is no relation between the US rate of growth and that of Italy: for instance, between 1959 and 1961 the growth-rate slows down in the USA but reaches new peaks in Italy. This indicates that there is a phenomenon of emancipation of the Italian economy from the American one: partly because Italian trading relations with other countries become relatively more important than the US–Italy

TABLE 2.1 A comparison of economic growth, 1950–63

	Average growth rate (%)	
	1950–58	*1958–63*
Japan	7.3	11.1
West Germany	7.8	5.7
Italy	5.3	6.6
France	4.5	5.6
USA	3.0	4.2
UK	2.3	3.5

Source: OECD, *National Accounts Statistics 1950–1968.* Note that the first figure for Japan refers to the period 1953–58 only and that the first figure for Italy refers to the period 1951–58 only.

one, partly because internal factors (e.g. labour costs) weigh more heavily.[3]

Having established this periodization we can now turn to a more detailed examination of the causes of the so-called economic miracle and the contributions that political decisions made to it.

The most widely-held view is that Italian economic growth was achieved thanks to foreign demand. According to this Italian development was essentially export-led. The increased competitiveness of Italian goods in the international market was achieved because Italian entrepreneurs faced lower labour costs than entrepreneurs in other countries, helped by the low value of the lira. In that period foreign demand did increase and this was due to American aid, American growth-rates and their effect on international demand, as well as technological progress, the cheap price of energy, especially oil, and the development of a mass market for consumption goods. These were factors which were, of course, common to all countries in the West. Italy happened to be favourably situated because, as we have indicated, she was able to control her wages bill.[4]

We shall return to the question of wages, but before this we need to examine the general hypothesis of Italian economic development as being export-led. For this we shall rely on Augusto Graziani's works, the most articulate exponent of this thesis.[5] As we pointed out in Chapter 1, if a country such as Italy wants to be active in the international market she must produce those goods the rich countries want. In order to do so she had to develop, virtually from scratch, the capabilities to compete internationally in the production of mass consumer goods, i.e. cars, light household goods and petrochemical products. The market for these industries was determined internationally. Home demand could not play a leading role, because home demand would depend on high wages and wages in Italy were low. Thus Italy has to develop the economic structure of a rich nation i.e. to produce the same kind of goods as a rich nation, but without having the living standards of a rich country. This is precisely how the industrial dualism of the Italian economy was exacerbated: the gap between exporting firms and home-oriented firms grew. Productivity in the export sector was high (because they faced foreign competition) whereas it was low in the home sector. This can be illustrated by Table 2.2. The food industry was essentially home oriented, the textile industry was at first home oriented and only later joined the export sector, the rest were all export oriented. Because profits were higher in the export sector self-financing was easier, that is, the firms operating in this sector could expand without any major need for loans. The exporting sector needed to maintain a high productivity, hence its investments were all directed towards capital-intensive production and thus did not contribute as much as it could have to an increase in employment. It was the 'backward' sector which really helped to bring down the rate of unemployment. This can be demonstrated by the fact that between 1951 and 1963 employment grew by 100 per cent in the retailing sector, 84 per cent in the building sector, but by only 40 per cent in the manufacturing sector.

TABLE 2.2 Annual growth of hourly productivity, 1953–63

	(%)
Food industry	4.6
Textiles	4.8
Engineering	8.6
Manufacturing	8.7
Chemical	10.8
Vehicle industry	10.9

It is apparent that Graziani's explanation allows us to re-examine the view that it was the poor wages of Italian workers which were the essential fuel behind the 'economic miracle'. It is true that Italian wages were lower than those of many of her international competitors, but they were not uniformly low. Wages in the expanding sector were higher than those in the backward sector: another instance of dualism. But Graziani points out another interesting feature: the growing dualism in the price structure leading to the distortion in consumption we mentioned at the beginning of this chapter. If we examine the internal composition of the aggregate level of prices we find that the prices of goods produced in the 'backward' sector tend to rise more rapidly than the home price of the goods produced in the export sector. This is essentially due to differences in productivity and efficiency. But what are the consequences of this pricing dualism? Graziani points out that the most immediate consequence was that some basic goods (such as meat) were becoming relatively more expensive than non-basic goods (such as television sets). Thus home demand for the goods produced in the dynamic sector increased. This helps to explain a paradox that many visitors to Italy find difficult to understand: the average Italian had a diet which was poorer than that of most workers in other European countries but had the same sort of household goods: cars, transistor radios, vacuum cleaners, television sets, etc. This distortion in prices coupled with the distortion in wages meant that Italian workers were demanding the same goods workers in other countries were demanding, i.e. goods produced in the dynamic sector.

This thesis illustrates rather well the relative integration of the Italian people into the quality of material life which was present in the West and for whom the American pattern of private consumption became the established model. The consequences of this for the territorial dualism which afflicted Italy can be immediately estimated: the North with its industries its mass consumption and its efficient exporting sectors integrated in the world economy represented one pole of development; the other was the South which provided the North with the labour force and was dependent on non-private, i.e. state, forms of accumulation in order to achieve similar standards of living. The importance of explanations such as that provided by Graziani is that they are not simply technical ones: they offer a framework for analysis which can be used to make connections between 'purely' economic factors and social and political ones. Graziani's export-led thesis, however, in spite of its undoubted appeal should be modified for a number of reasons.

First of all – as we shall see – the export-led thesis cannot be sustained for the period 1950–57. The integration of the Italian economy in the international system took some time: there were still protectionist tariffs against a whole range of goods and this favoured the development of exporting industries, while there were lower barriers against the imports competing with the 'backward' sector. After 1957, with the entry of Italy into the EEC, foreign demand becomes of paramount importance. But before then and until then it was home demand which led the way. The real boom in international demand occurs only after 1955, and it takes some time before post-war investment becomes really productive. It also takes some time before the weakness of the labour movement has an effect on the relative level of wages, an effect which is enhanced by the constant growth of productivity. The view that exports were a major cause of the 'miracle' is valid only for the post-1957 period not for 1950–57.[6] In 1958 the value of Italian exports was 4.7 per cent of the total value of all exports of the top fourteen industrialized countries (same as in 1940). But by 1963 this had reached 7.3 per cent.[7]

Furthermore the export-led thesis is also considerably weakened by the fact that the Italian balance of payments on current account (i.e.

goods and services) would have registered a large deficit throughout the period 1953–57 if it had not been for two items not related to the exporting capability of Italian firms: revenue from tourism and income from the money sent back to Italy by Italians working abroad. Despite this Italy suffered an average yearly deficit of over 85 million dollars in the period 1953–57, but this would have been a yearly deficit of 373 million dollars had it not been for foreign tourists and Italian emigrants. There was an average yearly surplus of $258 million in 1958–63, but it would have been an average deficit of $565 million but for tourists and emigrants.[8] It can thus be seen that, in spite of a remarkable growth of Italian industry, the economy as a whole derived considerable benefit from two 'industries', tourism and the export of labour, which are more typical of an underdeveloped country than of a modern advanced industrial country. The significance of these remarks is that they illustrate one of the chief peculiarities of Italian development: it was based in considerable part on the underdeveloped features of the country. These features do not constitute an obstacle to development, but, on the contrary, were part of the conditions for Italian economic growth as it actually took place.

By far the most outstanding 'underdevelopment' feature which served the need of development was the lower level of wages existing in Italy. We have already pointed out that this low level of wages was in part due to the large-scale unemployment existing in the 1950s – an agricultural reserve army of spare labour – and to the consequent weakness of the trade-union movement. This situation had the same effect that an 'incomes policy' would have had. In fact it was only in the 1960s, when Italian wages had reached a European level, that Italian decision-makers started discussing the possibility of introducing an incomes policy. Thus the subsequent attempt to intervene on the level of wages in the 1960s is not due to a sudden conversion to the principles of interventionism, but rather to the fact that the 'incomes policy' in existence was determined by indirect factors. Real wages were stagnant between 1950 and 1954 and between 1956 and 1961. Unemployment, which in 1950 was at 7.8 per cent, had decreased by 1960 only to 7.3 per cent, while the average unemployment in the rest of Europe was only 1.9 per cent, and this in spite of the emigration of 1.7 million Italians.[9]

Of course, low wages by themselves do not explain the competitiveness of Italian exports, let alone Italian economic growth. If that were the case we would not be able to explain why underdeveloped countries which can obviously rely on cheap labour were not able to follow the Italian example. Of the many differences between Italy and underdeveloped countries in general, one of the most significant in the sphere of labour is the fact that the general cultural level of the southern Italian peasant, however low it may appear to some, is already structured by the ethics and the 'mentality' of the technological world. It is this 'cultural' aspect which permitted the transformation of the southern peasant into a high-productivity, assembly-line proletarian in a couple of weeks, whereas such a transformation is unthinkable in a similar space of time in the majority of underdeveloped countries.[10] This cultural adaptability also means that the link between the towns and the countryside is not broken as it is frequently in underdeveloped countries. In the latter the modern sector is an island separated from the traditional sector, in Italy the exchange between city and countryside continues: the washing machines produced by a southerner working in the North can then be bought by his relatives who have remained in the village, and this purchase can be achieved also thanks to the portion of the wages the worker sends back.

The low-wage economy was largely due to the existence of a cheap supply of labour in the South. But this supply did not have 'natural' causes; it was politically determined. One of the features of this political intervention was the agrarian reform of 1950 which resulted from the agrarian revolts of the late 1940s. The agrarian reform was promulgated in 1950 when the government decided to distribute 40,000 hectares of land in Calabria. Another law later in the year redistributed land in all latifundia areas and yet another law established a fund for the rebirth of the South called the *Cassa per il Mezzogiorno.* The agrarian reform can be criticized on many counts: its application was partial because it covered only uncultivated land in the latifundia areas, high compensation was paid to the expropriated. As P. A. Allum has written:' ... it was a political operation to transform a part of the rural proletariat of the agro-towns into peasant proprietors which it hoped would turn them into defenders of the status quo. At the same time, it provided the machinery for their control; the land agencies [i.e. the *Cassa*, DS] were to exercise the new kind of patronage.'[11]

The *Cassa* did not develop the South. In fact it was not meant to do that. What it did was to prepare in the 1950s a reserve of potential labour by using its powers of intervention mainly in favour of what it defined as 'viable' farms. It expanded the market for northern industry by increasing southern incomes through a public works programme and established a new clientele system for the leading party of government, the DC.[12] In the first five years (1950–55) the *Cassa* established infrastructures in favour of agriculture (e.g. land-reclamation projects, subsidies for agrarian reform). The subsequent five years paved the way for the change in policy which resulted in the attempt (in the 1960s) to industrialize the South.[13] Thus throughout the 1950s the South was not conceived of as a terrain for industrialization.

The political reasons for the non-industrialization of the South depended on the assumption that land-owning peasants were more conservative than proletarians. It was thus necessary to keep them on the land and out of the factories. However, such a view, if pushed to the limits would have been disastrous for northern industry which would have been forced to subsidize inefficient farming and which would be deprived of a potential labour force. The government had to perform a delicate balancing act: after all the agrarian reform was conceived as a consensus-seeking operation. Thus the government protected only pre-existing capitalist farms and those created by expropriated landlords and enterprising farmers. Poor peasants, left on too small a parcel of land contributed to the take-off of the Italian economy in the period 1958–63 by massive internal migration. Thus government policy protected a section of the southern population and more or less forced the rest to seek a life away from the land. The strategy of public works programmes which was in the hands of the *Cassa* and other state agencies was meant to consolidate the infrastructures, strengthen the agricultural sector and develop tourism. This was the economic basis for a new coalition of interests in the South. State intervention could be accepted by the North because it developed a market in the South for northern produce without increasing the competitiveness of southern industry. It obtained the favour of southern interests because it helped to expand the building industry and developed a vast network of small peasant properties.

When internal migration soared, the extensive public works programme which had been undertaken on the basis of previous population levels had to be cut down. Furthermore, the population which did not emigrate to the North moved to the coast because it was there that there was more work, whether it was in the tourist sector, in the retail sector or in the small manufacturing sector. The State thus saw its main task as one of creating the infrastructure for private industry. It did not yet act in the South as an entrepreneur, but it helped the development of many small firms. In 1961 60 per cent of those employed in southern industries worked in firms employing less than ten people. This network of small enterprises which grew in the South was thus closely linked to a system of public spending and was hence indebted to local and national political interests.[14] Government action in the South helped the North more than it did the South. The moneys spent on the infrastructure, e.g. motorways, helped northern industries both directly because the North produced the materials used, and indirectly because it gave impetus to the demand for manufactured products (e.g. cars). Furthermore, the entry of southern labour in the public works system, because of the precarious nature of employment in the building and construction industries, left southern labour in a marginalized and exposed position. Those who had left their land to work in one of the *Cassa* projects could not return to it when the project was terminated: they had to move further north. Finally the public spending programme helped to sustain domestic demand for the products of northern industries.[15]

Thus this form of state intervention in the South, like all the previous ones in the preceding 100 years was subordinated to the interests of the ruling industrial economic groups. Both the agrarian reform and the

Cassa's public works programme contributed to the end of the latifundia system, the birth of small-scale peasantry and, hence, to new opportunities for leaving the countryside.[16]

The aggregate effects of state intervention signalled a constant decline in the importance of agricultural production. Even though productivity in agriculture increased by 44 per cent between 1951 and 1967 its proportion of the national income declined constantly: from 20–21 per cent in 1951 to 13–14 per cent in 1967. This decline was accompanied by an unprecedented emigration of agricultural workers: 2.5 million between 1951 and 1967. By 1963 Italy was self-sufficient only in three major agricultural products: rice, fruit and vegetables and wine. She produced less grain than France and West Germany, as well as less meat, milk and sugar.[17] The weakening of agriculture and its cost in terms of balance of payments were thus the counterpart to the low-wages policy of the government.

So far we have done nothing more than to establish the role played by the State in the determination of a low-wage system which permitted Italian entrepreneurs to enjoy a competitive advantage with respect to their foreign competitors. Nevertheless, low wages were not the only element in the growth of exports which, however, was not the only cause of Italian economic development.

The other causes can be established by disaggregating national income statistics.[18] The figures show that between 1951 and 1961 national income grew by 78.3 per cent while consumption grew by only 59.8 per cent. Thus the growth in consumption cannot account for the growth in national income. There must be other factors, namely public spending, exports and gross investments. We have already stated that exports began to play an important role only after 1957–8. When it comes to investments, which grew considerably (138.6% between 1951 and 1961), we must bear in mind that private, profit-seeking investments are due to a growth in demand or, at least to an expected growth in demand. This means that they cannot be classified as the primary cause of growth but, rather, as the result of growth in the national income.

What is it, then, that caused a growth in demand? Apart from foreign demand (which leads to exports) there can only be public spending and state investments, and as public spending did not grow any higher than the national income (i.e. state spending on education, health, armed forces, police, etc.) the central role must have been that of state fixed investment. Let us examine the figures given in Table 2.3. If we average it out we find that the rate of growth of investment in agriculture, housing and transport was a staggering 184 per cent. Let us take each of these sectors in turn:

Agriculture. Investments in agriculture were state investment or state-induced investments directed towards modernization.

Housing. The need for housing was due in part to war damage, in part to urbanization. Yet nearly 40 per cent of investment in housing received

TABLE 2.3 State-fixed investments, 1950–61 (in thousands million lire)

	Av. 1950–51	Av. 1960–61	Growth 1950/51–1960/61 (Absolute)	(%)
Agriculture	242	487	245	101.2
Housing	306	1,008	702	229.4
Transport and communications	278	848	570	205
All other sectors	790	1,610	820	103.8
Stocks	173	316	143	144.8
Total	1,789	4,269	2,480	138.6

state subsidies and the financial control of housing was such that the State was in virtual control of it. The expansion of the building programme was particularly marked in the period 1950–58 (before the export boom began).[19] It is true that the bulk of houses was built by the private sector, but the determinant move was a state initiative; the Housing Plan promulgated in 1949. The effect of the state housing policy was to encourage private investment in housing and much of this was of a speculative nature. It also created a strong link verging on corruption between local authorities and real-estate entrepreneurs. Housing plans were not integrated with public transportation. This meant that land distant from the inner city was not developed, thus forcing up the demand for houses as near as possible to the centre of towns and causing overcrowding.[20] Unlike the UK and the USA there was no major move towards suburban housing. In the UK, suburbs developed in part because of an efficient commuting system based on public transport. In the USA, where public transport was often non-existent, the geography of cities and their specific layout permitted the widespread use of private cars. Neither condition applied to Italy. There was no move towards extensive public housing. State intervention in housing enabled the private sector to take off, but was not coupled with public intervention directed towards improving the negative consequences of these policies.

Transport and communications. This sector includes roads, air transport, railways, radio and television, telephones and the merchant navy which are all state owned or part-owned. Here again public investments led the way and interventions such as the motorway programme gave a formidable impetus to the private sector.

Thus the economic miracle was in large part due to the activity of the

State, not in competition with private enterprise but as a major element in its growth. The influence of neo-liberal thinking could still be felt in the monetary management of the economy and in the Bank of Italy, but for what were essentially political reasons the DC could not behave like a traditional *laissez-faire* political party. It had to use, however reluctantly, what were in fact Keynesian policies of macro-economic intervention. These in turn were not determined by any commitment to a particular economic school, but by the need to establish a solid consensus not only with respect to the private sector but also with respect to large sectors of the population. Anti-communism and religious piety could not be the only cement for the new political and economic power bloc the DC was forming in Italy, jobs had to be found in every village and town. At the same time state intervention did not follow a 'plan' along the French model of indicative planning. The State intervened and massively, but there was no plan. Intervention was conceived as an instrument of social control, as a way of preventing the growth of the Italian Communist Party (PCI), as a way of ensuring the electoral basis of the DC and as a way of providing private enterprise with favourable conditions for growth. In the formation of this new political power bloc the use of the State was essential.

Even though there was no real plan, the concept of planning as such began to make headway. Even in the early 1950s there was a recognition that the spontaneous evolution of the Italian system could not resolve the dualism between North and South. It was in this context that the left wing of the DC succeeded in preparing in 1954 the so-called Vanoni Plan (from the name of the Minister under whose auspices the plan was prepared, Ezio Vanoni). Rather than a plan this was a document which established three general objectives for the next ten years[21]:

1. The creation of 4 million new jobs in the non-agricultural sector.
2. The narrowing if not the outright elimination of the income differential between North and South.
3. Equilibrium in the balance of payments.

In order to reach these objectives the economy would have had to grow by at least 5 per cent a year. In fact the economy grew by a rate slightly over 5 per cent, and the balance of payments was in equilibrium after 1958. However, non-agricultural employment grew by only 2.6 million units and the gap between North and South was as wide as ever: southern per capita income as a percentage of average per capita income was 62.7 per cent in 1951 and 62 per cent in 1963.

The interventions of the State through the Istituto per la Ricostruzione Industriale (IRI) and the Ente Nazionale Idrocarburi (ENI) – the state hydrocarbon company – and the abolition of all protective tariffs in 1957 which culminated in Italy's entry into the EEC had far more effect than the planners. In order to eliminate the gap between North and South something more than the good intentions of the Vanoni Plan would have been necessary: namely that the rate of growth of southern incomes be twice as big as the rate of growth of northern incomes (i.e. 8% against 4%). In order to achieve this, total investment in the South would have had to have been twice as large as investment in the North.[22] This would have entailed the most rapid and intense industrialization of the South. Only a command economy could have accomplished that in the 1950s in Italy. Only a different model of development could have achieved the ambitious objectives of the Vanoni Plan, but this would have required a quite different political framework. In the circumstances the Vanoni Plan remained a dead letter. The State, however, already controlled much of the 'commanding heights' of the economy through the expanding system of state holdings. In 1952 IRI was in control of the three 'banks of national interests' and hence of the foundations of the banking system. Furthermore, it controlled 60 per cent of cast iron and iron mineral production, 60 per cent of armaments and munitions, 25 per cent of precision engineering, 25 per cent of electricity, 60 per cent of the telephone system and the Radiotelevisione Italiana (RAI) (then still the only radio broadcasting system, television was introduced later under the RAI). By 1955 IRI had 187,000 employees as well as a vast number of shareholdings in private firms from chemicals to paper and printing, from building to motorways and hotels.[23]

By 1962 IRI was the second industrial group in Europe, second only to the Royal-Dutch-Shell Petroleum Company.[24] At first the expansion of the group followed the principles of intervening to save private firms from bankruptcy. It was the creation of ENI in 1953 which forced IRI to adopt a more dynamic posture.

The motivation for the establishment of ENI differed markedly from the reason behind the establishment of IRI: IRI had been conceived by the Fascist State as a temporary 'rescue' operation, while ENI was founded in order to give the State the exclusive rights over the extraction of methane gas in the Po Valley. The opposition of private enterprise was very strong, since this was the first time the State had attempted to acquire full control over a natural resource. The form of this intervention was a company entirely owned by the State. Ente Nazionale Idrocarburi was led by an imaginative and dynamic man, Enrico Mattei, a former Resistance partisan and a member of the DC. Mattei had been able to use his connections within the left wing of the DC to protect ENI, but quickly and thanks to the considerable political and economic resources at his disposal he was able to become relatively autonomous from the State. With the birth of ENI, the Italian state-holding form of public intervention becomes an authentic *system* of state participation in industry, the so-called 'parastate' system. The expansion of this system coincided with the rapid period of growth of the Italian economy: in 1959 one-fifth of all investments came from this sector, by 1962 it accounted for one-fourth of all investments and for one-third by 1964.[25] Ente Nazionale Idrocarburi expanded horizontally, particularly in sections of the economy which were controlled by only one or two private firms who were therefore less able to monopolize the market. Hence ENI also fulfilled the function of anti-trust legislation.[26]

The political autonomy of IRI and ENI was quite clear with regard to Parliament and government. However, they worked in close connection with the DC, exploiting its factional struggle. Furthermore, because they provided considerable employment and commanded enormous resources, they also provided a terrain for the expansion of party clienteles and the share-out of jobs and positions both within the parties of the governing coalition (i.e. the parties of the Centre until 1963) and within the factions of the DC. Thus the guarantee of the permanence of the system of state participation was increasingly connected with the permanence of the DC at the centre of the political system.

There was little cooperation or organic connection between ENI and IRI, and neither of them became the vanguard of Italian industrial growth. However, Italy derived considerable benefits from them. Thanks to ENI's attempt to bypass the oil cartel of the seven largest international oil companies, Italy was able to negotiate direct deals with oil-producing countries and thus obtain access to sources of cheap oil, one of the fundamental conditions for European economic growth. Moreover, ENI and IRI reorganized the port of Genoa, strengthened the industrialization of north-eastern Italy (the triangle Venice–Mestre–Porto Maghera, one of the centres of the petrochemical industry and a DC stronghold), strengthened steel production on the north-western Tirreno coast and petrochemicals in Sicily.[27] All this, however, was done in a haphazard way and without any clear national plan for economic development. The achievement of ENI and IRI was that they succeeded in establishing those industrial infrastructures (cheap steel, cheap petrochemicals, a motorway system, cheap energy) which allowed rapid Italian economic growth. As the President of the Banca Commerciale (one of the big three banks) Raffaele Mattioli wrote in 1962:

> One of the most remarkable achievements of IRI was this: ... IRI, without any expropriation or nationalizations has saved the whole of free enterprise. Practically without noticing it, IRI as it consolidated itself and expanded the field controlled permanently by the State has protected and ensured the effective and long-term survival of private enterprise.[28]

Thus the public sector, instead of competing against private monopolies and/or adopting a strategy in favour of collective needs, ensured instead the expansion of the private sector.[29] The other economic instruments at the disposal of the State, such as monetary policy and fiscal policy could not be used or were not used in favour of economic growth.

Monetary policy formally depends on the Treasury, but is in practice under the control of the Bank of Italy which not only is very independent from the State but is also run by anti-interventionists. After the deflation of 1947 which contributed to the end of the post-war inflationary spiral and which helped to ensure a regime of low wages, the Bank of Italy continued its restrictive policy until 1955. Between 1955 and 1963 monetary policy was less restrictive. This, in fact, did not matter very much: a restrictive monetary policy seeks to influence interest rates on the assumption that high interest rates will contain demand and thus help to reduce inflation and/or will benefit the balance of payments. This depends, however, on the centrality of interest rates and hence of bank lending as the fuel with which to activate economic growth. By the mid-1950s, however, the level of profitability was so high in the private sector that much of new investment was due to the reinvestment of existing profits. In other words firms did not borrow as they were able to generate the money internally. Thus monetary policy neither helped nor was it an obstacle to economic growth.[30]

Monetary policy comes into its own only as a counter-cyclical policy, i.e. when the economy moves into a depression. This happened when the 'economic miracle' came to a close in 1963 and the authorities counter-attacked with a harsh deflation. As for fiscal policy it has proved to be a most unreliable instrument in Italy mainly because direct taxation, not being very progressive, has little automatic anti-inflationary effects (progressive taxation has an automatic anti-inflationary bias because as incomes are pushed up by inflation a greater proportion of wages and salaries are hit by taxation. This reduces the proportion of disposable income, hence reduces the growth of private consumption and hence of demand). This disadvantage could have been partially removed by a prompt intervention of the fiscal authorities, but the fact that the burden of taxation in the Italian case takes the form of indirect taxation removes from fiscal policies much of their clout. This also means that profits and incomes from rents and self-employment are not hit as much as they should be, not least because there is widespread evasion. Again this is not a 'natural' factor. It is, rather, a conscious decision of the authorities. The tax-evaders are on the whole the professional bourgeoisie, the small-and medium-size entrepreneurs as well as speculators and real-estate operators who constitute one of the central foundations of the social and electoral base of the DC.[31] It is thus essentially for political reasons that monetary policy has been the privileged instrument of economic policy of the Italian authorities. It must be added that most European countries too favoured monetary controls, particularly Belgium and West Germany, while the UK stood out alone for relying heavily on fiscal manipulation. Other countries adopted some elements of planning either by sponsoring investments (France) or some forms of incomes policy (Sweden, the Netherlands).[32]

We have so far illustrated the State's contribution to economic growth and sought to account for the kind of intervention and 'non-intervention' that paved the way for the 'economic miracle'. At least until 1960 there was very little opposition to the government on the labour front. The Left, excluded from power and increasingly divided could do very little. The trade unions were divided too and had to face the ever-growing influx of non-unionized labour from the countryside and a level of unemployment which constituted a formidable obstacle for an active and dynamic labour movement. But what of private enterprise? While from the tehnical and economic point of view it was able to modernize itself and to become more efficient and more productive, the same cannot be said for its politics. Its fundamental outlook was profoundly anti-trade union, an understandable policy but also a short-sighted one for it should have realized that Italian trade unions would eventually be able to reassert themselves, particularly as the era of massive unemployment was coming to an end and the southern reserve of labour was being reduced. The only long-term trade-union policy private industry adopted was that of trying to deepen the divisions within the labour movement: it sought to strengthen the Catholic trade union (the CISL) and the social-democratic one (the UIL) against the CGIL (socialist and communist) by sacking communist shop stewards and trade unionists or shifting them to the most demanding jobs or to self-enclosed sections of the plants.

The short-sightedness of Italian entrepreneurs also manifested itself in their policies with respect to the parastate sector: it opposed ideologically any extension of the State in the economy. We have already mentioned in Chapter 1 the Sinigaglia Plan on steel which encountered the outright opposition of the employers' association, the Confindustria, and of the steel tycoon Giorgio Falck. Such opposition grew as Enrico Mattei, the chairman of ENI, decided to expand horizontally into territory dominated by the giant Montecatini: petrochemicals, plastic and synthetic rubber. The Confindustria even allied itself with the seven giant oil companies, the 'Seven Sisters', against ENI when this moved into oil.[33] Yet, as we have seen, the growth of the state sector was to the economic advantage of private enterprises or, at least, of some of them. By the end of this period of exceptional growth the Italian economy was dominated by giant private firms: Edison in electricity, Fiat in cars, Olivetti in typewriters and office machines, Pirelli in rubber products, Snia Viscosa in textiles, Montecatini in chemicals.

The process of economic concentration which accompanied this growth also took the form of transforming many small- and medium-sized firms into real dependencies of the large firms. This was the case particularly in the car industry dominated by Fiat. In fact any study on political power in Italy must give a major place to Fiat which in this period became a vast empire whose economic decisions would influence politics as well as economics. In the first place Fiat increased production by 400 per cent between 1950 and 1961; it was an authentic monopolist as it controlled 90 per cent of car sales in Italy (no single car-manufacturing company in the world had such a formidable base in its home market). Productivity at Fiat increased by 126 per cent between 1950 and 1960.[34] These figures still do not give us an idea of the political power wielded by Fiat. Let us then consider the economic/political effect of Fiat's most important decision: the mass production of the Fiat '600' in 1953. The chain reaction is remarkable: it has been calculated that by 1963 20 per cent of investments in sectors other than the car-manufacturing one were directly due to Fiat. Not only small- and medium-sized firms were affected but also large ones: ENI, the steel industry, chemicals. Every 1,000 lire produced by Fiat generated an increment of production of nearly 2,000 lire in the economy as a whole and an increase in exports of 210 lire.[35] As the car industry expanded it produced greater demand for motorways, for oil, plastics, rubber, steel. In a sense it could be said that Fiat 'planned' the Italian economy. Furthermore, Japanese cars were successfully kept out of Italy until the 1980s.

Finally, profits between 1953 and 1960 increased by 45 per cent in the car industry and by 54 per cent in the chemical industry which thus established themselves as the leading sectors because the average growth of profit for that period was 28 per cent. But it must not be thought that the development of the Italian economy was a great victory for private capitalism alone. They and the state sectors were not the only forces which were the protagonists of the 'miracle'. Landed property and real-estate companies grew in unison with private industrial capital and became ever more intertwined with it.

Profits grew so rapidly in that period that not all entrepreneurs reinvested them in industry, many sought to use them for speculative reasons in the land and housing market. This was also true of self-employed professionals who had a considerable amount of cash at their disposal thanks to widespread tax evasion. At the same time thanks to urbanization there was a constantly growing demand for houses in urban centres. We have already explained that, unlike the UK and the USA, urban centres were the most sought-after place of residence. This means that housing decreases in value in proportion to its distance from the centre. As the city expands the value of the agricultural land immediately surrounding it becomes more expensive because it is in the front line of future housing investment. As it is sold by farmers and bought by real-estate speculators it provokes 'ripple' effects in both directions: it forces up land and house values all the way to the centre of the city as well as the value of the outlying agricultural land. Thus the layout of the city reflects the class structures: in the centre, the rich and professional bourgeoisie and top bureaucrats, then in successive concentric circles those employed in the tertiary sector of the economy, white-collar workers, then factories and factory workers living in public housing and then, finally, the agricultural areas and the farmers.[36] Of course this is the general pattern: rent control legislation ensured that there were still pockets of low-income families living in the centre of cities, but there was certainly no room for the masses of agricultural workers who arrived in the urban conurbation to find work.

This process of private funding of housing with state and local subsidies as well as tax concessions contributed to the asymmetrical development of luxury housing against housing for low-income groups. This is understandable in the absence of a determined effort by central government for a more balanced approach to housing: to build a luxury house in the centre of town creates proportionately more profits than houses for industrial workers. Thus the years of the 'economic miracle' if they were good years for industrialists were golden years for real-estate entrepreneurs. We mentioned that profits between 1953 and 1960 for the car and petrochemical industries increased by about 50 per cent, but average rents in the whole of the country increased by 100 per cent and in northern urban areas they increased by 300 per cent. This occurred in a period when retail food prices increased by 33 per cent and wholesale prices by 13 per cent.[37] Wages in the non-agricultural sector, on the other hand, increased by 23 per cent between 1955 and 1960.[38] This was the economic balance sheet of the relation of forces in Italian society as the 'economic miracle' was drawing to a close.

REFERENCES AND NOTES

1. De Cecco, M. (1971).
2. Salvati, M. (1973).
3. D'Antonio, M. (1973), pp. 12–14.
4. Castronovo, V. (1975), p. 408.
5. Graziani, A. *et al.* (1969); see also Graziani (1969); and his introduction in Graziani (1972). The export-led model is based on the pioneering work of Kindleberger, C. P. (1964). The best application of the export-led model to Italy available in English is Stern, R. M. (1967).
6. Salvati, M. (1977), p. 103.
7. Castronovo (1975), p. 407.
8. My figures on the basis of the discussion and the figures in D'Antonio (1973), p. 202.
9. Castronovo (1975), p. 407.
10. De Cecco (1971), p. 982.
11. Allum, P. A. (1972), pp. 118–19.
12. D'Antonio (1973), p. 236.
13. Ibid, p. 238.
14. Graziani (1972), pp. 55–7.
15. Fabiani, G. (1977), p. 158.
16. D'Antonio (1977), pp. 49–50.
17. Coda-Nunziante, G. and De Nigris, M. (1970), pp. 200–5, also in Graziani (1972), pp. 174–7.

18. The following remarks and discussion on the composition of investments are based on a memorandum by G. Ackley published for the first time in Graziani (1972), pp. 156–65. Michele Salvati (1977, p. 104) makes the same points.
19. Castronovo (1975), p. 404.
20. See Graziani (1972), p. 20.
21. Valli, V. (1979), p. 110.
22. C. Napoleoni in Graziani (1972), p. 201.
23. Castronovo (1975), p. 422.
24. Ibid. p. 425.
25. Colajanni, N. (1976), pp. 17–18.
26. Castronovo (1975), p. 422.
27. Ibid., p. 426.
28. Quoted in Villari, L. (1975), vol. 2, p. 672
29. Castronovo (1975), p. 480.
30. D'Antonio (1977), p. 44.
31. Ibid., p. 46.
32. Aldcroft, D. H. (1978), p. 190.
33. Castronovo (1975), p. 421.
34. Figures in Castronovo (1975), pp. 429–30.
35. Ibid., p. 431.
36. Silva, F. and Targetti, F (1972), p. 24.
37. Figures in Castronovo (1975), pp. 419–20.
38. Figures calculated on the basis of ILO (1965).

Chapter 3

FROM 'MIRACLE' TO CRISIS, 1963–1969

The crisis of the system of alliances based on the centrist coalition of the Christian Democratic Party (DC) begins not after the end of the 'economic miracle', but in the middle of it. Towards the end of the 1950s the DC sought an increased cooperation with the Socialist Party (PSI) whose pact of unity with the Communist Party (PCI) had been rescinded following the events of 1956 (de-Stalinization and the Soviet invasion of Hungary). Fearing a coalition government centred on an alliance between the PSI and the DC, the Liberal Party forced a government crisis in February 1960 with the open intention of sabotaging the negotiations and strengthening the right wing of the DC. In April of that year Fernando Tambroni formed a government entirely made up of Christian Democrats. In the Chamber of Deputies that government was able to obtain a majority only thanks to the support of the Monarchist Party and of the neo-fascists. Throughout Italy there was a strong popular reaction led by communists and socialists. The police reacted and fired on the crowd in several cities. The Tambroni government fell thus demonstrating the impossibility of reorganizing the alliance system of the DC on the basis of support from the Right. Thus there could now be only one solution: the 'opening to the left,' i.e. a DC–PSI coalition. These were the main steps towards the 'Centre-Left' government:

1. 22 July 1960: Amintore Fanfani (DC) forms his third government with the external support in Parliament of republicans and social democrats (i.e. these parties still vote for the government but without being in it). At the last minute the PSI abstains.
2. March 1961: the Congress of the PSI approves an 'opening to the left'.
3. January 1962: the Congress of the DC approves an 'opening to the left'.
4. February 1962: Amintore Fanfani forms his fourth government with the abstention of the PSI.
5. 21 September 1962: the Chamber of Deputies approves the bill

      nationalizing the electricity industry: it is the *de facto* sign that the new coalition can work.

6. A counter-offensive by the right wing of the DC following the increase in communist votes at the elections of April 1963. Fanfani and Aldo Moro (the leading proponents of the Centre-Left) try and fail to form a new government because of PSI reaction.
7. Transitional government led by Giovanni Leone made up of Christian Democrats only (Summer 1963).
8. October 1963: PSI Congress approves the formation of Centre-Left government.
9. 4 December 1963: The new Centre-Left government coalition is launched. The Prime Minister is Aldo Moro, the deputy Prime Minister is Pietro Nenni leader of the PSI. The left wing of the PSI forms a new party, the Socialist Party of Proletarian Unity (PSIUP).

Thus it took more than three years from the opening of the negotiations to change the dominant coalition. The dates we have given show that the initial impulse for this process of realignment cannot be traced to the end of the 'economic miracle'. Nevertheless, there is no doubt that one of the causes of the move away from the centrist coalition which dominated Italy since 1947 was the fact that the revitalization of the trade-union movement in 1960 showed that it was necessary to reconstitute the Italian political system in a way which would divide the Left. The incorporation of the socialists in the sphere of government as junior partners in a coalition in which two minor parties would also be present (the Republican Party and the Social Democratic Party) meant that the DC was prepared to share some of the power it had accumulated with others, if, by doing so, it could be guaranteed the continuation of its position of centrality in the political arena. The isolation of the communists was one of the aims of the formation of the new coalition, but as the 'economic miracle' was coming to an end it became increasingly clear that the process of economic development had left open a number of problems and questions whose resolution entailed the expansion of the social basis of government.

That the existence of unresolved problems was an acknowledged fact can be seen by looking at the literature of the period. In their book *Ideas for Economic Planning* two of the leading theorists of the Centre-Left coalition, Giorgio Fuà and Paolo Sylos-Labini pinpoint the problems with great accuracy.[1] They recognize that among the achievements of the 1950–63 period there was the fact that unemployment, had, by 1963, been tackled fairly successfully. Nevertheless, there existed a number of structural distortions which pervade all fields of economic activity, from agriculture to the structure of employment, from the pattern of consumption to the differential in incomes between the various regions of the country, from the retail sector to industry. The data confirm the existence and persistence of this gap, whether we look at incomes, production or productivity. Besides these well-known structural problems there also was a new problem, namely an inflationary tendency: in 1960 it was 2.7 per cent, in 1961 2.8 per cent, in 1962 5.1 per cent and in 1963 7.6 per cent. Furthermore, even though total productivity in manufacturing industry grew at a rapid pace for the first time since the war such growth was inferior to the growth of total wages (i.e. basic wages plus any addition to the pay packet due to productivity bonuses, overtime, etc.).[2] What this means is that the existing link between productivity and wages had been broken. Until then it was necessary for wages to grow at a lower rate than productivity so that the subsequent growth of profits could finance the improvements in plants and machinery and hence productivity. The only way open for an increase in both wages and productivity is through technological innovation. But for the Italian economy, open to the world as it was and is, this is an expensive strategy: technological progress is an external factor because Italy imports know-how; innovations come from outside, they have to be paid for, outside, deepening Italy's dependence on international constraints.[3]

Thus the crisis which underlined the political realignment to the left had not only structural aspects but also contingent ones: a crisis of profitability which led to the end of the self-financing of enterprises. The revival of working-class militancy had led to a profit squeeze. In 1962 the trade unions had sufficiently recovered their strength (partly due to the full employment conditions achieved in the North) to obtain the first large-scale wage rises since the post-war period: while the average annual increase in wage rates was around 4.4 per cent in the 1954–61 period, it jumped to 10.7 per cent in 1962 and to 14.7 per cent the following year. So far we have listed some of the problems which had been singled out by the decision-makers and which had been used in order to promote a realignment of political forces.

Let us now examine the elements which brought the 'economic miracle' to an end in greater detail. It has been suggested that one of the causes of the end of the 'miracle' was the fact that Italy had reached a situation of full employment. Yet in 1963 Italy still had 2.5 per cent unemployment and if we compare Italian developments with West Germany and the UK we can see that it had still a relatively high level of spare labour (see Table 3). What these figures do not show and cannot show are changes in 'disguised' unemployment, i.e. that the decrease in unemployment is due not to the growth of employment but to the lowering of the participation of the population in the labour force (e.g. women abandoning the labour force) or due to the increase in emigration facilitated by the free market of labour established by the EEC. In other words the increase in wages was not due to full employment *per se*, but to the fact that emigration deprived the Italian North of a proportion of the reserve male labour force.[4]

Furthermore, there was a downturn in Italian agriculture and contraction in employment in sectors such as clothing and shoe

TABLE 3.1 Unemployment (percentages)

Year	West Germany	United Kingdom	Italy
1955	5.1	1.1	7.6
1956	4.0	1.2	9.4
1957	3.4	1.5	8.2
1958	3.5	2.0	6.6
1959	2.4	2.2	5.6
1960	1.2	1.6	4.2
1961	0.8	1.5	3.5
1962	0.7	2.0	3.1
1963	0.8	2.4	2.5
1964	0.7	1.7	2.7

Source: ILO (1965).

manufacturing. This meant that employment decreased in sectors employing marginalized and casual labour while employment increased in the 'modern' sectors which were better organized from a trade-union point of view. It is this pattern in the labour market which caused the upturn in wages.[5] We can also look at it from another point of view: as women left the labour force, families depended increasingly on a single breadwinner, usually male, and this stimulated the militancy of the male labour force. So when we say that full employment had been reached we should amend it by emphasizing that full employment had been reached in the North, among the male labour force and in the advanced sectors of the economy. Table 3.2 shows the effects of this renewal of trade-union militancy on wages. As we can see there were two wage explosions in this period, 1969 and 1970, both due to the trade-union militancy of the preceding year.

The effect of the strikes of 1962 was to diminish the effectiveness of one of the conditions which had made Italian enterprises competitive: low wages. Hitherto Italian enterprises had been able to increase production through an increase in employment, now there was essentially only one avenue open (apart from causing a slow-down in wage increases in a tightening labour market): the expansion of production through an expansion in productivity. Wages in 1962 and 1963 had for the first time outstripped productivity: the answer of Italian capitalism in the successive years would be to try to increase productivity without increasing employment. What the period 1963–69 showed was that it was no longer possible to solve the problems of the Italian economy thanks to the passivity of the labour movement.

Italy had entered the EEC with some clear structural handicaps: constant emigration, scarcity of primary products, particularly sources of energy, low productivity in agriculture and poor technology. This was compensated by the ability of Italian entrepreneurs to contain costs

TABLE 3.2 The effects of trade-union militancy on wages 1960–71

Year	Yearly percentage of increase in		Million of hours lost in strikes
	Real Wages	Money wages	
1960	5.4	10.8	46.3
1961	5.9	11.1	79.1
1962	6.9	16.4	181.7
1963	11.1	21.6	91.2
1964	7.1	11.9	104.7
1965	4.1	5.5	55.9
1966	4.9	6.9	115.8
1967	5.1	10.6	68.5
1968	5.9	8.7	83.9
1969	5.4	10.1	302.6
1970	14.09	16.9	146.2
1971	9.14	15.1	103.6

Source: Based on data from ISTAT.

thanks to the low level of technological innovation necessary to produce household electrical goods and other Italian exports, and thanks to low wages.[6] This, however, left Italy dangerously exposed to foreign competition from some Third World countries (which could compete on the terrain of low technology and cheap labour), and from the advanced countries (which were able to impose a much stricter connection between exporting ability and technological progress, e.g. Japan and West Germany).[7] Italy resorted to a dual strategy – deflation and state intervention.

While the new ruling coalition was planning a systematic intervention in the economy using all the instruments available as well as planning the creation of new ones, the Bank of Italy – always in charge of monetary policy – was continuing its traditional deflationary line in direct continuity with the Einaudi policies of 1947. In September 1963, less than two months before the official entry of the PSI into the governing coalition, the Bank of Italy imposed a harsh credit squeeze. Its effects were immediate. Firms found it more difficult to borrow from the banks. Investment decreased by 8.6 per cent in 1964 and by 7.5 per cent in 1965[8]. Demand decreased and a depression ensued with consequent negative effects on employment which fell by 2.5 per cent by 1965 (by 4% in the industrial sector alone).[9] There was a slow-down in internal migration and a decrease in the share of wages in the Gross National Product (GNP). As usual those firms which were hit the most were those oriented towards the home market, while firms oriented towards exports such as chemicals and engineering were hit the least.[10] Those who favoured the credit squeeze as a way of tackling inflation assumed that inflation was principally due to wage rises and, as the wage rise of 1962–63 seemed to have been a once and for all affair, they assumed that the inflation spiral was a short-term phenomenon which could be contained by a drastic if painful credit squeeze. Others believed that inflation and the balance of payments deficit which accompanied it were due to structural imbalances in the Italian economy and the lack of planning. Among the latter we find the chief sustainers and proponents of the Centre-Left.

From the point of view of the authorities the credit squeeze had had the merit of slowing down inflation, readjusting the balance of payments and, more importantly, dampening down the militancy of the trade unions which renewed the labour contracts of 1966 with remarkable acquiescence. Nevertheless, it had become accepted in government circles that it was necessary to initiate some form of planning. Readers will recollect that the Vanoni Plan of 1954 (see Ch. 2) had remained a dead letter; however, planning as a concept had not been completely abandoned and even before the formal launching of the Centre-Left, the Budget Minister, Giuseppe Pella, nominated in March 1961 a commission chaired by G. U. Papi which included both entrepreneurs and trade unionists. This was the beginning of a long saga of attempted planning which we shall try to summarize.

The Papi Commission was based on the concept of indicative planning which involved the projection of future public spending and state intervention so that entrepreneurs could tailor their plans in accordance with expected government policy. By August 1962 the framework established for the Papi Commission was abandoned as inadequate for the kind of intervention the economy required. The new Budget Minister, the republican Ugo La Malfa, in a famous 'Note' appended to his main report identified three structural imbalances in the Italian economy: between agriculture and industry, between North and South and between public and private consumption. To resolve these imbalances the following framework was suggested[11]:

1. To cut down on funds given to projects which did not expand productive capacity (e.g. public housing).
2. To increase forced saving through taxation.
3. To plan the quantity and the direction of both private and public investment.
4. To obtain the cooperation of the trade-union movement for a policy of wage restraint in exchange for an improvement in social services (a proposal which would have required, presumably, a modification of item 1).

This was the first time that a leading government spokesman discussed the structural problems of the Italian economy and proposed ways of eliminating them. The domination of liberal economists seemed to have come to an end. La Malfa nominated three commissions: one to deal with tax reforms, one to deal with monopolies and the third was to become the foremost planning body to be chaired by Pasquale

Saraceno, a Catholic economist deeply committed to planning. The following may give the reader an idea of the saga of Italian planning in the 1960s.

The Saraceno Commission met throughout 1963 and included among its members experts, industrialists and trade unionists. By January 1964 the report was ready and the new Budget Minister, the socialist Antonio Giolitti, accepted it in June 1964. The plan, now called the Giolitti Plan could not be approved in Parliament because, by then, there had been a change in government. Finally the new government (still a Centre-Left coalition) appointed a new Budget Minister, Giovanni Pieraccini, who accepted the plan in 1966. This plan, now the Pieraccini Plan, was approved by Parliament in July 1967 even though the plan was for the five years from 1966 to 1970. The Pieraccini Plan went beyond the framework established by La Malfa: it dealt not only with the 'three structural imbalances' but also with the question of 'social investments' (e.g. health and education). The aims of the Pieraccini Plan were the following:

1. Full employment. This would entail an increase in the non-agricultural labour force of 1.4 million.
2. The increase in the rate of growth of agricultural production and the narrowing of the gap between farm and non-farm incomes.
3. The reduction of territorial imbalance through the creation of a proportionately greater number of industrial jobs in the South than in the North.
4. A new pattern of employment which would favour the satisfaction of collective needs over private ones.

In order to achieve this it would be necessary to have an annual increase in incomes of 5 per cent while maintaining price stability, balance of payment equilibrium and free trade. The plan had not been conceived as a self-contained piece of legislation. It was the equivalent of a new economic deal, an attempt to reverse the direction of economic affairs by obtaining the consensus of those strata which had not significantly benefited from the 'economic miracle'. It signified, in other words, a fundamental change in economic conception symbolized by the debate over the interpretation of Article 81 of the Constitution. This article established that any bill entailing new expenditure must indicate how the money was to be raised. Until 1961 the ruling interpretation was the liberal one, namely, that there could be no deficit spending, in other words the government could not borrow in order to cover the proposed expenditure except in the short term (i.e. until 'real money' would be raised from, say, taxation). The liberal economist and politician Luigi Einaudi had asked for the insertion of this paragraph specifically in order to ensure that politicians would not seek popularity and votes through the use of public expenditure.[12] In 1961 this would be challenged by the Keynesian-interventionist front led by La Malfa. The new interpretation asserted that a balanced budget could be obtained through deficit spending provided this sought to stimulate the use of unused national resources, thus increasing the wealth of the nation and, indirectly, the Treasury.[13]

Savers, however, were deserting the national money market and were beginning to send their money abroad. So at one and the same time the State found that it needed to borrow considerable sums and that savers were not forthcoming with the cash. What was needed was a new system to channel funds into banks and direct them towards both public and private investments. The State, now committed to planning, could have created a new institution which would have supervised the financial intermediaries (banks and financial institutions). No such institution was created. Instead the defeated neo-liberals inside the Bank of Italy were able to ensure that the control of the financial system would remain in the hands of the Bank of Italy.[14] Thus the planning debate of the early 1960s was resolved with a political compromise and, although the planners seemed to emerge as the victors, the neo-liberals kept a right of veto through their control of the financial system. The effects of the compromise were, as we have seen, the apparent contradiction between the policies of a centre-left government, which sought to intervene in a reforming direction and the credit squeeze of 1963 imposed by the Bank of Italy. Short-term policy remained under the control of the conservative elements (the anti-interventionist neo-liberals), the long term was left to the reformists: the 'future' not the present was to be planned by the Left. Unable to establish any links between the present and the future, between short-term crisis management and long-term economic restructuring, the Centre-Left government was never able to implement its proposed reforms except for the nationalization of electricity. But even this reform resulted in an unexpected compromise between reformists and anti-planners: generous cash payments for the shares hitherto held by the electricity companies.[15]

The vast amount of cash thus generated provided the impetus for a spate of mergers and take-overs. The creation of the new state electricity company (ENEL) brought the telephone system under state ownership. Then ENEL began to diversify outside the electricity sector and to behave as another state holding company: it acquired shareholdings in Olivetti and in Montedison (itself a result of the 1966 merger between the chemical giant Montecatini and the former electricity giant Edison). Thus the formation of ENEL gave added impetus to the expansion of the state-holding system, gave rise to a new generation of state entrepreneurs whose names would dominate Italian industry in the 1960s and 1970s: Giuseppe Petrilli, Pietro Sette and Eugenio Cefis. At the same time the DC extended its control over the state sector partly because its base in agriculture was decreasing and partly because control over a sector of industry could help the party to satisfy the employment aspirations of migrant workers from the South.[16] Thus a reform which would have had to play a leading role in the restructuring of the Italian economic system, played a far more decisive role in the expansion of the power of the DC.

The interconnection between political power and economic intervention is just as visible in the domain of state intervention in agriculture. The first agricultural plan, or 'Green Plan,' was promulgated in June 1961. Its aims were to consolidate efficient farms and to raise both productivity *and* employment on the land – an absurdity in the conditions of the time.[17] The sums which the State was ready to provide were very large. Nevertheless, small farmers were unable to make ends meet and still found it preferable to leave their lands and go to the cities to find employment. Thus the first Green Plan did not achieve its formal objectives: what it did was to enable some southern farmers to survive and thus contain the flood of emigration. In any case the solution of the 'Southern Question' could not be seen purely in terms of agriculture, but only in terms of the correct relation between agriculture and industry. Thus two possible strategies were discussed in the early 1960s:

1. Agriculture as the foundation of economic development.
2. Agriculture to be subordinated to export-oriented firms. This assumed that international demand would go on expanding.

It was this second strategy which was adopted. Agricultural productivity would grow not because of structural intervention in agriculture, but simply because internal emigration would continue towards export-oriented firms. Public .expenditure would ensure the localization of industry in the strongest areas while agriculture would be helped only where it was already efficient (as in the first Green Plan).

As we stated in the preceding chapters the agrarian reform of 1950 had resulted in the development of small private holdings. The reform and subsequent funding had also enabled the old agrarian classes to transform themselves into capitalist farmers. They managed to retain a modicum of competitiveness within the EEC even though they were unable to meet national needs. What happened in the 1960s is that international factors became even more important for agriculture. The development of the Common Market Common Agricultural Policy (CAP) had a decisive impact in Italy. The CAP's pricing policy is applied throughout the Common Market in a homogeneous manner, but its effects are very differentiated: it affects farms of varying sizes in different ways.[18] The effects of the CAP are even more serious in Italy because, unlike other European countries (especially France and West Germany), Italian agriculture is polarized between many small farms and a few very large farms. Small farmers cannot apply large-scale economies and cannot therefore enjoy the advantages of CAP pricing policies. Furthermore the CAP pricing policy favours crops which can be found in northern and western Europe rather than in Mediterranean Europe. While northern Italian export-oriented industry derived considerable benefits from the EEC, no equivalent benefits were possible for agriculture either in terms of modernization or improvements of agricultural incomes. Furthermore, Italy had to contribute to the agricultural funds and hence to the support of the French and Dutch farm prices where agriculture was and is more efficient than in Italy. The expansion of the EEC regional budget which would devote funds to the poorer areas of Europe was prevented by the opposition of West Germany and France and, in the 1970s, by the increased competition for this fund due to the presence in the EEC of countries with marked regional problems (the UK, Ireland and Denmark).[19] In fact it would be difficult to conceive of a free-trade policy which would not cause an expansion of strong areas and contraction of weak areas.

As a result of these policies thousands of small farms disappeared while the larger farms increased their size by a total of 800,000 hectares. In 1950 the agrarian reform had distributed 700,000 hectares, taking them away from the landlord.[20] Ten to twenty years later these were won back by those same landlords now transformed into capitalist farmers.

The subordination of agricultural development to industrial development was no longer the unintended effect of the *laissez-faire* of the 1950s. It had now become the overt strategy of the interventionism of the 1960s. This new strategy entailed a novel approach towards the South: industrialization. The new industrial policy for the South had two political motivations:

1. To enable local entrepreneurs to become fully-fledged industrialists instead of remaining craftsmen or farmers.
2. To attract northern investment.[21]

This new strategy was based on a system of incentives which established in the South favoured areas of development in Bari, Brindisi, Cagliari, Salerno and Taranto draining off aid from other areas, thus creating a new dualism between development and underdevelopment within the South. These large public projects were very often the creation of state enterprises: Istituto per la Ricostruzione Industriale (IRI) established through Italsider giant steelworks near Taranto while Ente Nazionale Idrocarburi (ENI) located large refineries in Sicily. These large-scale technologically advanced plants had no connection with the rest of the southern economy. They were a sort of colonial enclave with little if no contact with small local firms. They established, on the contrary, a direct connection with the North. Their economic isolation from the rest of the southern economy earned them the appellation of 'cathedrals in the desert'. Furthermore, these firms were able to obtain considerable funds from the State in the form of subsidies, low-interest or interest-free loans as well as direct grants as a part of invested capital (in some areas as high as 20%).[22]

Given these considerable financial benefits big capital was quick to establish a 'compromise' with those social groups and those political forces (governing parties) which controlled public spending in the

South. Thus the growth of state-dependent southern social strata which established clientele relations with the governing groups could go hand in hand with the partial industrialization of the South. The clientele system was not a remnant of an underdeveloped society. On the contrary, it fed on and grew with state intervention in the South. The Cassa per il Mezzogiorno began to finance basic large-scale enterprises, both private and public: electricity, steel, gas, chemical, paper – all industries which are fairly capital intensive and which contribute little to employment.[23]

Investment in the South did not do much to mop up unemployment. This problem was tackled through the expansion of the bureaucracy and of the public purse. By the beginning of the 1970s 30.4 per cent of all salaries and wages in the South were due to employment in the public administration sector, while the Italian average was 20 per cent. Conversely, while in Italy as a whole industrial wages and salaries were 47 per cent of all incomes, in the South this was only 33 per cent.[24] Clearly the chief source of employment in the South was increasingly dependent on central and local government. This can best be seen by examining Table 3.3. The massive decrease in employment in agriculture was partly due to the change in emphasis in the direction of state intervention in the agricultural sector. This became clearer with the second Green Plan (1966): small farmers were to be ditched and public intervention went increasingly towards electrification and irrigation projects which were meant to favour existing entrepreneurs in rural areas rather than the marginal farmer.[25]

Another channel had to be found for small farmers. The funds which had been withdrawn from the agricultural budget reappeared in a new form, disablement pensions, which increased at a phenomenal rate in the mid 1960s; it is easy to understand why. Unlike old-age pensions disablement pensions depend on 'subjective' factors such as a certificate from a compliant doctor employed by the pension fund controlled by the small farmers and funded by the State. By 1974 the pension funds paid disability pensions to nearly 1.5 million small farmers against 625,000 for old-age pensions.[26] That disablement pensions were used for political reasons is evident from the comparative statistics revealed in recent studies: while in the northern province of Mantova in 1973 there were only 53 disability pensions for every 100 old-age pensions given to small farmers in the southern provinces of Enna, Benevento, Campobasso and Frosinone (to mention but a few) the ratio was 10,000 disability pensions for every 100 old-age pensions.[27] Between 1970 and 1975 public expenditure on all pensions trebled and amounted to more than 10 per cent of Gross Domestic Product (GDP). By 1975 there were 12.6 million pensioners of which 5 million were in receipt of disablement pensions.[28]

The relative failure of industrialization in the South and the diminution of employment on the land thus brought about a considerable expansion of the 'protected sector' in the southern

TABLE 3.3 Employment in the South, 1951-70

	1951		1961		1970	
	thousands	*%*	*thousands*	*%*	*thousands*	*%*
Agriculture	2,774.3	51.9	2,203.5	39.4	1,615.0	29.0
Industry (inc. building and construction)	1,210.3	22.6	1,601.1	29.0	1,795.1	32.3
Tertiary	983.8	18.4	1,282.2	23.0	1,542.7	27.7
Public employees	378.7	7.1	482.2	8.6	611.4	11.0
Total	5,347.1	100	5,588	100	5,564.2	100

Source: D'Antonio (1973), p. 256.

economy: a sector where the State played the leading role through direct use of public spending (pensions), through tax concessions for the location of industry, through direct state investment (IRI and ENI) and through the expansion of the bureaucracy. The Centre-Left coalition decision to resolve the 'Southern Question' quickly became the political cover for an operation which sought to protect the South from the worst consequences of the end of the 'economic miracle'. The growth in public expenditure was increasingly seen as proof of the lack of 'industrial vocation' of the South. There were demands that intervention in the South should stop and that the State should concentrate on the North.

Yet all the efforts of the State did little to protect the South. The recession of 1964–65 (engineered by the credit squeeze of 1963) meant that there was little northern investment in the South in spite of state aid, of low wages and weak trade unions. There was instead a flight of northern capital to the EEC. Industrial concentration in the North meant that it obtained a proportionately larger share of public funding for works programmes than the South. So, in 1965, the *Cassa per il Mezzogiorno* could expand its financing of the South only after the North had been given guarantees of similar state funding. Finally the drop in national demand meant that northern industry attempted to expand its trade with the South, thus weakening those southern industries which already existed and whose conditions of existence depended on local demand.[29] The income gap between North and South was still great in 1967 although, when compared with 1950, it was narrowing: if in 1950 southern per capita income was 40 per cent of northern per capita income, by 1967 this had become 48 per cent.[30]

Northern industry did not react to the decrease in profitability through an increase in investment in the South, exporting capital. At home the crisis of profitability was resolved not through capital investment but by the reorganization of the work process: more overtime and a speed-up in assembly lines. This was the fundamental strategy adopted to resolve the crisis.[31] It depended on the possibility of 'squeezing' the existing labour force. This strategy depended, in turn, on the fact that the trade-union militancy of 1962 had been short-lived and that the reserve of labour available was still considerable.

The fact that even state investment in the South was capital intensive meant that internal migration continued even though there was comparatively little increase in employment in the North.[32] This can only mean that existing employed labour in the North was being displaced by the fresh recruits to the northern labour force.

The chief type of labour to be displaced was female labour. According to official figures female employment *decreased* by 1.1 million units between 1959 and 1967. Female labour was expelled from agriculture because of the general shrinkage of employment in agriculture. It was expelled from industry because of the competition from migrant male labour. Male labour in agriculture did not decrease at the same rate because the effects of state intervention and of EEC policies (the Mansholt Plan) was to favour the expansion of capitalist farms which determined a growth in the number of day labourers. The proletarianization of the rural labour force thus followed the pattern of employment in industry: a preponderance of male labour. Furthermore, the crisis in the textile industry, a traditionally large employer of female labour, accelerated this tendency. It should be added that Italy was the only industrialized country in Europe to exhibit the dual feature of growing industrialization and a *decrease in female employment.* Massimo Paci, who has contributed the best study available on the structure of the labour market in Italy in the 1960s, explains that internal migration did not raise overall activity rates (i.e. the proportion of the employed labour force to the total population) precisely because of this substitution effect.[33] Furthermore, he shows that migration also contributed to the lowering of activity rates in the South: often male workers left behind their families – women, children and the old. These groups, deprived of their most productive labour, could no longer fend for themselves. They became increasingly dependent on remittances from the North and state aid. Even when the entire family moved to the North the situation did not improve from the point of view of female participation in the labour market. There were limited opportunities in non-agricultural jobs due to the lack of technical training for women, the inadequacy of social services such as child care and the shrinking of handicraft activities and of the textile industries. There was also an aversion to working outside the home both on the part of women themselves and of their male family members.[34]

Behind the expulsion of the female labour force from production there are not only factors of an 'objective' economic nature and ideological elements in favour of the continuing subordination of women, there are also political decisions. Given the considerable increase in public spending and the outright creation of semi-fictitious employment by the State, one could have expected that some resources be diverted to the creation of more employment opportunities for women through a network of child care centres and training programmes. Yet this did not occur. At this stage one can do little more than speculate as to the political reasons behind this inadequate response. Could it be that the ruling coalition feared that a rapid entry of female labour into production would further disrupt the foundation of the family (already profoundly modified by industrialization and emigration) thus generating social pressures difficult to control? Or that the tensions provoked by higher male unemployment would have had greater social and political consequences? In other European countries female employment was on the increase throughout this period partly thanks to the growing introduction of part-time labour, but part-time labour was resisted by the Italian trade-union movement.

The specificity of the Italian case is probably due to the concurrence of ideological, social and political factors which did not exist to the same extent in comparable countries such as France. But it was not only female labour which was excluded, the same fate was suffered by male labour over 45 years of age and below 25. The changes in the structure of activity rate per age and sex can be seen from the figures in Table 3.4.

While the decrease in female participation in the labour force was partially counteracted by the rise in male incomes, the decrease in employment opportunities for young people took two forms: one 'private', that is, the continued permanence of young people in their

TABLE 3.4 Specific activity rates by age-group and sex in 1960 and 1970

	Male		Female	
Age-group	1960	1970	1960	1970
14–19	67.3	38.4	45.3	28.9
20–4	78.3	69.4	48.3	43.3
25–9	96.2	93.9	36.2	33.2
30–4	98.1	98.2	34.4	27.7
35–9	97.6	98.2	34.3	29.9
40–4	96.7	97.3	33.5	30.8
45–9	96.0	95.0	31.9	29.2
50–4	92.8	90.7	30.5	25.9
55–9	86.5	81.1	24.2	18.3
60–4	60.5	48.2	17.9	10.6
More than 65	30.0	12.9	8.5	2.6
Total	81.2	73.1	31.7	24.8

Source: Podbielski (1974), p. 127, ISTAT figures.

parents' home (giving rise to problems associated with the so-called 'generation gap') and one 'public', that is, the growth in educational opportunities. There is in fact a close relationship between the increase of public spending in general and the decrease of the population employed in productive activity and there is an even closer connection between the decrease in youth employment opportunities and public spending in education. Schools begin to be conceived as places which can absorb labour which would otherwise be unemployed and, after schools, the universities too become a 'parking place' for otherwise unemployed intellectual labour.

The concurrence of an expansion in the public sector with a general tendency towards capital-intensive investment determined a remarkable growth of the tertiary sector in Italy.[35] It should be added that this development of the tertiary sector also determined a considerable expansion of the so-called *rentier* sector closely connected to real-estate speculation. This development has been partly caused by the lack of a sustained public housing programme (virtually abandoned after 1963) but also by the growth of highly paid elements of the professional classes and of the higher echelon of the state bureaucracy, as well as the development of a strong managerial class. The high incomes controlled by these strata enabled them to invest money in real estate and/or spend it on luxury housing and second homes.[36]

Thus the changes brought about by the end of the 'economic miracle', the capital-intensive strategy adopted by entrepreneurial groups, and by the growth of the public sector and of state intervention, were considerable. But their effects were to be even more far-reaching than what has been suggested so far. Much of the 'economic miracle' had been based on the growth of small firms, often set up by former workers. These were now in considerable difficulties. In spite of government subsidies the crisis of 1964–66 took its toll. In fact the crisis would have been even more dramatic than this had the rest of the world economy been in a recession, but international demand was still strong enough to sustain Italian exports. Furthermore, the increase in wages due to the trade-union struggles of 1962 meant that the home market was not as depressed as it would otherwise have been.[37]

The spate of mergers which followed the crisis increased the concentration of Italian industry. Between 1966 and 1967 29 private firms owned directly or indirectly 34 per cent of all shares while the top 100 firms (out of 60,000 firms in manufacturing industry) controlled 40 per cent of all exports.[38] As Castronovo points out, Italian industry began to look like an iceberg: at the top there were three large public enterprises (ENI, IRI, ENEL) and five or six private firms – Fiat, Pirelli, Snia Viscosa (textiles), Italcementi (cement) and Falck and Finsider (steel); at the bottom there were 72,000 small- and medium-sized firms employing between 11 and 500 workers.[39]

How did Italy emerge from the crisis of 1964–66?

The economy picked up again but thanks to productivity gains rather than new plants. Productivity was achieved through the speeding up of the work process, the reorganization of existing plants and 'rationalization' through mergers. The profits thus generated were, on the whole, exported rather than reinvested at home. Public spending, as in other advanced countries, continued to grow. It was not financed through an increase in direct taxation, but through an escalation in employers' and employees' contributions and other forms of indirect taxation. Thus the burden fell disproportionately on low-income groups (employers' social security contributions are, *de facto,* a tax on employment as well as a cost which – in that period – found its way to price increases). After the once-and-for-all increase of 1962, wage increases were roughly matched with productivity until 1969. This temporary wage truce had the same function as an incomes policy. Instead of using direct means to control incomes, as the Labour government did in Britain (1966) the Italian government, though raising the threat of a statutory incomes policy, preferred to use familiar indirect means – deflation and internal migration. These techniques of control of industrial relations could no longer work in Italy. By 1969, when the short-lived recovery was coming to an end, deflationary policies were difficult to pursue. To succeed they would have needed to be implemented over a long period of time and be even more severe than in 1963. The very high level of industrial conflict which occurred in the 'hot autumn' of 1969 meant that the labour movement had become too strong to be defeated with traditional methods.

The 'hot autumn' was the most acute social conflict since 1947. There were 302 million hours of strikes in 1969 and again 146 million in the following year (see Table 3.2). The causes of the conflicts were varied and here we cannot do more than list them:

1. The most often quoted cause was the speed-up of the assembly lines and the intensification of the work process. This had brought about a worsening in working conditions. In this context it is significant that the demands of the trade unions were not purely about wages: the most popular slogans and demands were all concerned with non-monetary issues such as the quality of life at work.

2. A general dissatisfaction with the quality of life *outside* the factories contributed to the strength, unity and politicization of working-class demands. The congestion in urban centres due to urbanization and the waves of migration had reached crisis conditions. There were considerable pressures on public services, health, education and housing.[40]

3. The State seemed unable to resolve any of these problems, in spite of the many promises made by the politicians of the Centre-Left coalition. The growth in spending in the public sector was badly administered and took the form of subsidies, extension of bureaucracy and payment to clientele groups. At the same time

there was a lack of public investment towards the social services and housing.

4. Economic policy seemed to be indecisive: the saga of attempts at planning showed that the divisions within the ruling groups prevented a clear and dynamic approach. Financial and economic policy was further paralysed by the existence of four decision-making centres: the Ministries of Finance, Treasury, Budget and the Bank of Italy.[41]

5. There was a profound dissatisfaction with the entrepreneurial classes, much admired during the years of the 'miracle' and now increasingly considered greedy and devoid of a sense of national responsibility. The paradox of a country which exported both labour and capital played a role in the lack of popularity of entrepreneurs.

6. There were changes in the composition of the labour force.[42]

As we mentioned there were fewer women and fewer workers over 45. The labour force was becoming increasingly made up of workers between the ages of 25 and 45. It was also more homogeneous than before as older skills became supplanted by new methods of production. This younger, male working class included, however, an important proportion of people who had left their land five, ten and in some cases fifteen years before. They had expected to be among the beneficiaries of the 'economic miracle'. Instead they had seen their working conditions deteriorating, and few improvements in housing, health and the education of their children. With the decrease in female employment these male workers were supposed to be the sole breadwinners. They had been employed in factories long enough to have lost their initial fear 'to make trouble', but they had not been employed so long as to be able to remember the repression in the factories which had occurred in the period 1949–55. As we shall see in the next chapter, their militancy took not only government and employers by surprise but also the organized labour movement (the trade unions and the PCI and the PSI). This 'new' working class was more open to questions of equality and social justice; they fought against differentials and for a better deal.[43] They were, of course, at the bottom of the pile; they had the worst jobs, the longest hours, the worst and most unhealthy forms of housing. If they had been the only ones to strike then the movement of 1969 would not have had such major political repercussions. It would have been a movement of the 'wretched of the earth', of marginalized workers. Instead it was able to march united with the bulk of the working class and create a situation of semi-permanent labour conflict which transformed the Italian labour movement from a subordinate element of the Italian political system into one of its chief actors.

In this situation deflation was no longer a feasible option. The working-class movement, particularly the engineering workers, had acquired a novel self-confidence which rendered a massive 'guided'

63

depression impossible. The dominant groups would increasingly resort to price inflation as a means of lowering the real costs of labour. This strategy was facilitated by the inflationary spiral which would hit the Western economies after 1972 and by the end of the international system of fixed exchange rates (devaluation of the dollar in August 1971).[44] But this, as they say, is another story which belongs to the next chapter.

REFERENCES AND NOTES

1. Fuà, G. and Sylos-Labini, P. (1963).
2. Silva, F. and Targetti, F. (March 1972), p. 17.
3. De Cecco, M. (Oct. 1971), p. 983.
4. Valli, V. (1979), p. 72.
5. Ibid. p. 73.
6. Castronovo, V. (1981), p. 417.
7. Onida, F. (1977), p. 70.
8. Valli (1979), p. 123.
9. Castronovo (1981), p. 461.
10. Graziani, A. (1972), p. 71.
11. Castronovo (1981), p. 456–7.
12. Falzone, V., Palermo, F. and Cosentino, F. (1976), pp. 231–2.
13. Amato, G. (1976), p. 132.
14. Ibid. p. 135.
15. Forte, F. (1966), extracts in Graziani (1972), pp. 209–10.
16. Castronovo (1981), p. 463.
17. Amato (1976), p. 41.
18. Fabiani, G. (1977), p. 165.
19. Castronovo (1981), pp. 498–9.
20. Fabiani (1977), p. 166.
21. Castronovo (1981), p. 446.
22. D'Antonio, M. (1973), pp. 238–9.
23. Valli (1979), p. 107.
24. D'Antonio (1973), p. 239.
25. Amato (1976) p.52.
26. Ibid, p. 60.
27. See Amato (1976), p. 71. The most detailed work on Italian pensions is Castellino, O. (1976).
28. Reviglio, F. (1977), p. 117. In the UK, a country with a population comparable to Italy the sum of all those in receipt of invalidity and disablement benefits as well as those in receipt of war pensions in 1975 was just over 1 million – see Department of Health and Social Security (1975).
29. Graziani (1972), pp. 73–4.
30. Saraceno, P. (1972) p. 261.
31. This is the thesis which informs Michele Salvati's *Il sistema economico italiano: analisi di una crisi*, (Salvati, 1975).
32. Employment in southern industries as a proportion of total employment

in industry actually decreased between 1961 and 1971, see D'Antonio
(1973), p. 238.
33. Paci, M. (1973).
34. Podbielski, G. (1974), p. 126.
35. Vainicher, M. E. (1977), p. 57.
36. Garavini, S. (1974), pp. 68–9.
37. Graziani (1972), pp. 71–2.
38. Castronovo (1981), p. 461.
39. Ibid., p. 465.
40. Graziani (1972), pp. 74–5.
41. Castronovo (1981), p. 468.
42. Ibid., p. 475.
43. Ibid., p. 476.
44. D'Antonio (1977), pp. 57–8.

Chapter 4

THE CRISES OF THE ITALIAN ECONOMY, 1969–1985

The 'hot autumn' of 1969 is a historic date in the development of post-war Italian society. Its significance cannot be underrated even if we limited ourselves to its economic effects. A periodization of the post-1945 period would single out the years 1963–69 as the period in which, at one and the same time, the crisis of the 'model' of economic development which had led to the 'economic miracle' becomes manifest (1963) and irreversible (1969).

The economic importance of 1969 can be seen by listing of the following facts.[1]

1. Increases in wages before 1969 were matched by increases in productivity. After 1969 wages increased at a rate higher than the cost of living index and higher than productivity.
2. In the 1960s hourly wages increased in Italy at a rate which matched the increases in other countries of the Organization for Economic Cooperation and Development (OECD): 10 per cent in Italy, 9 per cent in OECD. After 1969, and throughout the 1970s hourly rates in Italy increased yearly by 20–25 per cent, double the average of the OECD countries.
3. Inflation rates in the 1960s in Italy were in line with the rest of the OECD, but after 1973–74 Italian rates are, on average, twice those of the OECD countries.
4. Between 1969 and 1970 alone, labour costs increased by 16 per cent.
5. In manufacturing industry money wages rose by 9.1 per cent in 1969 and by 23.4 per cent in 1970. Real wages, of course, rose by much less because of the increase in the cost of living index.
6. The share of the national income going to wage-earners went up from 56.7 to 59 per cent and in industry this share went up from 60.7 to 64.1 per cent.

What does this tell us? First of all that in terms of productivity and inflation rates Italy no longer follows the general pattern of OECD countries. But, and this is the second point, this 'deviation' from the norm of the advanced capitalist countries brings the average purchasing power of Italian workers on a level with those countries. The result is to destroy the main advantage of Italian entrepreneurs: low wages. Having lost this advantage Italy remains a special case, but one which has new characteristics.

The 'hot autumn', however, was not only about wages. It occurred at a time when the whole of Italian society seemed to be in upheaval. The student movement had become a major political phenomenon and, although it never reached the peaks of the French equivalent in May 1968, it shaped, either directly or indirectly, the crisis of Italian society: from terrorism to the women's movement, from dissent within the Church to the birth of a host of small left-wing parties and to the radicalization of large groups of intellectuals and middle-class radicals. Furthermore, as we shall see in subsequent chapters, 1969 also caused profound changes in the organization of the labour movement, in the trade unions and in the political parties.

The 1969 movement also achieved results which would ensure that the increase in wages obtained could not be reversed easily by the kind of counter-offensive of the industrialists which had been a hallmark of the 1960s. In 'qualitative' terms it obtained the following.[2]

1. A greater working-class control over the use of the labour force in factories. After 1969 it would be far more difficult for entrepreneurs to increase productivity by devices such an increase in the speed of the assembly lines or by a reorganization of the labour process.
2. Workers were able to acquire a greater degree of control inside the factories which made them more independent both from the trade-union hierarchy and from the entrepreneurs. Changes had to be negotiated at shop-floor level.[3]
3. Entrepreneurs could no longer use 'marginal' labour for the lowest and less skilled jobs inside the factories to the same extent as before. This was in part due to the decrease in female employment but it was also due to the fact that workers had obtained a uniformity of contracts and wage levels which did not exist before.
4. The strength of the labour movement was such that the government had to pass a new law in 1970, known as the Workers' Charter (*Statuto dei Lavoratori*) which strengthened considerably the bargaining power of the workers and made illegal a number of anti-trade-union practices.
5. It was now far more difficult to sack workers, both because of the strength of the movement and because of new legislation.
6. There was a shortening of the working week and overtime was abolished in a number of large firms.

Entrepreneurs were ill-equipped to face this challenge. The strategy they had adopted in the 1960s backfired: they had reduced the volume of productive investments and increased productivity by squeezing the labour force. Now they found themselves left with a rebellious labour force and obsolete plants. They could not hope for an expansion of international demand. Approaching on the horizon were the years of world-wide inflation, dollar crisis, energy crisis and momentous changes in the relationship between the industrialized North and the underdeveloped Third World. The Italian economy entered this period of crisis with a political system which had relied for its stability on a constant economic growth. There was a void of ideas and, in this void, the first instinct of the financial authorities was to try once more, to use their traditional instrument: deflation.

The increase in labour costs due to wage rises had caused an increase in prices. Unlike 1962–63 when the small firms operating on the home market had been the first to increase prices, this time it was the export-oriented sector which passed on the increase in wages to their customers at home and abroad. This could now be done because inflation was also hitting the other industrialized countries and the increase in prices did not entail a decrease in the competitiveness of Italian firms. However, the balance of payments was in deficit not only because of an adverse balance of trade but mainly because of a sustained flight of capital. In itself this was nothing new: after the nationalization of electricity there had been a constant export of capital. But in 1969 this flight of capital had reached massive proportions partly because of high interest rates abroad and partly because of a widespread desire to avoid taxation. Thus the deflationary policy of the authorities was also intended to raise Italian interest rates and make it less attractive for business to send their money abroad. The credit squeeze of 1969 was not very effective. Aggregate demand for consumption goods fell a little, but there was no increase in investment and this meant that the long-term problem of re-equipping Italian industry was not tackled. Once more short-term objectives of monetary stability prevailed over longer-term ones of industrial regeneration.

At this stage it will be useful to explain briefly the kind of economic theory which inspired the Bank of Italy, the leading monetary authority.[4] Its central assumption was that entrepreneurs wished to maintain stable profit margins and, whenever costs increased they would attempt to transfer this rise on to prices. This strategy was likely to encounter internal and external obstacles. Internally, that is on the home market, competition from other firms made it more difficult for any single firm – at least in the short run – to increase prices. Abroad the possibility of price increases was limited by the behaviour of other firms whose own labour costs had not increased as much as Italian labour costs. Thus for the Bank of Italy Italian prices were relatively inflexible because of the degree of international integration of the Italian economy.

But there are other ways of maintaining intact your profit levels. If you cannot increase prices you may be able to increase productivity: the same amount of labour can produce more at similar prices. Internally you can increase sales because the increase in wages would have entailed an increase in demand and, externally, you would be able to keep up or even undercut foreign competition. The problem with increasing productivity (if you cannot discipline your labour force) is that you need to increase investment. You can do that in two ways: either by financing out of profits, or by borrowing from the banks. But if you borrow you add interest rates to your costs. Thus the Bank of Italy held the view that increases in wages brought two kinds of pressure on the economy: an inflationary pressure because they stimulated an increase in prices, and a movement towards a recession because they caused a decrease in investment (the self-financing option was more difficult because the increases in labour costs would reduce the self-financing capability of firms). In other words, wage increases are a 'bad thing'. In the course of the 1970s the Bank of Italy reached the conclusion that monetary intervention (credit squeeze, deflation, etc.) has only a negative application: it could reduce aggregate demand but not encourage investment.

There was another option open: an incomes policy. Although this was no doubt the preferred option it was impossible to apply. There can only be two kinds of incomes policy – voluntary or statutory. A voluntary incomes policy was not on the cards because the trade unions were unwilling to accept it unless it were part of a major package of internal reforms which would have entailed a great increase in public spending. A statutory policy required a docile labour force which was hardly the case in Italy in the 1970s. Thus there remained a single option to be pursued in order to enable firms to maintain their levels of profitability: internal inflation and devaluation.

Domestic inflation usually redistributes profits to the advantage of the larger and more efficient firms, but does not necessarily alter the overall level of profits. To ensure that inflation would not have negative repercussions on foreign trade it was then necessary to devalue the lira so that the external prices of Italian goods remained competitive. The problem with constant devaluation is that it has important inflationary effects. This is so because once exporters realize that devaluation can go on for ever they will not be so resistant to price rises, knowing that every upward movement in prices will be followed by a matching decrease in the foreign exchange value of the currency. Furthermore, a devaluation of the lira may well make Italian exports relatively cheaper, but it certainly makes Italian imports more expensive and makes it easier for domestic producers to put up prices and this too pushes up the inflation rate.[5] Price-control experiments were repeated on and off throughout this period with fairly disappointing results.

The strategy of inflation–devaluation also failed because in 1973 the energy crisis exploded when the Organization of Petroleum Exporting Countries (OPEC) was able to impose a massive increase in oil prices.

It becomes clear that the main difficulties faced by the Italian economy in this period were due not only to its having lost its central pillar of low wages, but to its having become totally interdependent with the international economic system. We could rephrase its predicament in the following way: the decision to open the Italian economy to the outside world depended for its success on international competitiveness, this in turn depended on low wages. By the early 1970s Italy was integrated into an international economic system but could no longer rely on low wages. The option of reintroducing protectionism was never seriously considered by Italian political parties, whether of the government or of the opposition. The main argument against protectionism was that, in essence, it was too late: international constraints were by then too great.

Of course it could be argued that the level of international integration did not have to reach such massive proportions. Economic development did not have to be based so strongly on exports. The home market could have played a more important role. Agriculture did not have to be left to fend for itself with the result that Italy became an importer of food. Italy could have played a more important role in EEC agricultural policy instead of trailing behind the French and the Germans, and could have made a more significant attempt to modernize its administration and restructure its agriculture instead of using such a small proportion of the 'Guidance Fund' of the EEC agricultural policy (which meant that Italy used a lower percentage of this fund than any other EEC country).[6] That the level of international integration of the Italian economy had increased massively can be seen from Tables 4.1 and 4.2.

In order to sustain this level of participation, an economy which is so integrated must possess some special advantages. From a geographical point of view Italy could have acted as a link between the markets of northern Europe and those of the Mediterranean. Yet its geographical position also meant that it faced competition from both the Mediterranean south (olive oil, wine and citrus fruits) and from the rest of Europe (manufactured goods).[7] Besides that, Italy suffered from a number of structural handicaps, the main one being the lack of natural resources in relation to its population. The UK has oil, gas and coal. Norway has oil. France and West Germany have coal *and* fertile soil. The Netherlands has gas and fertile soil.[8] Italy has no oil, no gas, no coal,

TABLE 4.1 International trade, 1958–74

	Imports as % of GNP	Exports as % of GNP	Imports + exports as % of GNP
1958	11.6	10.6	22.2
1970	18	17.2	35.2
1974	29.8	23.7	53.5

TABLE 4.2 International trade, a comparison

	Imports + exports as % of GNP in 1974
UK	60.5
Italy	53.5
France	42.1
W. Germany	41
Japan	30.5
USA	14.2

Source: Peggio (1976), pp. 38–40.

and vast areas are difficult to cultivate (e.g. mountain areas), although here the main culprit is a backward productive structure.

These structural handicaps, whether due to natural and objective factors or to past governmental mistakes, could perhaps have been partially compensated by a policy of attracting foreign investment. Here Italy could offer the industrial structure of an advanced country, a skilled labour force and wages which were still lower than those of most advanced countries. In fact in the 1970s there was a much greater intervention of multinational companies than had occurred in the previous decade. But this intervention took the form of acquiring existing firms, of using state subsidies and low-wage labour without resulting in any considerable investment in advanced technology.[9] On the contrary, it could be argued that such intervention made it more difficult for Italy to develop new technologies. Research and development was carried out abroad, in the USA, in West Germany and in Japan. Production requiring low-technology inputs was diverted to Italy. The growth of multinational companies tended to accelerate the international division of labour and production was diversified following the logic of using factors of production at the lowest costs at world level. Thus Italy's position in the international division of labour constantly deteriorated.

This process was further accelerated by what was probably the most significant change in the conditions of international trade which occurred in the 1970s: the shift in the terms of trade towards the producers of primary products and, in particular, towards the oil-exporting countries. This shift meant that industrial countries now had to export much more in order to acquire those primary products they needed for economic growth. Hence a number of Italian industrial and agricultural products faced greater competition on world markets (as well as on the home market). Italy had to export more and more. An obvious strategy (adopted, for instance by France) was to produce products with a high technological content, but Italian industry was not equipped for this.[10]

71

How did other countries react in the period 1971–75? The USA had been facing throughout the 1960s massive foreign competition. It reacted by devaluing the dollar in 1971 and 1973. It decreased its commitment to finance other countries' development and this meant that military spending too was decreased in South-East Asia. By 1973 the US balance of trade was no longer in deficit and the USA became competitive again in many sectors. This encouraged foreign investments, particularly from West Germany and Japan.[11]

West Germany became the leading motor of the European economy: its export trade accounted, by the mid 1970s, for one-third of all EEC exports. Similarly, in Asia, Japan became the pillar of a new Far Eastern industrial development which included the network of the 'newly industrialized countries' of South Korea, Singapore, Taiwan, Hong Kong as well as the Philippines and Thailand.

Thus the devaluation of the dollar had profound effects on the international economy: the strong (Japan and West Germany) grew stronger, and the weak (Italy and the UK) grew weaker. The USA which had a high rate of inflation before the OPEC price rise dealt with it by relying on a prices and incomes policy while reflating the economy, thus accelerating inflation in the USA and in the rest of the world. Inflation in the USA had the effect of depreciating the value of the dollar with respect to other leading currencies, and low interest rates in the USA meant that there was a massive outflow of capital from the USA to Europe and Japan.[12] The presence of this enormous monetary mass which constituted the Eurodollar market contributed to the inflationary spiral in Europe which was – with the significant exception of West Germany – higher than in the USA.

The devaluation strategy was adopted in 1973 as Italian inflation rates reached a comparatively high level. This was also the year of the first massive increase in oil prices. The devaluation of the lira proceeded constantly throughout this period against all other currencies, as can be

TABLE 4.3 Rates of consumer price increases in six major industrialized countries, 1970–81 (in %)

	1970	1971	1972	1973	1974	1975	1976	1981
USA	5.9	4.3	3.3	6.2	11.0	9.2	5.8	11.0
Japan	7.2	6.3	4.8	11.8	22.7	12.2	9.3	3.9
France	5.2	5.5	5.9	7.3	13.6	11.8	9.6	13.9
W. Germany	3.7	5.3	5.5	6.9	7.0	6.9	4.6	6.5
Italy	4.9	4.8	5.7	10.8	19.1	17.2	16.7	18.7
UK	6.4	9.4	7.1	9.1	15.9	24.2	16.8	11.4

Source: For 1970–80 – IMF and Parboni (1981) p. 79: for 1981 Financial Times, 14 Nov. 1981.

seen by Table 4.4 which indicates the amount of Italian lire needed to purchase one unit of foreign currency.

The 1973 fluctuation of the lira had differentiated effects on the Italian economy. Firms depending on imports for their production suffered, exporters did relatively well. There was, however, a huge increase in public spending which helped the recovery. This lasted only until 1974, the year in which Italian inflation rates became the highest in the West. Since then Italian inflation has remained at a very high level, occasionally conceding this unwanted leadership to other countries, usually the UK.

After 1973 the problem arose of covering the ever-growing deficit in the balance of payments. International loans, and particularly West German loans were used frequently, but there was also another Bank of Italy credit squeeze which, as usual, hit the large firms much less than the small- and medium-sized firms. This new credit squeeze stopped the recovery dead in its tracks and initiated the most serious economic crisis of the post-war period.[13]

Let us now take a look back at the gradual slowing down of the Italian economy and at the kind of reorganization which occurred in the 1970s.

TABLE 4.4 Foreign exchange rates, 1972–85

Currency	1972	1973	1975	1977	1979	1981	1983	1985
US $	583	602	652	882	848	1202	1638	2081
Swiss franc	152	191	252	368	476	658	751	749
Sterling £	1460	1478	1447	1540	1627	2316	2402	2365
French franc	115	134	152	179	188	211	198	207
German mark	183	227	265	380	422	534	605	634
Yen	1.94	2.16	2.20	3.30	4.07	5.52	6.92	8.11

Source: Bank of Italy, 1972–78; *Financial Times*, 1981; *La Repubblica*, 25 Nov. 1983; *Financial Times*, 20 Mar. 1985.

The average rate of growth of the national income dropped from 6.56 per cent in the period 1959–63 to 5.96 per cent in the years 1964–70 and to 3.36 per cent in 1970–74. The average yearly rate of growth of industrial production dropped from 9.07 per cent in the period 1959–63 to 6.20 per cent in 1964–70 and to 3.38 per cent in 1970–74. Finally the ratio of investment to income, that is, the amount of lire one needs to invest in order to obtain 1 lira increase in income, went up from 3.76 in 1959–63 and 3.50 in 1963–70 to 6.32 in 1970–74.[14] Clearly it was necessary to re-equip Italian industry. One of the chief problems, however, was that this re-equipment required a major restructuring. The industries which had been the keystones of the 'economic miracle' were successful not so much because of any special flair on the part of Italian entrepreneurs, but because they were based on low wages and a low level of technological content, as was the case with typical Italian exports such as textiles, clothing, shoes, furniture and household goods. Italy has thus been able to adapt itself to the spaces left open in the international economy. In so doing, however, it would, in all probability, face the competition of newly industrialized countries of the Third World which have low wages, and would find it more difficult to produce those goods where a high technological content is necessary. For goods with average technological content, such as machine tools, cars, oil-related products, rubber and metal goods, only in two cases (cars and oil-related products) was there adequate technical progress. For goods with *high* technological inputs (electronics, aircraft, scientific and precision instruments, computers, high-quality chemicals, microprocessors) only plastics and chemical goods kept up with international competition and were adequately catered for. Italy's dependence on foreign technology can be demonstrated by the fact that in 1972 it imported 152,000 million lire worth of patents but exported only 27,000 million.[15]

Such restructuring around high technology would have required state intervention of a different calibre: efficient and ruthless. But by the 1970s the state sector had become a political instrument in the hands of the Christian Democratic Party (DC), its economic functions were subordinated to the policies of enabling the survival of that party and the kind of economic structures which had grown with it. The path of high technology was never seriously considered. There remained, apparently, one avenue: the attempt to circumvent the gains achieved by the working class in 1969–70 by reorganizing the system of production in such a way as to maintain the production of traditional goods while resisting Third World competition. To put it in a simpler way: how was it possible to go on producing clothing and shoes by maintaining relatively low cost while enhancing their quality and those fashionable characteristics which could enable them to compete with Hong Kong and Taiwan?

The answer was the decentralization of production. Production was shifted from large industrial groups to an array of small firms and cottage industry. Employment in this sector assumed various forms: domestic labour, underemployment, juvenile and even child labour, casual and part-time labour and even prison labour. The pressures towards this decentralization of production and the creation of a second, 'hidden' or 'black' economy were essentially two:

1. Escape from trade-union constraints: labour payments in the 'black economy' did not have to correspond to wage rates offered in the 'open' sector. Health and safety regulations could be easily circumvented and there are fewer or no strikes.
2. Escape from the full burden of taxes, by avoiding paying employers' and employees' contributions which are the highest in Europe.[16]

Thus an increasing proportion of the labour force began to work in conditions which are reminiscent of the low-wage economy typical of the 1950s. This situation is all the more easily accepted because the wages generated in the 'black' economy are usually added on to those in the 'open' sector. It is often the case that while the male worker continues his employment in the 'open' sector the other members of the family are employed in the 'hidden' sector. Their pay is considered an addition to the pay of the men. It can thus be low. There is also the growth of the so-called *doppiolavoro* (second job): the reduction of overtime enabled many workers to take a second job where they did not pay any taxes or contributions.

It is difficult to estimate the size of the 'black economy'. The state statistical office (Istituto Centrale di Statistica) has estimated that the number of people who are employed, even though they are not officially registered as such, is between 1 million and 3.5 million. To these should be added all second 'unofficial' jobs. It is also difficult to assess how far this problem is specific to Italy. It has been pointed out that Italy has used little foreign labour and that, in a sense, the 'black economy' is the Italian version of immigrant labour. The proportion of foreign labour in EEC countries is around 7 per cent and in West Germany and France the proportion is of 10 per cent.[17] Of the 6 million foreign workers employed in EEC countries only 1.5 million come from other EEC countries. The importance of foreign labour is not only that it can be exploited more easily, but that it is far more flexible and mobile. When it is no longer usable it can simply be got rid of. Resident labour is better protected and nowhere more so than in Italy (in the 'open' sector, of course): equal pay, daily hours worked, lower retirement age, greater difficulties in laying off workers, etc. Statistics of the OECD show that the rate of withdrawal from the labour market is lower in Italy (particularly after 1974) than in the USA, Sweden, France and the UK.[18]

The effects of the decentralization of production towards the hidden sector permitted Italy to achieve a growth-rate which, though inferior to that of the 'economic miracle', was higher than that of most industrial advanced countries of the OECD. In 1980 Gross Domestic Product (GDP) increased by 4 per cent against –0.2 per cent in the USA, 1.4 per cent in France, –1.4 per cent in the UK, 1.9 per cent in West Germany. Only Japan (+4.2%), Portugal (+4.7%) and Finland (+4.9%) did better.[19] This was in no small part due to the fact that between 1973 and 1979 the sectors of the economy which expanded were, with the exception of the chemical industry, sectors where there is a strong presence of 'black labour' such as leather, shoes, clothing and furniture.[20]

Once more the South did not derive any particular benefit from this development. The small- and medium-sized firms of the 'hidden' sector were located, on the whole, in the Centre and in the North. The larger firms, both public and private, had decreased the rate of growth of their investments partly because of the financial crisis they were undergoing, partly because of the heavy losses encountered by some (e.g. steel due to world overproduction and Japanese competition). This serious crisis meant that they were not likely to invest more in the South and that state resources which could have been used otherwise had to be directed towards enabling existing firms to pay their debts or reorganize existing plants.[21]

The problems of the South were further multiplied by the failure to restructure agriculture. As a result Italian food imports from the rest of the EEC increased at a steady rate (sixteen times since 1957), while agricultural exports since then increased by only three or four times).[22] In 1972 the EEC established some directives for the modernization of agriculture and the training of agricultural producers. Marginal farmers no longer obtained funds to modernize their farms but to enable them to sell their land. Thus the public bodies which had been instituted in order to help smallholders had now to get rid of them. One way of doing this was for the Ministry of Agriculture to transfer some of its former functions to the regional authorities which had been instituted in 1970. But the Ministry resisted this proposal for political reasons: the Ministry wanted to continue to give subsidies to those organizations and associations with which it had been connected for years and with which it had established a dense clientele network often based on personal relationships. From the point of view of the Ministry what mattered was the danger that any transfer of funds would decrease the powers of patronage of the Ministry. The result of this essential internal struggle between centre and periphery was a compromise: the regions obtained some resources and the Ministry kept all powers of guidance and coordination and, more importantly, control of the funds to be used as compensation to the marginal farmers for the sale of their lands.[23]

The absolute priority always given to political matters over economic ones reflected not only the deepening Italian crisis but also the internal crisis of the DC. Economic decision-making acquired more and more the characteristics of warring feuds. The very concept of planning lost the reformist significance it had had, at least formally, under the Centre-Left governments of the 1960s. Now public investments in the state sector, rather than responding to an industrial strategy, reflected the interests of the public entrepreneurs themselves who used them as joint ventures with politicians of the governing parties. Having created the state-holding sector as relatively autonomous from parliamentary control, the DC now found that it had created authentic centres of power with which it had to negotiate. These centres of power used the economic resources at their disposal for political ends. For instance when, in the 1970s, the state mining company (EGAM) acquired shipbuilding shares it did so not because it needed to diversify into shipping but because it wanted to get hold of the newspapers belonging to the shipping owners.[24]

Thus the interconnection between the leading groups of the public sector and the ruling political bloc became closer. The political power of the public corporations was not established by law but relied on the connection established with particular factions within the DC. With the expansion of the State, the political cadres of the DC increasingly occupied economic positions in banks, credit institutions and, of course, economic institutions such as the *Cassa per il Mezzogiorno* and public corporations. This process is of course not unique to Italy: there is everywhere a constant intertwining between business and politics. The difference is that in some countries, such as the USA, it is business that 'colonizes' politics and not the other way round.[25]

How did the entrepreneurial world counteract this tendency? At the ideological level the employers' association, Confindustria, stressed the need for an efficient modern state based on the principles of managerial and technical efficiency which would appeal to the new middle classes against the paternalism of the DC.

The criticism of the DC by big business centred on the following points:

1. Private enterprise is being squeezed by a spendthrift government, by high wages and by excessive trade-union power.
2. Public spending is inefficient and simply transfers resources through the banks to the State. The consequent enlargement of economic activity does not generate profits and/or new investment.
3. Employers' contributions to social costs are too high.
4. The index-linked scale of wages whereby wages will go up as prices go up squeezes profits.

An examination of the complaints levelled by private enterprise anywhere in Europe or North America would show that there is nothing specifically Italian about these complaints. However, in most other countries public spending is identified with the Left. In Italy it is identified with the DC, and there is no alternative to the right of the DC, at least not within the established constitutional system. Gianni Agnelli, the President of Fiat, and the most lucid representative of big business, encapsulated the problem facing Italian entrepreneurs when he explained that the agreement established between private enterprise and the DC could work as long as each kept to his side of the pact: the exercise of political power to the DC and economic growth to private enterprise. However the DC, in order to exercise political power had to maintain mass support, and had to organize public spending accordingly. The consequence of this is that, according to Agnelli, private enterprise had to begin to involve itself directly in politics.[26] The analysis focuses on only one aspect of the problem, but it is not far off the mark. The strategy, however, is Utopian: it assumes that the political problem of establishing a mass consensus could be better achieved by a clearly capitalist party (presumably it would have to be a 'regenerated' DC). This party would still need to use public spending in order to achieve the massive investment that a regeneration of Italian industry requires. There would have to be a time-lag during which the social strata currently subsidized would be left to fend for themselves. This would either destabilize the political system from the right or bring to the fore the only alternative to the DC within the constitutional system: the Italian Communist Party (PCI).

The DC adopted a different strategy: to foreclose the communist option by attempting to involve that party in the DC system of government. This was the strategy adopted during 1976–79 when the PCI was offered (and accepted) a subordinate role in political decision-making. The strategy was only partially successful because the Communists pulled out before they became too deeply enmeshed in the DC system.

The political and economic strategy of private enterprise in the 1970s was also unrealistic because its analysis assumed that there is an organic contradiction between the 'healthy' forces of private enterprise and the economic activity of the state sector.[27] Apart from the fact that the Confindustria itself had, by the mid 1960s, been converted to the concept of planning and that Agnelli himself, on the morrow of the 'hot autumn', had recognized the central importance of trade-union involvement in economic decision-making, it is simply not true that the state sector has operated against the interests of private business. The crisis of accumulation which hit Italy in the 1970s was also due to the fact that private capital was invested abroad where returns would be higher, or invested at home but in non-productive use such as real estate. State subsidies and public works programmes were often directed towards the creation of energy inputs and primary products which supported the production cycles of big business. Furthermore, private firms and high income groups enjoyed a *de facto* low tax burden because of massive tax evasion and the widespread possibility of tax avoidance.[28]

Is true that the 'restructuring' of private firms by decentralizing production towards small firms thus expanding the 'hidden' sector marks the development of market conditions outside state control (really 'free' enterprise). But the growth thus generated can be achieved precisely because of the much-criticized inefficiency and lack of authority of the Italian State. This free market restructuring, coupled with the expansion of public spending, further exacerbated the distortions of the labour market. The level of activity rate (defined as the percentage of the population in the labour force) is lower in Italy than in most other advanced countries, as was the case in the 1960s as well. The same can be said about the participation rate of women in the labour force: it is still exceptionally low, although it is difficult to assess the extent to which the expansion of the 'black' economy has entailed an increase in relative female employment. Furthermore, if we examine the distribution of labour in the Centre–North and in the South we can note the continuing disequilibrium.

Between 1973 and 1976 (see Table 4.5) the economy of the South and

TABLE 4.5 Distribution of employment in the South and North, 1972–6

Year	Labour force (thousands)	Agriculture (%)	Industry (%)	Building and public works (%)	Tertiary (%)	Unemployed (%)
(a) The South						
1972	6,127	28.13	15.84	12.17	38.55	5.28
1973	6,140	27.42	16.27	11.77	39.33	5.19
1974	6,157	26.52	16.87	11.61	40.53	4.45
1975	6,192	25.19	16.98	11.51	41.24	5.05
1976	6,336	25.15	16.88	11.11	41.57	5.27
(b) The North						
1972	13,835	11.36	33.42	7.89	44.61	2.69
1973	13,934	10.80	33.61	7.63	45.43	2.50
1974	14,118	10.46	33.85	7.45	46.19	2.02
1975	14,205	9.88	33.51	7.29	46.90	2.40
1976	14,305	9.33	33.33	7.09	47.45	2.78

Source: Our figures on the basis of the SVIMF7, Report on the South, 1976.

that of the North exhibit the following similar traits: a decrease in employment in agriculture; a small decrease in employment in the building industry and in public works; an increase in employment in the tertiary sector and a fairly stable level of unemployment. The two most striking differences are firstly, after the tertiary sector agriculture is still the largest employment sector in the South while industry is the largest in the North and, secondly, unemployment in the South is roughly twice as large as unemployment in the North.

Another important difference between North and South is given by the variance of participation rates. Those employed as a percentage of the potential labour force were, in 1975, 31.5 per cent in the South and 38.9 per cent in the North. The equivalent statistics for West Germany in 1974 was 42.2 per cent, for France 39.9 per cent and for the UK 42.9 per cent.[29] Thus participation rates in the north of Italy did not show a significant variance with those of industrialized countries. It is the southern statistics which modify the Italian total and which show, once more, the historical failure to unify Italy.

With the constant shrinking of the agricultural sector the traditional reserve army of labour which was at the disposal of the Italian economy had virtually disappeared.[30] It is in this period that there is for the first time in Italian history an entry of foreign workers, particularly from

Ethiopia, Somalia, Libya, Egypt and the Philippines. These, however, essentially found employment as domestic workers and on the periphery of the 'black' economy. A new important component of the reserve army was urban-based youth which was exercising increasing pressures on the labour market. Thus a greater number of young people were in fact encouraged to stay on at school and to enter the universities which by then were operating an open-door policy. The consequence of this process was to increase the percentage of young qualified unemployed. According to official figures in 1978 there were in Italy 1.5 million unemployed. Of these about half were looking for their first job. Unemployment in the South was 9.9 per cent while in the North it was 6 per cent. Male unemployment was 4.7 per cent while female unemployment was 12.6 per cent. Of those between the ages of 14 and 19, 31 per cent, and of those between 20 and 29, 14 per cent, were unemployed.

The rate of unemployment for those leaving school at 18 (13.9%) was higher than the unemployment rate of those who had left at 14 (9.3%) or before (4.3%) This is, of course, a vicious circle: those with higher qualifications want jobs in the 'open' economy where they can be better paid and obtain more secure jobs. But employment in this sector is either stagnant or is given to those with some work experience, often gained in the hidden economy. There is thus a transfer from the 'black' economy to the 'open' one. Younger entrants in the labour market cannot accede directly to the 'open' sector and their qualifications make them reluctant to enter the 'black' sector.[31]

Obviously the constant growth of the supply of graduate labour has had the partial effect of containing the levels of salaries among white-collar workers and, in general, throughout the 1970s, of decreasing income differentials between salaried workers and wage-earners. The push towards equality, however, has been chiefly determined by the operation of the *scala mobile,* the indexation of wages. According to the formal model of wage indexation there is an automatic mechanism whereby earnings increase in such a way as to match the rate of inflation. In practice, this occurs only in part because of the way in which the mechanism works and because the increase in pay occurs only after the increase in price. When this mechanism was instituted in 1952 it had the effect of maintaining and, in some cases, widening the differentials. The 'egalitarian' policies of the trade unions forced a revision of this mechanism in 1975 when it was established that incomes would be increased by a fixed and equal amount of money. This has the result of lowering differentials the greater the inflation rate. For instance, suppose Martini earns 10,000 lire a month and Rossi earns 20,000 lire, and suppose each percentage point of price rise determines an increase of 2,000 lire. If inflation is at 10 per cent there will be a 20,000 lire increase across the board. The relative position after adjustments will be that Martini earns 30,000 lire and Rossi earns 40,000 lire. The differential in real terms is smaller: before the rise Rossi earned twice as much as Martini, after, only one-third more. The overall narrowing of differentials can be seen in these figures on income distribution in the province of Modena (see Table 4.6).

The trend towards equality was, however, counterbalanced by an increase in differentials within certain categories of workers. In certain cases, firms would increase the payment of fringe benefits to senior executives in order to maintain or extend existing privileged positions. Thus in 1978 at Fiat the effect of the *scala mobile* and the wage-bargaining round which had been centred on the principle of 'equal increase for all' would have produced a differential between basic and maximum wages of 100 : 143. To compensate for this loss on the part of the better-paid executive, Fiat increased their salaries so as to establish a differential of 100 : 247.[32] However, with the exception of senior executives it would be true to say that for the entire sector which is subject to international competition (virtually the whole of private manufacturing industry and some state enterprises) the differentials narrowed considerably. In sectors which are not export-oriented, such as banking and insurance and national monopolies such as electricity, large differentials were maintained. Among local government employees there were abnormal and unjustified differentials even between workers doing exactly the same jobs. A parliamentary investigative commission has revealed that an employee of a northern region would be paid by the regional government an average of 5.1 million lire a year, in central Italy 5.4, in southern Italy 5.7 and in Sicily and Sardinia the average is 5.9.[33] A more up-to-date study is that of A. Accornero and F. Carmigliani (1978). This revealed that the average income of a regional employee was inversely proportional to the average income in the region as a whole: the higher the income per regional employee the poorer the region.[34] More significantly there is the fact that a porter employed in a private manufacturing firm can earn between 4 and 7 million lire a year (1976 figures), if employed by a regional government the same person can earn anything between 2.7 million and

TABLE 4.6 Ratio between incomes in the Province of Modena (skilled industrial worker = 100)

	1971	1974	1977	1978
Skilled worker	100	100	100	100
Agricultural worker	72	72	94	100
Elementary-school teacher	158	152	116	116
Dustman	149	136	145	153
Junior doctor (hospital)	608	457	280	245
Consultant (hospital)	1,093	781	481	409

Source: Valli (1976), 1979, p. 154.

8.4 million lire, but porters in the Italian Chamber of Deputies can muster a yearly income of between 8.5 and 17 million lire.[35]

These differentials are a divisive element and favour the growth of corporative unions which negotiate outside the framework of agreements established by the leading three trade-union confederations. In some sectors they constitute *de facto* clientele groupings which have established special links with factions of the political parties forming the ruling coalition. But the differentials were also a reaction against the tendency towards equality which, in many cases had been seen as excessive.

The tendency towards equality through the indexation of wages has also been seen as a major factor towards the increase of Italian labour costs. The rate of growth of these has been higher than any other European country with the exception of the UK (but absolute labour costs in both these countries are, if anything, lower than those in West Germany, France, the Netherlands, Denmark and Belgium). We are talking, obviously, of labour costs measured in national currencies. The devaluation of the lira has been such that if we were to convert all measurements of labour costs into say, dollars, the Italian rate of increase would be slightly below average.[36] Nevertheless, employers are concerned with internal prices, with how many more lire they have to pay their employees.

The argument about the cost of labour has dominated Italian debates on economic policies at least since the beginning of the 1970s. The government's three-year plan for 1979–81 (the Pandolfi Plan) isolated the cost of labour and the ever-increasing growth of public spending as the key problems facing the Italian economy and as the central internal causes (the major external cause being the high cost of energy) diverse phenomena such as the constant depreciation of the lira, the decrease in competivity, stop-go policies and many others.[37]

The document is silent on other possible factors which have contributed to the depreciation of the lira and the high level of inflation such as high interest rates and the flight of capital.[38] It is thus not surprising that it indicated three conditions for the achievement of high rates of growth, an increase in employment and the development of the South. The plan's objectives were:
1. To reduce the proportion of public spending of the GDP.
2. A freeze of increases in *real* wages.
3. An increase in the mobility of labour.[39]

To refuse to adopt this strategy, affirms the plan in its opening paragraph, is tantamount to 'giving up staying in Europe'.[40] It was in order to 'stay in Europe' that is, in order to keep up with the rest of Europe that the Italian government, against the advice of the majority of economic experts, decided to join the system of exchange rates known as the European Monetary System.

In 1983 the socialist leader, Bettino Craxi, became Prime Minister.

The economic programme he adopted was intended to lower inflation rates and bring Italy to the levels of its foreign competitors. During 1984 Italy's inflation decreased from 15 per cent to 10.6 per cent, Italian exports to the USA increased by a record 46 per cent and the Italian economy as a whole grew by 2.8 per cent instead of the 2 per cent which had been forecast. The gap between Italy and its competitors, however, was not bridged. In the top seven industrialized countries the rate of growth was 5 per cent rather than the forecast 3.3: the USA grew by 7 per cent (rather than 4.5), France and West Germany by 1 per cent over the forecast, Japan by 1.5 over the forecast. All countries increased their exports to the USA thanks to its record balance of payments deficit and the strength of the dollar which made all other countries' products very cheap. As for the decrease in the rate of inflation, the Craxi government's major success, this was in line with the general trend in the industrialized countries. In absolute terms, however, Italian inflation rates were still over twice as high as the average of the OECD countries. As for unemployment, this was 10.3 per cent in 1984, second, among the top seven, only to the UK.[41] Thus not only the gap remains but the vicissitudes of the Italian economy are far more dependent on the international economic cycle, and particularly on the US cycle, than on the decisions of the government.

While it is true that Western Europe is made up of economic systems which are strongly interconnected it is also true that their economic features are different. Even if the economic problems are similar, the same policies cannot always be adopted. Thus Italy cannot follow the deflationary policies that West Germany has adopted since 1973 because unlike West Germany, Italy has a high rate of unemployment, massive regional problems and it has no surplus foreign workers to send home.[42] This does not mean that a common approach to solving common problems cannot be arrived at. This would mean joint participation in establishing different policies. For this to be achieved it would be necessary, however, that the Italian authorities adopt a more decisive approach in matters of foreign affairs. Similarly, in order to achieve the objectives of the plan with respect to labour costs and labour mobility, it would be necessary to reach an understanding with the trade-union movement. Such an understanding would entail a different mode of ruling the country, a different attitude towards the PCI and possibly a different political system.

In the epoch in which the State has acquired responsibility for the economic process the traditional separation between economics and politics, typical of the nineteenth-century Liberal State can no longer exist. It would have been impossible to write this brief history of the Italian economy without constantly referring to specific political determinations of economic affairs. Every single economic decision has had to be made on the basis of the kind of consensus, whether of an active or passive kind, that such a decision would create, mould, change or reinforce. Ultimately, political consensus rests on social groups and social classes and their organizations. We shall deal with these in Part II, and we shall leave to Part III the system of political institutions and political parties.

REFERENCES AND NOTES

1. Baratta, P. *et al.* (1978), p. 4. See also figures in Castronovo, V. (1975), p. 476.
2. Castronovo (1975), p. 477.
3. Garavini, S. (1974), p. 29.
4. This analysis of the economic assumptions of the Bank of Italy relies on Graziani, A. and Meloni, F. (1980), pp. 59–80.
5. Valli, V. (1980), p. 89.
6. Amato, G. (1976), p. 55.
7. Onida, F. (1977), p. 75.
8. Ibid., p. 73.
9. Peggio, E. (1976), p. 51.
10. Colajanni, N. (1976), p. 12.
11. Onida (1977), pp. 70–1.
12. Parboni, R. (1981), pp. 79–80.
13. Valli, V. (1979), p. 135.
14. Figures in Colajanni (1976), p. 8.
15. Castronovo (1975), p. 482.
16. Garavini (1974), p. 60.
17. Cantelli, P. (1980), p. 51.
18. Ibid., p. 88.
19. National Accounts of OECD in the *Financial Times,* 7 Dec. 1981.
20. See figures in Cantelli (1980), p. 81.
21. Valli (1980), pp. 99–100.
22. Fabiani, G. (1977), p. 167.
23. Amato (1976), pp. 62–4.
24. Ibid., p. 101.
25. Garavini, S. (1977), p. 28.
26. Colajanni (1976), p. 46.
27. That there is such a contrast is the thesis asserted in a best-selling book by two leading Italian journalists: E. Scalfari and G. Turani *Razza padrona. Storia della borghesia di stato,* (Scalfari and Turani 1974).
28. Garavini (1977), pp. 27–8.
29. Valli (1980), p. 105.
30. Fabiani, G. (1980), p. 3.
31. For this analysis see Valli (1980), pp. 151–2.
32. Trentin, B. (1980), p. 3, interview by B. Ugolini. The figures are official Fiat figures.
33. Figures in Baratta *et al.* (1975), p. 109.
34. Accornero, A. and Carmignani, F. (1978), pp. 122–5.
35. See figures in Baratta *et al.* (1975), p. 109.

36. See figures in Filosa, R. and Visco, I. (1980), p. 108.
37. 'Piano 1979–81. Una proposta per lo sviluppo una scelta per l'Europa', in Nardozzi (1980), p. 28.
38. See Valli's critique of the Pandolfi Plan in Valli (1979), pp. 140–4.
39. 'Piano 1979–81. Una proposta . . . ', in Nardozzi (1980), pp. 39–40.
40. Ibid., p. 23.
41. Data in *La Repubblica* 3 Jan. 1985, p. 2, in Visco, V. (1985), p. 1 and in Barclays Bank (Dec. 1984).
42. Valli (1979), pp. 165–6.

Part Two
SOCIETY

Chapter 5:

SOCIAL CLASSES

Part I of this book has been devoted to an overview of Italian economic development and has attempted to offer a historical perspective on its integration in the world economy, its rapid industrialization and the consequent effects of it: crisis and further unequal development. It is already apparent, even without examining any data, that there has been a significant shift from agriculture to the industrial sector. Not only is this not peculiar to Italy but it is, in a sense, a tautology: any process of industrialization involves, by definition, a shift of population from the countryside. We are not, however, dealing simply with two sectors of the economy: industrial and agricultural production. There is a third sector, populated overwhelmingly although not exclusively by intermediate groups usually termed the 'middle classes'. Furthermore, these 'middle' groups can also be found in both the manufacturing sector (e.g. artisans) and in even greater numbers in the rural economy (e.g. independent small farmers or peasants).

It is thus immediately apparent that when we talk about the classification of the population we can use essentially two criteria: distribution in terms of broad occupational definitions, for example manufacturing, agriculture and services, or stratification in terms of social class, for example upper class, middle class and working class. One can of course use other criteria, for example income levels. This would be important if we wanted to know whether Italy is becoming a less unequal society in terms of income while an analysis in the distribution of the levels of purchasing power would also tell us whether Italy is becoming a richer society.

Here we want to concentrate on the stratification of the population in terms of social classes and then examine briefly the distribution in terms of occupational sectors. The reason for insisting on social classes is that it is politically important. In spite of the rise of social 'subjects' which cut across classes (e.g. women and youth) political parties tend to define their strategy and their demands in terms of specific classes. For example the Italian Communist Party (PCI) defines the working class as the main protagonist of progressive social change, as the class whose aspirations it seeks to defend and promote, but it also recognizes that the working class needs to establish alliances with other classes and, in particular with the 'middle strata'. If, however, an analysis were to establish that the middle strata are being constantly 'proletarianized', then the whole concept of class alliances would become more problematical. Let us take another example: the Christian Democratic Party (DC) is said to rely on a mechanism of consensus in which the middle strata play the central and crucial role. If that is so, then it would be in the interest of this party to maintain the strength and expansion of this sector, or, alternatively, to adopt a different political strategy. It is thus not surprising that one of the most important attempts to analyse social classes in Italy, that of Paolo Sylos Labini, caused much controversy.[1]

Sylos Labini borrowed his central concepts from the classics of political economy, the works of Adam Smith and David Ricardo, who had divided the population in terms of the origins of incomes: incomes from profit (capitalists), from rent (landlords) and from wages (workers), but they were also perfectly aware that an important section of the population derived its income from its independent activity (artisans and farmers). Sylos Labini thus proposed the following classifications:

1. *The ruling class,* or bourgeoisie. This included both capitalists and large landlords as well as the managers of enterprises and leading professionals.
2. *The middle classes.* This was further subdivided into three categories: the 'relatively independent petty bourgeoisie' (farmers and sharecroppers, artisans, shopkeepers and small business people, small professional people); the salaried petty bourgeoisie (white-collar workers and teachers, technicians, etc.); special categories (priests and nuns, military personnel).
3. *The working class.* This includes the industrial working class, agricultural labourers, manual workers employed in services and transportation, domestic servants, shop assistants, construction workers, etc..

Sylos Labini's work spans a considerable period of time: from 1881 to 1971 and is based principally but not – as we shall see – exclusively on census reports. We shall deal only with the post-war period (see Table 5.1).

It is, however, of interest to state briefly Sylos Labini's conclusions from the broader 1881–1971 study[2]:

1. The most important result is that, since 1881, there has been a massive expansion of the salaried middle class (2% in 1881) and a major contraction of the independent petty bourgeoisie (41% in 1881).
2. The relative weight of the whole of the middle classes with respect to

TABLE 5.1 Distribution of population by social class, 1951–71

	1951 (%)	1961 (%)	1971 (%)
Bourgeoisie	1.9	2.0	2.6
Middle classes	56.9	53.4	49.6
1. Salaried	9.8	13.1	17.1
2. Independent	44.4	37.2	29.1
3. Special cat.	2.7	3.1	3.4
Working class	41.2	44.6	47.8

Source: Sylos Labini (1974), p. 156.

the working class has not changed very much (1881: middle classes were 45.9% and working classes 52.2%).
3. The top bourgeoisie is fairly stable (1881: 1.9%).

In fact the most interesting changes are those since 1951. In that year the middle classes were at the peak of their growth, they contract thereafter. The salaried petty bourgeoisie increases in the twenty years between 1951 and 1971 more (in absolute percentage points) than in the previous seventy years. The relatively independent petty bourgeoisie, which had increased during the fascist period to 47.1 per cent decreased rapidly between 1951 and 1971. But the most interesting changes are those which occur *within* the classes and subclasses. The bourgeoisie appears to be fairly stable, but this disguises a decrease in the number of landlords and an increase in the numbers of entrepreneurs and managers.

The decrease in the percentage of the relatively independent petty bourgeoisie is due exclusively to the contraction in the numbers of farmers (from 30.3% in 1951 to 12.1% in 1971); shopkeepers and artisans in fact increase.

The decline in the agricultural working class is very evident between 1951 and 1971 (from 11.8% to 6.2%), but this is not a new phenomenon: it was 35.6 per cent in 1881 and has declined ever since.

The industrial working class (including building workers) moved from 18.7 per cent in 1901 to 22.9 per cent in 1951, not a spectacular increase. It then grew rapidly to 33 per cent by 1971.

What all these figures reflect is something we already knew from our overview of economic development: a massive shift from the countryside to the town.

We have hitherto used Sylos Labini's figures. As we stated earlier his work caused a certain amount of debate and controversies. We shall want to give a brief look at these before proceeding, on the basis of his figures and of those of others, to examine in a more detailed manner the changes which have occurred within each category.

The first problem concerning the statistical analysis of social classes is that concerning the validity of the data themselves. Antonio Chiesi points out that the main sources of statistics (ISTAT, DOXA, Bank of Italy) are all open to serious criticism.[3] Others, such as Paolo Ammassari lament that the study of social classes in Italy began in a serious way only in 1968. Previously it was in the hands not of sociologists as apparently it should be, but in those of historians and these tended to be suspicious of 'positivist' approaches because of their Crocean or Gramscian–Marxist formation.[4] Sylos Labini does not always make his own statistical sources clear. He used for most years the census data, but he could not use these for 1971 because they were not yet available. So he used instead the *Yearbook of Labour Statistics 1972* and built his 1961 tables also on the basis of the *Yearbook*.[5] If he had used the census of 1961 for the 1961 statistics, he would have obtained a different set. The differences are considerable, as Luca Ridolfi has demonstrated in Table 5.2. The data are different but the categories and the construction of these categories, i.e. their definitions, are identical in both cases. The result is that if you use the census data you get a significantly larger working class and a significantly smaller middle class than if you use Sylos Labini or, to put it numerically, with the census data you get an extra 1.4 million workers and 1.8 million fewer middle-class people.

TABLE 5.2 Census versus Sylos Labini social class data (1961)

	Census data (%)	Sylos Labini data (%)	% difference
Bourgeoisie	2.1	2.0	−0.1
Middle class	45.2	53.4	+8.2
Working class	52.7	44.6	−8.1

Source: Ridolfi (1975), p. 74.

The other problem with Sylos Labini's class analysis is a familiar one: the question of demarcation lines. A doctor could be in the bourgeoisie if he/she is a famous practitioner with a wealthy clientele, or a 'relatively independent petty bourgeois' if he/she is a modest country doctor, but the demarcation line is usually not so clearly delineated. Furthermore, there is the problem of 'mixed' status, for example a factory worker with a plot of land.

Finally, broad categories such as those used so far disguise quite different social conditions: the relatively independent petty bourgeois could be an affluent jeweller in the centre of Rome or Milan or someone with a stall selling plastic jewellery at a local market. Let us then examine a study which further differentiates within classes and which establishes categories different from those examined so far.

Carlo Trigilia uses a concept of bourgeoisie which is identical to that of Sylos Labini, but 'his' middle classes are divided into *white collar* and *independent middle class* (same as Sylos Labini but excluding independent 'precarious' or 'casual' activity; this is to be included in the *casual proletariat* and they are mainly small farmers). There is then a class called the *central proletariat* which includes all workers, urban and rural, employed in firms employing more than ten people. Finally, there is the *marginal proletariat;* this is divided in the 'peripheral' proletariat (workers in firms employing less than ten workers), and the 'casual' proletariat which includes small farmers, stall-holders, other casual independent workers and labourers.[6]

This subdivision would probably, on further investigation, give rise to as many problems as Sylos Labini's subdivision, and, anyway, does not disprove what is generally known and evident from his figures. They, however, offer a more detailed and hence more accurate picture. The main findings are in Table 5.3. A careful study of Table 5.3 will show that:

1. The bourgeoisie expands, but more in the North than in the South

TABLE 5.3 Economically active population per social class (%)

	1951			1961			1971		
	Italy	North	South	Italy	North	South	Italy	North	South
Bourgeoisie	2.1	2.2	1.9	2.2	2.4	1.9	3.2	3.3	2.6
I. Independent									
middle class	37.0	37.2	37.0	26.1	26.3	25.9	17.4	18.1	19.1
Agriculture	28.5	28.7	28.2	18.2	17.4	19.8	9.5	8.0	12.9
Industry	4.0	3.8	4.5	3.8	3.9	3.8	3.9	4.6	2.4
Tertiary	4.5	4.7	4.3	4.1	5.0	2.3	5.0	5.5	3.8
II. White collar	10.7	11.9	7.8	13.9	15.7	10.3	21.5	23.3	17.8
Private sector	4.2	5.3	2.0	7.3	9.1	3.6	11.9	14.3	6.8
Public sector	6.5	6.6	5.8	6.6	6.6	6.7	9.6	9.0	11.0
III. Central									
proletariat	17.0	21.9	7.6	21.5	27.0	10.1	25.1	30.6	12.8
IV. Marginal									
proletariat	33.2	26.8	45.7	36.3	28.6	51.8	31.8	24.7	47.7
Peripheral	4.6	3.9	6.2	7.1	8.9	3.4	7.7	9.2	4.2
Casual	28.6	22.9	39.5	29.2	19.7	48.4	25.1	15.5	43.5
Agricultural	*11.8*	*6.3*	*22.4*	*9.4*	*3.2*	*21.8*	*5.8*	*1.6*	*15.5*
Industrial	*10.7*	*10.4*	*11.2*	*12.0*	*9.4*	*17.3*	*9.7*	*6.3*	*17.3*
(construction	*4.9*	*4.2*	*6.4*	*7.4*	*5.2*	*11.6*	*5.4*	*3.4*	*10.0)*
Tertiary	*6.1*	*6.2*	*5.9*	*7.8*	*7.1*	*9.3*	*9.6*	*7.6*	*10.7*
Total	100	100	100	100	100	100	100	100	100

Source: Trigilia (1976), p. 262.

2. There is a very large decrease of the independent middle class in both North and South, but in agriculture this class decreases more in the North than in the South, in industry it increases in the North and decreases in the South and in the tertiary sector it increases more in the North than in the South.

3. The number of white-collar workers more than double, but the increase in the South is greater than the increase in the North and this is mainly due to the expansion of white-collar jobs in the public sector in the South, i.e. due to the extension of the central government (Rome) and local administration. However, the main impetus behind the increase in white-collar jobs *overall* is due to the private sector.

4. The central proletariat increases far more in the North than in the South.

5. Overall the marginal proletariat does not change significantly between 1951 and 1971. However, the 'peripheral proletariat' increases considerably in the North while it actually decreases in the South (this consists of workers in firms employing less than ten people). The casual proletariat decreases in the North and increases in the South. The southern increase in the casual proletariat is entirely due to the increase of the casual workers in the tertiary and industrial sectors because there is actually a decrease in casual workers in agriculture.

I think it is now possible to go beyond the simple statement that the chief characteristic of Italian development has been the shift from agriculture to industry. The pattern of transformation of social classes has quite specific contours in northern Italy and contrasts sharply with the South. The largest single class in the North is the 'central proletariat' (30.6% in 1971) while the largest single class in the South is the 'casual proletariat' (43.5% in 1971). The 'surplus' population in the South is expelled from agriculture, does not find an outlet in industrial enterprises in the South and is thus in part 'exported' towards capitalist enterprises abroad or in the North. Those who stay are absorbed in the tertiary sector of the independent middle class, in the white-collar private sector, in the casual tertiary sector and in the casual construction industry. All these sectors which absorb otherwise unemployable southern labour are all 'politically protected' sectors. This political protection derives from the control on the public purse exercised by successive DC governments.

In the North industry absorbs southern labour, expels female and older male labour and, when it enters into a crisis in the 1960s, it restructures itself through an increase in productivity and a further expulsion of labour. This excess labour in the North finds a place in the expansion of white-collar jobs in the private sector, but also in the decentralization of industry towards smaller units of production (the 'home' of the peripheral proletariat). There is a considerable expansion of small firms who are *de facto* satellites of the larger units (this is achieved through a wide system of subcontracting to small 'family' firms, often women working at home).

Thus the changes in social classes respond not only to an economic logic but also to a political one which joins together North and South in a pattern of reciprocal exchange of political and economic tasks whereby the South relates to the North as an area of *dependent development*.

The policy of southern industrialization was directed towards capital-intensive large-scale production (see Chs 3 and 4) with little impact on southern employment. Nevertheless, it is sufficient to expand purchasing power (further expanded by the increase in state jobs) and hence the market. This market attracts the products of northern industry. Traditional southern industry which is small-scale and inefficient, cannot compete, particularly as it now faces an increase in labour costs (wages, etc.). Small firms are forced out of business and their excess labour emigrates north, abroad or finds a home in marginal urban employment, particularly in the construction industry and in the tertiary sector.[7]

The upshot of this rather complex process of political and economic development is a growing internal differentiation of southern society both in the geographical and in the occupational sense. The inland areas of the regions of Molise, Basilicata and Calabria are clearly backward areas, they are devastated by emigration, and what employment there is, is in an under-capitalized and poor agricultural sector; in local government jobs there is hardly any industrial proletariat. In the coastal areas of the islands, Abruzzi, Campania and Apulia you have large-scale industrial developments and peripheral areas which depend on the industrial sector. As Trigilia points out, 90 per cent of state funds towards southern industry between 1961 and 1971 went to these coastal area.[8] Between 1971 and 1981 the percentage of those employed in industry and agriculture in Italy decreased, the tertiary sector grew to include half the active population (see Table 5.4). Furthermore, even among those employed in industry the shift in these ten years has been

TABLE 5.4 Employment by sector, 1971 and 1981

	1971 (%)	1981 (%)
Agriculture	17.2	11.2
Industry	44.4	39.8
Others	38.9	49.0

Source: Grussu (1984), p. 36. These figures have been elaborated by the CRAS on the basis of census data and ISTAT figures.

away from blue-collar workers (see Table 5.5). Thus the numerical importance of the working class is in diminution and Italy is fast becoming a 'post-industrial' society like other advanced Western countries.

As can be seen, if the discussion on social classes had remained stuck at the general level of the three broad classes we would not have been able to say much more than that Italian industrialization has followed the general pattern of more 'advanced' countries. We would have been able to use the figures to substantiate the hypothesis that economic development follows the same pattern and the same logic everywhere: from the countryside to the towns. But the key difference between Italy and the other European countries is the centrality in Italy of the 'Southern Question'.

All Italian governments since Unification have had to grapple with this question and their actions have tended to shape economic and social development.

TABLE 5.5 Occupational distribution in industry, 1971 and 1981

Industry	1971 (%)	1981 (%)
Managers + white collar	12.4	16.3
Workers	74.2	70.4

Source: Weber (1981), p. 190.

Thus – as Picchieri points out – the contraction of the peasants slowed down precisely when they were felt to be needed for the purposes of political stabilization by the fascist authorities in the 1930s and by the DC in the 1950s.[9] Contrary to all 'economic laws' the number of small shopkeepers not only has not decreased but has actually increased, and this was largely due to the intervention of the political authorities.[10] The resistance of small shopkeepers could be, at least in part, due to the backwardness of the retailing system. What, undoubtedly, it feeds on is the lasting ambition of many workers, particularly those whose memories of an independent occupation is still recent – i.e. workers from the countryside – to set up shop on their own, 'to be their own bosses'.

The overall expansion of the middle classes outside the rural sector (the middle classes as a whole, including the peasantry, as we have seen actually contracts) is also due, according to Sylos Labini, to the fact that the big bourgeoisie, being numerically small and needing allies, has tended to facilitate the expansion of these groups.[11] Clearly, we should not assume that this is a conscious objective envisaged by the top social class. What this means, however, is that one must be careful not to conclude that the sole aim of the DC is the political protection of various middle strata groups.[12] Christian Democratic economic policy is also directed to help and protect large private firms through fiscal and monetary means, through public investments in key sectors such as steel and motorways. Conversely, the political protection of middle strata groups is also achieved by forces other than the DC; it is achieved by economic means by oligopolies who are able to confer advantages on a whole range of economic activities that is, to confer incomes higher than those accruing to others engaged in similar activities but in non-oligopoly sectors.[13]

Furthermore, there is also an economic pay-off. Middle-class incomes in the years of the 'economic miracle' constituted the necessary home market for those household goods which the export-oriented private firms needed. A home market constituted essentially by working-class incomes would have entailed higher labour costs, thus wiping out the competitive advantages of Italian industry. Middle-class incomes which did not depend on the private manufacturing sector were highly functional to the 'economic miracle'.

Alessandro Pizzorno, who sustains the above thesis, also points out that the political strength of the Italian middle classes can also be detected if one considers the singular fact that virtually all government crises in the 1950s were provided by either one or the other of the three small parties who were usually in government with the DC: the Social Democrats, the Liberals and the Republicans and that these three parties have an electorate which is virtually entirely composed of middle-strata groups.[14] The working class and its parties, Socialists and Communists, were in opposition, the rural groups were kept quiet with a piece of land and public works programmes, while the middle classes were the only groups which could disturb the rapid advances of the Italian entrepreneurial classes.

Once again it is necessary to remind the reader that the middle classes did not expand as such. What expanded, apart from the shopkeepers (and in this case the numbers are not significant), were the white-collar sectors. These expand all over Europe. The distinctive trait of the Italian situation is that the working class expands. The overall contraction of the middle classes would have been even higher if shopkeepers had decreased (as they should, at least according to received opinion), if the middle class had not been protected and if the government had not expanded white-collar jobs in the public sector.

Some maintain that one should avoid concentrating excessively on the middle classes because what is peculiar about post-war Italian economic and social development is the expansion of the working class.[15] One should add that such an expansion continued throughout the 1960s while the participation rate of the population in the labour force had dropped from 43.3 per cent in 1960 to 35.9 per cent in 1972 (the biggest drop in the OECD countries). In fact the expansion of the industrial sector in terms of the labour force employed in it was second only to Japan. At the same time as there was a constant transfer of people from the agricultural sector to the industrial sector, there was also a strong emigration. In other words the expansion of manufacturing could not mop up all 'surplus' labour from the countryside. Here we get nearer to one of the central particularities of Italian economic development. It is the only one of the advanced industrial countries which sustained a rapid economic development while exporting labour instead of importing it, as was done by virtually all of Italy's main competitors in Europe.

Emigration has been a phenomenon which has been virtually uninterrupted except for the 1930s throughout the history of modern Italy. Between 1861 and 1973 26 million Italians left Italy and – up to 1965 – about 6 million returned. Initially (1876–1910) emigration was from the Veneto region towards the American continent, mainly Argentina and Brazil (about 1.5 million) and from the South to the United States (6 million).[16] In the same period there was also some emigration to the coal-mining regions of Europe, Belgium, France, Germany and the United Kingdom. After 1922 the USA stopped immigration from Italy, but in spite of that and in spite of obstacles on the part of the fascist authorities emigration continued throughout the 1920s: 2.5 million left mainly to France and Argentina.[17]

The post-war period saw a massive emigration. Between 1946 and 1973 7.1 million people left Italy, but net migration (i.e. the difference between emigration and returned emigrants) was 3 million. Initially (1946–54) there was a certain balance between emigration towards other European countries and that directed towards other continents, but after 1955 Italian emigration was essentially European; its main destination was Switzerland, France (up to 1958) and West Germany.[18] The emigration towards West Germany and Switzerland was essentially male, on short contract, working on assembly lines, construction and in services such as catering and cleaners.

The export of labour continued thus until 1973. In that year for the first time in the history of modern Italy more Italians returned home than left Italy: between 1973 and 1978 the 'balance of labour' showed a gain of nearly 68,000 people.[19] At the same time as this emigration in reverse occurred there was another novel phenomenon: Italy began to import foreign labour. An estimated 350,000 foreign workers, mainly from the Horn of Africa, the Philippines and Egypt arrived in Italy – and virtually all of them illegally.[20] The return of Italian emigrants was mainly due to the international economic crisis which hit construction and manufacturing, particularly assembly-line work in the car sector. This led countries such as West Germany to 'unload' some of its redundant labour force by sending them back, foreign workers being the first to be sacked.

The advantage gained by economies such as the West German one is certainly remarkable. In the years of its economic miracle, it imported cheap labour when needed. At the outset of the recession it was able to dispense with such labour. But what of Italian industry? During its period of fast economic growth it was also able to import labour, but it was imported – so to speak – internally, that is, from the South. Internal Italian migration acquired, from the very beginning, a form of permanent 'immigration'.[21] The workers who left the countryside for the northern industrial triangle Milan–Turin–Genoa had equal citizenship rights. They could not be politically discriminated against or isolated by language barriers or fear of being expelled. Furthermore, Switzerland or West Germany had saved all the expense of educating the imported workers. As many came when young and able-bodied and without their families, they saved the host state expenses associated with schooling, pensions, health services, etc. In other words, foreign workers were putting into the economy far more than they were getting out of it in terms of social services.[22] But in Italy the southern 'immigrants' were there with their families, their needs, their possibility of influencing political organizations and trade unions and, in 1969, they could be in the forefront of the events leading to the 'hot autumn'.

The importance of the 'Southern Question' appears once again: its reserve army of labour fed the Italian 'economic miracle' and when this came to an end the tensions remained, grew and exploded.

REFERENCES AND NOTES

1. Sylos Labini, P. (1974). For other contributions see: Calza Bini, P. (1973); Maitan, L. (1975), Braghin, P., Mingione, E. and Trivellaro, P. (1974).
2. Sylos Labini (1974), see pp. 27–34 and Table 1.2, p. 156.
3. Chiesi, A. (1975), pp. 214–15.
4. Ammassari, P. (1977), p. 16.
5. This was only made clear in a letter sent by Sylos Labini to the journal *Quaderni Piacentini* and published in no. 60–1, p. 129.
6. Trigilia, C. (1976), pp. 260–1.
7. Ibid., pp. 278–9.
8. Ibid., p. 279.
9. Picchieri, A. (n.d.), p. 97.
10. Sylos Labini (1974), pp. 29–30 and Barbano, F. (1979), p. 189.
11. Sylos Labini (1974), p. 85.
12. Cassano, F. (1979), p. 19.
13. Sylos Labini, P. (1975), pp. 174–5.
14. Pizzorno, A. (1974), p. 336.
15. Ammassari (1977), p. 66.
16. Isenburg, T. (1980), p. 336.
17. Ibid., p. 341.
18. Birindelli, A. M. (1976), p. 180.

Chapter 6

NEW SOCIAL SUBJECTS

The social subjects we are interested in have two chief characteristics: first of all they transcend and cut across classes and, secondly, their mode of organization and their political behaviour cannot be easily captured or enclosed within those of political parties. They thus represent a double challenge: they disrupt the pattern of class politics which is a specific feature of European (though not American) political history and they challenge the central role of political parties as forms of organization of political society. They do so not only because they are not class aligned and hence not party aligned, but also because they refuse to distinguish between a private sphere of life where 'politics' is kept out (e.g. inter-personal relations) and a political sphere which keeps the domain of the 'private' out of it. The two social groups I am talking about are *women* and *youth*.

Women and youth are to be examined as 'new' social subjects. Obviously what is 'new' about them is not the fact of their existence. What is new about them is that they have come to be identified as *political* forces and yet they do not organize themselves in a traditional political manner: in centralized formal organizations.

WOMEN

It is clear that if we can talk of women as 'social subjects' it is because there is a women's movement. This arose, in Italy as in most West European countries, in the 1970s. One should really speak of a 'rebirth' if it were not for the fact that older types of feminism were either those of small groups of women whose existence was virtually ignored by women at large, or movements seeking to enter existing forms of organization in politics (e.g. the movement for women's suffrage) and thus did not pose a threat to the existing system of organizing political life.

Italian feminism drew its chief ideological inspiration from the American women's movement, that is from the country with the most-developed system of sectional politics or 'pressure-group' politics and the least-developed system of class-oriented politics in any of the advanced industrial countries. This could not be otherwise: the Italian political tradition did not offer much to women. In the market-place of ideologies there was a version of catholicism which did offer a role to women, but a subordinate one (the role of the homemaker and of the mother), there was a version of Marxism, which, in spite of the enrichments brought about by thinkers such as Antonio Labriola, Antonio Gramsci and the communist leader, Palmiro Togliatti, was still concerned essentially with the forging of alliances between social classes as organized by specific political parties.

Another major influence on the formation of Italian feminism was the student movement of 1968. This movement was, among other things, the expression of a social conflict which could not be defined in terms of class, but it was also a movement which at one and the same time expressed a critique of authority and of accepted forms of organization and behaviour while reproducing – within itself – the subordination of women.[1] Thus those radical women who were attracted to the politics of the students' movement perceived fairly early on that there was a marked contradiction between the aspiration of the movement in general and its patriarchal form of organization.

There were also some structural preconditions behind the women's movement such as an increase in female education which would make women more competitive with men in a number of occupations and a decrease in the birth-rate which meant that women were anchored to domestic chores for a shorter period of time.[2] But the main reasons must be found in the increased complexity of women's roles in society and their relation to it. The institution which was at the centre of women's struggle was the family, but the family was no longer the main institution within which women could find their place in society. More women were entering the labour market. This entry was, however, occurring at a rate which was much lower than that of other Western countries (see Part I, Ch. 3). In fact, female employment even fell during the 'economic miracle' as women were substituted by young male migrant workers from the South. This did not take place through the deliberate sacking of women workers, but by taking advantage of their high turnover in the labour market, i.e. the fact that their initial entry into it is a temporary one (i.e. it is interrupted by pregnancy and child-rearing).[3] The rise in the standard of living facilitated their being kept out of the labour market. The wages earned by male workers increased and this maintained and reinforced the division of labour between the male breadwinner and the female homemaker. When the 'miracle' was over, women began to return to the labour force, but they tended, on the whole, to take jobs in the so-called 'hidden economy' of casual labour and small family firms (cottage industry, subcontracted labour, sweat-shops, etc.).

These processes lead to the growing complexity of women's roles. The role which is assigned to them is that of the caring and loving role of the good wife and good mother. There is, however, also a need for extra income, women now *need* to work and this makes it more difficult to fulfil their assigned family role. This tension is felt by virtually all working women. The necessity for women to work is further accelerated by some of the changes in the family in Italy in the post-war period. The most visible quantitative aspect of this change is the decrease in the size of the family itself, from 3.97 persons in 1951 to 3.18 in 1976 and the concurrent decrease in the average number of income-earners in the family (from 2.3 in 1900 to 1.7 in 1951 to 1.5 in 1961 to 1.2 in 1971 to 1.1 in 1976).[4] This means that instead of two or three workers in a family you now often get only one. Children increasingly leave the family home when they can work and marry earlier. Census data show that there is a sharp decrease of the 'extended' family (defined as being made up of a married couple, their children and other relatives) while there is a growth of households made up of one person only, of childless couples and of those whose children have left the home.[5]

In 1971 households made up of five or more members were nearly twice that of one-person households. Between 1971 and 1981 one-person households have increased by 5 per cent (from 12.9 to 17.9% of all households). Households made up of six or more persons have gone down from 9.7 to 5.4 per cent of all households. In the North one-person households are twice as many as large households. As an average the Italian family is made up of three persons but, between 1971 and 1981, this type of family has declined.[6]

As the extended family declines there is a parallel growth of the Welfare State. This, albeit very partially, begins to provide a range of services previously offered by the family, e.g. care of children and old people. The services of the Welfare State, however, are available only if there is an individual who is prepared to engage in the necessary bureaucratic practices needed to obtain these services, whether bringing the children to a nursery or filling in forms. This role is seen as natural to women: it is an extension of their role of 'loving and caring homemakers'. At the same time, women are also expected to compensate where public services fail. Finally, the extension of the consumer society and the constant and dramatic decrease in the self-sufficiency of the household (compare a peasant family with an urban family which must purchase virtually everything it needs) adds on another task for women: the purchase of private services.[7] To sum up, women work before they have children, then they abandon their work in order to look after their children, then they often return to work, while they must function as the agents of the Welfare State within the family (purchaser of public services), as the agents of the consumption sector of the economy within the family (purchaser of private services), and they compensate for the deficiencies of the Welfare State. They often work in whatever peripheral, casual or marginal jobs are available if the man's wages cannot provide for the family needs. Furthermore, they must also fulfil their traditional roles of procreators and homemakers (household chores, cooking, etc.). Compared to this the life of the man is a rather simple one: work, leisure and sleep.

The complex life-cycle of women is thus characterized by three phases: (1) pre-child-bearing employment; (2) domestic labour when children are under 6; and (3) when children go to school, when they do both domestic labour and extra-domestic paid employment.[8] This also means that when women enter the labour market they know that there will be an interruption (phase 2) and that when they re-enter it they will be subjected to the specific conditions of phase 3. The prospect of an uninterrupted career is thus seldom available to women. Furthermore, paid employment during the long phase 3 must be adapted to the requirements of their domestic commitments. Thus women tend to 'prefer' jobs such as nursing (which can be done at night), cleaning offices early in the morning, schoolteaching, etc. These are also jobs which are, in a sense, an extension of the traditional 'caring and loving' role of women.[9]

Women's employment has thus tended to be concentrated in the services sector, but they have also acted as substitute land workers as male labour left the countryside for the towns. In 1951 out of 100 people working in agriculture 24.6 were women, but by 1976 31.6 were women. The female labour force in industry (as a percentage of the male) dropped from 21.9 to 20.1 between 1951 and 1976, while in the tertiary sector it increased from 29.9 (1951) to 36.7 (1976).[10] Between 1977 and 1982 the female labour force in the tertiary sector increased by 23 per cent and more in the South (+32%) than in the Centre-North (+18%) while the male labour force increases in the tertiary sector by only 11 per cent.[11] These figures do not reflect the extent to which women are concentrated in the service sector, because many of those working 'in industry' are in fact working in the service sector of industry. This sector is, generally speaking low paid, less trade unionized and technologically very backward at least until fairly recently.[12] A recent survey shows that only 22.5 per cent of women have a full-time job, while 5.8 per cent have only casual employment and 71.8 per cent do not work.[13] However, it has also been calculated that women represent 70 per cent of the unofficial labour market which suggests that, in practice female participation in the labour force may not be so different in Italy as in other industrial countries.[14]

One of the effects of the nature of the female labour market is that working women earn far less than working men. Table 6.1 shows a sample survey taken in 1976–77 on the differences in earnings between men and women.

TABLE 6.1 Monthly income by gender 1976–77 in 1000 lira

	Less than 120 (%)	120–200 (%)	200–270 (%)	270–350 (%)	over 350 (%)
Male	8.4	20.6	32.2	22.3	16.4
Female	24.5	33.3	16.7	17.6	7.8
Total	12.7	23.9	28.1	21.1	14.2

Source: Mannheimer and Sebastiani (1978), p. 25.

If we examine women's employment in various categories of the service sector we find that, without exception, they tend to be concentrated in the lower-paid jobs. Thus in the Civil Service they have the less secure jobs.[15] It is true that there has been an improvement: while in 1953 there were only 2.6 per cent of women in the top Civil Service grades, by 1975 this had gone up to 12.8 per cent. Overall female employment in the Civil Service jumped between 1953 and 1975 from 10.4 to 31.9 per cent; this, however, has occurred concurrently with a lowering in the prestige of Civil Service occupations.[16] It has been found, in fact, that women, unlike men, are attracted to Civil Service jobs not because of status but because of the security of tenure some of them might be able to enjoy – a pension, the hours of work and welfare schemes as well as the formal criterion of 'equality of opportunity'.[17]

If we take the 1971 Census data on professional employment we are faced with a clear illustration of the systematically subordinate position of women in modern Italian society. According to the data there are 1.6 million people belonging to what the Census calls the 'liberal, technical and scientific professions'. Of these 41 per cent are women, nearly half. Women make up 66 per cent of the teaching profession, but as you examine the various categories within this profession, you find that the proportion of women is inversely related to the prestige and income of the job: 79.4 per cent of elementary-school teachers are women, as are 63.7 per cent of middle-school teachers, 49 per cent of high-school teachers and 21 per cent of university teachers (within this section they are concentrated among the non-tenured staff). The same story can be told for the health profession of which 49.9 per cent are women, but this is due to the fact that they are in the majority in the largest categories – nursing staff (67%), assistants and technicians (85%). Only 8.7% of doctors are women ('loving and caring' but also well paid).

As in other European countries and in North America the central institution which defines women's general role in society, the family, has shown signs of instability. The concept of 'the crisis of the family' has become common currency in sociological literature and it has become increasingly difficult to talk of the 'typical' family (say, a gainfully employed husband, a housewife and a couple of children). The available figures, do in fact suggest that in quantitative terms there is a basis for a crisis of the family. We can observe a decline in the number of marriages from 7.1 per thousand inhabitants in 1950–52 to 5.9 per thousand in 1978. In fact this collapse is entirely due to the years 1972–78, marriages actually went up until the early 1970s. Presumably there has been a marked increase in 'common law' marriages. There has also been an increase in illegitimate births (from 2.4% of all births in 1961 to 3.6% in 1978) and the number of legal separations has gone up from 11.2 per 100,000 inhabitants in 1952 to 40.8 per 100,000 in 1978.[18]

So far we have simply delineated some of the general preconditions for the rise of the new feminist movement: the growing complexity of women's role, their marked subordination in the work-place, the impact of American feminism, the student movement of 1968, the crisis of the family, etc. The history of women's entry into politics, however, does not start in the 1960s. Before then women, or at least some women, were organized, but were organized by others. Under fascism the State sought to organize the subordination of women around their central role of 'devoted spouse and exemplary mother' using instruments such as the *fasci femminili* (not very successfully) and finding ideological reinforcement in the papal encyclical *Casti connubi* (1931) which was the fullest statement by Pope Pius XI on woman as wife and mother.[19]

Subsequently, women took part in the Resistance and in 1943 some of them formed the Gruppi di difesa della donna which became the Unione Donne Italiane (UDI). The UDI included Communist, Socialist, Liberal and Action Party (a radical republican party) women, but no Christian Democratic (DC) women. Thus, behind the first political organization of women in liberated Italy you had political parties and especially the Italian Communist Party (PCI).[20] There was no independent organization of women. The campaign for the extension of the suffrage to women was a muted affair, mainly because all the political parties agreed; those of the Left supported female suffrage for ideological reasons, the DC supported it because they would benefit the most.[21]

The two leading parties perceived the need to cultivate women's support fairly early on. The PCI had no base among women as such. Its natural base, the organized working class, was essentially male both because of male prejudice among trade unionists and because there were few women in occupations organized by the trade unions.[22] The PCI had thus to rely on UDI, but this was not a successful organization. In spite of its claim of being independent from the PCI (Socialist women were in it too), it never succeeded in being anything more than an extension of the PCI, at least until the late 1970s. Its membership dropped from its high point in 1950 of 1 million to 200,000 in 1960.[23] The PCI had always had a smaller proportion of women members than the DC, roughly 25 per cent against roughly 36 per cent, but it certainly did more to promote the advancement of women in the party than the DC. In 1972 there were 7.2 per cent of women in leadership positions in the PCI against 2.3 per cent in the DC. By 1976 the gap had grown (13.1% in the PCI against

2.0% in the DC).[24] In the Chamber of Deputies elected in 1983 19.9 per cent of PCI deputies were women (38 out of 198) against 2.6 per cent for the DC (6 out of 255) and 1 out of 73 for the Socialist Party (PSI). The total of women corresponded to 7.9 per cent of all deputies – more than twice those in the British House of Commons. The highest office in Italian politics ever held by a woman was held by Nilde Jotti, a communist leader, when she became President of the Chamber of Deputies in 1979.

In spite of its inability or unwillingness to promote women, the DC always had the largest number of female cadres. It was greatly helped by an organization of the Church, Azione Cattolica (AC). This organization was based on the parish and not on the party, it was thus not 'party-political' and this presented a distinct advantage. Azione Cattolica was open to members of both sexes, but women always prevailed: in 1946 AC had 151,000 men and 370,000 women, by 1969 it had 183,000 men and 459,000 women.[25] As seen in Table 6.2, this corresponded to the fact that women have been and are more regular churchgoers than men while the overall number of regular churchgoers has been constantly declining.

TABLE 6.2 Regular Church attendance by gender, 1956–75

	Men (%)	Women (%)
1956	57	80
1961	45	51
1973	29	37
1975	25	35

Source: Weber (1981), p. 190.

The first basis of the DC among women was thus the Church and AC. There is a difficulty, however, in organizing women politically while holding the ideological position that they should stay at home, which is exemplified by Pius XII's call to AC women to get out of 'the trenches of home and family' in order to defend the home and the family.[26]

The DC was always conscious of the strategic importance of the family and has always attempted to defend what it defined to be its traditional values. Thus when a divorce bill was successfully introduced in Parliament in 1970 it voted against the bill and proceeded to organize a referendum for its repeal. The DC threw all its strength and resources into the battle on divorce. The attempt to repeal the divorce law failed: only 40 per cent supported the DC. Many women, including many DC women voted against the law. The referendum on divorce was one of the most important defeats of the DC in the post-war period. For the first time it could not count on some of its 'collateral' organizations (as pro-DC institutions are called): AC refused to support the DC on divorce, the Catholic trade-union movement, the CISL, refused to give any indications to its members on how to vote, the pressure group of socialist-Catholics 'Christians for Socialism' as well as the Association of Italian Christian Workers (ACLI) upheld the principle of the non-interference of the Church in state matters.[27] The theme of autonomy from political parties which had been one of the central aspects of the women's movement had an effect on the PCI's women's organizations: the UDI rejected to some extent the cautious line of the PCI (which tried to defuse the referendum, before fighting it) and linked itself with the demands of the feminists.

The decisive role of women in defeating the referendum to abrogate the divorce law has been confirmed by surveys. Italian electoral results are given for every single polling station, which makes it easier to verify the behaviour of relatively small, homogeneous segments of the electorate. Thus the result of a polling station in the northern town of Ivrea (54% against the abolition of divorce) could not be defined in any other terms but startling when we consider that the bulk of the voters for that particular polling station was made up of nuns from the local convent. Research in maternity hospital polling stations in three Italian towns revealed clear pro-divorce majorities: 80.7 per cent (Bologna), 71.2 per cent (Turin) and 84.2 per cent (Florence).[28] Using the same maternity hospitals and comparing voting in general elections, Marina Weber established that in the period 1968–76 there was a shift to the Left on the part of women of child-bearing age which was more pronounced than the shift to the left for Italy as a whole: 'In all three centres the PCI obtained a gradual increase in its share of the vote and one which was higher than that achieved nationally. The DC vote declined in all three centres by a greater amount than its national performance.'[29]

Even women who were members of the DC were, to some extent, influenced by a feminist orientation. They were not only responding to the birth of an ideology, but also to some of the changes which were occurring in Italian society. The very existence of consumerism led many women to enter the labour market and caused a conflict between consumerist aspirations and their designated role in the traditional family.[30] Lidia Menapace draws a portrait of DC women: they tend to be more 'conservative' on formal political questions, but they are in favour of some sort of compromise between the housewife role and the wage-earner role by defending the expansion of part-time work; they toy with the idea of 'wages for housework' in order to protect the role of the housewife. Many may be against divorce and abortion, but they demand legal equality between men and women and more educational facilities for women.[31]

As a result of these pressures both the DC and the PCI united to pass a reform of family law (1975) which changed some of the more anachronistic aspects of Italian legislation: the concept of adultery as a criminal offence was abolished, legal separation could be obtained when the marriage had broken down and no longer, as it used to be the case, only when one of the two parties was 'guilty', children born out of wedlock were given the same rights as 'legitimate' children. In 1977 a law was passed against sexual discrimination.[32] In 1978, against strong DC opposition, a law legalizing abortion was passed by the Italian Parliament and the attempt to reverse it with another referendum was clearly defeated with a majority of 67.9 per cent.

The women's movement was not simply confined to legal changes. It presented itself as a major challenge to the organization of politics and the dominance of political parties. As it arose when the country moved to the Left (1968) it sought from the very beginning to demarcate itself from old conceptions of left politics. It criticised in particular the PCI, which had revealed itself unable to tackle the 'woman question' in a decisive manner.

The original form of organization of the women's movement was the small 'consciousness-raising' group within which women could rediscover themselves and could found a new concept of femininity. The slogans which were at the centre of women's struggles emphasized the desire to reappropriate a world which had been colonized by men: *Donna è bello* ('Womanhood is beautiful', clearly imported from the USA and derived from the black slogan: 'Black is beautiful') and *L'utero è mio e lo gestisco io* ('The womb is mine and I use it as I wish') which emphasized control: the Italian word *gestire* implies control and is normally used in the sense of ruling a country or running an enterprise.[33]

Fifteen years or so have elapsed since the birth of the new feminism in Italy. There is little doubt that it has scored some remarkable successes both in the domain of ideas and in the institutional field. Nevertheless, it too, like virtually every other political organization in Italy, from the political parties to the trade unions, is in crisis. The small consciousness-raising group does not offer a terrain for an institutional struggle. On the one hand modern feminism criticizes institutions (parties, legislative assemblies, etc.), yet at the same time it accepts the fact that the legal changes which are necessary require the intervention of these institutions. The forms of organization of the women's movement do not permit it to have direct access to sources of power and institutional change. In this situation it can only act as a pressure group and thus subordinate itself to the mediation of institutions such as political parties. Another problem, related to this and present also in a number of other industrial countries, is that the forms of organization of the women's movement make it difficult to establish a positive relation with other movements. In other words, the question of 'alliance' is not only a problem for other parties and organizations such as trade unions, but it is also a problem for the women's movement itself. As Maria Luisa Boccia wrote: 'No social subject transforms its aspirations into a political project ... unless it is able to have a positive relation with other subjects and other movements.'[34]

YOUTH

The existence of a 'youth question' is as controversial as the existence of a 'woman question'. The debate usually centres on whether the internal differentiations within the age-group 14–24 are so considerable as to render any attempt to subsume all its members under the general category of youth quite meaningless. There are, however, numerous elements which also indicate that even the differentiations can have a meaning only if we acknowledge that sometime during the post-war period there emerges – not only in Italy but in the whole of the industrial world and in many urban centres of the 'Third World' – a category of people which exhibits specific economic, political and cultural characteristics and which have in common the fact of 'being young'.

We have already noted that in Italy the participation rate of the population, that is, the ratio of the labour force to the population, has fallen more rapidly than in most other industrialized countries. This reflects the fact that new jobs are not being created in proportion to the growth of the population. Potential entrants in the labour force therefore find it more difficult to find a job. If, in 1960 the participation rate of males between 20 and 24 was 78 per cent (48% for females), by 1973 it had fallen to 66 per cent (43% for females).[35] Thus an increasing number of young people had to delay their entry into the labour force and thus 'choose' to remain in education or to be unemployed. The demand for education has thus an 'objective' basis, but it could also arise because there was an effective expansion of the 'supply' of education. The authorities had assumed that the rapid economic growth of the late 1950s and early 1960s would continue and various official reports (e.g. the SVIMEZ report of 1961) had stressed that more highly qualified people were needed and that education had to expand accordingly.[36] As we know the rapid growth of the period of the 'economic miracle' had come to an end around 1963 and yet education, particularly university education, expanded throughout the 1960s (as in the rest of Europe and North America). Thus the educational sector had become increasingly a 'parking area' (as it was called in Italy) for otherwise unemployed young people, and at the same time it constituted a terrain where employment could be provided for otherwise unemployed graduates (teachers and researchers).[37]

The expansion of education not only increased the numbers of educated young people but also changed qualitatively the nature of education in Italy. At the end of the fascist period Italian univers. were essentially élite institutions and not, as they subsequently became, the focus for the aspirations of millions of young people. The function of the universities under fascism and under the liberal regime which preceded it was the ideological and cultural reproduction of a narrow ruling class.[38] An élite of students was taught by an élite of teachers.

With the birth of the Italian republic the pressures for mass education multiplied. All main political parties were in favour of it. The PCI maintained that it was necessary to expand education and higher education not only because this was necessary in a democratic society, but also because it was one of the main means of bridging the technological gap which existed between Italy and its main international competitors[39]. The DC and the PSI, particularly in the years of the Centre-Left, expanded education not only because they expected a concomitant expansion of the productive system, or because it would keep the number of young unemployed down, but also in order to meet the expectations of their own supporters and of the population at large. In any case the expansion of the State and its economic and welfare institutions *did* require the production of greater numbers of graduates.

Given the inability of the labour market to absorb the increasing number of graduates the qualifications of the average unemployed person grew, as shown in Table 6.3. The main reason behind graduate unemployment was the fact that while education expanded the share of graduates taken up by industry began to fall after 1961. In that year Italian industry took up 16.9 per cent of graduates. By 1964 this fell to 4.4 per cent, then it went up again to 12.5 per cent in 1969 only to fall to 5.7 per cent in 1976.[40] By 1980 there were 1.25 million unemployed aged

TABLE 6.3 Correlation between educational level and unemployment, 1960 and 1971

Educational level	% of unemployed looking for first job	
	1960	*1971*
Degree	2.7	6.3
High school diploma (18 years of age)	30.8	36.3
School-leaving certificate (14 years of age)	28.4	31.4
Primary school (10 years of age)	38.1	25.7
Illiterates	–	0.3

Source: CENSIS IV, *Rapporto sulla situazione economica e sociale del palse*, Rome, 1972, cited in Vacca, G. (1973), p. 49.

29 and of these 40 per cent had a degree or a higher

hemployed youth do? In the North there is plenty of casual
w stable jobs. Young people there tend to accept casual
;e it is clearly seen as a stop-gap measure. Many of them
tudy while working because university attendance is not
compulsory. In the South the rate of youth unemployment is twice that
of the North. The little casual labour there is highly exploitative and is
not seen at all as 'temporary'. The fear is that once it is accepted it
becomes permanent. Consequently, it is not sought. In the North
unemployed youth tend to accept these kind of jobs because they feel
that sooner or later they will obtain a 'decent' job. In the South most
young people are on the constant look-out for a safe and secure job, and
this is usually a public sector job.[41]

Youth unemployment is not particular to Italy; however, in Italy it
has occurred for a longer period than in other European countries: it
began in the 1960s, whereas in for example, France, Sweden and West
Germany it appeared in the 1970s. Furthermore, Italy shares with
'late-comer' countries such as Spain and Greece a particularly high rate
of graduate unemployment and, finally, youth unemployment is much
higher in Italy than in most other European countries with the exception
of Belgium.[42] In 1980 youth unemployment (youth being defined as
those under 24) as a percentage of the labour force was 27.5 in Italy, 14.7
in France, 10.6 in the UK and 4 in West Germany (OECD figures).

As we have seen previously, the statistical averages disguise the
unevenness of the problem. As shown in Table 6.4 unemployment rates
are much higher in the South. According to figures from the Ministry of
Labour, in 1979 the public sector was able to provide permanent
employment in roughly similar proportions in both North and South,
whereas the private sector provided employment opportunities mainly
in the North.[43] Thus in the South a permanent job means, in most cases,
a public sector job. Once again the State must intervene to compensate
for the inability of the private sector to provide adequate employment
opportunities in southern Italy.

So far we have established the fact that youth is a group which has
been particularly exposed to the problem of unemployment, or, to put it

TABLE 6.4 Unemployment rate for the 14–24 age-group in 1979
(North/South)

Northern regions	(%)	Southern regions	(%)
Piedmont	20.7	Campania	38.2
Lombardy	15.6	Calabria	40.5
Veneto	17.2	Sicily	33.6

Source: ISTAT (1989).

differently, youth has been particularly hit by the crisis of Italian economic development. Of course this, on its own, does not prove the existence of a 'youth question'. What we want to do now is relate the question of the labour market to the question of the expansion of education. We have already noted that there is a relation between the lengthening of the period of study and the growth of youth unemployment and that the expansion of Italian universities was essentially an expansion in terms of number of students admitted. As the actual structures of the universities are not adequate for the number of students registered it is practically impossible for all students to attend classes regularly, consult with their teachers, use the library, etc. In practice less than 20 per cent of university students actually attend courses.[44] Because of the ease of access to university (the school-leaving diploma enables a student to register at any Italian university of his/her choosing), Italian students are *de facto* part-time students who study on their own and use the university building only during examinations. The paucity of student grants or of cheap student loans means that students are even less economically independent than their American or British counterparts. They are forced by economic necessity either to rely on their families for a long period of time (Italian degrees take between four and six years, but on a part-time basis it would obviously take even longer), or to have some form of temporary employment, or both. The kind of temporary jobs students find tend to be the sort of casual, marginal and 'black economy' jobs that other young people find. Thus there is a trend towards the homogenization of most young people at a lower 'subproletarian' level.[45] The transformation of universities into part-time institutes, and the ease of access to them occurred as a result of the students' struggles of the late 1960s (one of the main student demands was for 'open access' against the traditional élitism of the universities). This coincided with the decentralization of Italian large firms and the development of small firms as *de facto* extensions of the former. Thus the new labour market for youth was formed at the same time as there was an objective necessity for young people to find temporary jobs.

One of the effects of the expansion of education, of the growth of youth unemployment, of the growth of a new labour market for young people based on casual labour has been to lengthen the period of time when young people stay with their families. In a sense the period of 'youth' has been lengthened. Traditionally the life-cycle was one whereby someone moved fairly rapidly from childhood to adulthood. The period of childhood was characterized by schooling. When this finished there began the period of work which lasted until old age. Marriage occurred fairly early on.

The lengthening of the period of 'youth' and the increase in the length of the period spent with one's own family was not only due to structural facts such as the expansion of education and the changes in the labour

113

market, but also to specific Italian cultural patterns which make it very difficult for young people, especially young women to live on their own. In addition to this there is also a chronic housing shortage.

Thus the 'generation gap' which has fascinated sociologists throughout the industrial world has manifested itself in a particularly virulent manner in Italy.[46] The traditional functions of the family, that is, the protection of its members against the 'big wide world' and the control over their life-styles, could not be carried out in the same way when the family was no longer dealing with children but with young adults. The family acquired a new function: the economic defence of its members. Young people stayed with their families because they needed to. As they stay longer with their own families and do not leave to form other families they have more time in which to challenge the very institution of the family, to develop an anti-familial ideology, to develop different cultural ethics, particularly a new sexual ethic. Add to this the impact of urbanization and migration, the consequent disruption of traditional patterns, the influence of foreign models of behaviour, particularly American, and we have the development of new forms of age-based solidarity. This solidarity is different from the traditional one based on the family as well as from the more modern one based on the place of work (e.g. trade unions and professional organizations). It is this particular set of circumstances which gives rise to a specific condition: 'youth'. In conjunction with this we have, in Italy as well as in the rest of the industrial world, the formation of a specific youth market based on cultural forms such as music and clothing. This market can exist for two reasons: young people have some income of their own thanks to their limited participation in the labour market and they receive some money from their parents. Parents are able to give this money because the standard of living of the average family has increased, and are willing to do so because money helps to resolve, at least temporarily, the increasingly strained parents/children relationship.

The formation of a 'youth condition' takes everywhere at first essentially cultural forms. These have an international aspect; they unite young people not only across regional divides, but also across countries. This is made possible by developments in technology and particularly the media. In fact for all this to happen it is necessary for the economic system to be able to produce cheap records, cheap clothes and to transmit via radio and television the new music and the new modes of speech. The formation of this youth condition occurred in the 1960s as television became universal in Italy and as small transistor radios became available at a low price to virtually anyone.[47]

The influence of the United States of America in all this cannot be underestimated. The USA exports to the rest of the world, particularly the urban-based world (even across the divide of the Iron Curtain) not only the technical infrastructure for the construction of a youth culture, but also the main cultural forms themselves, not to mention the sociological language with which to decode and understand them. In the course of the 1960s in Italy, more than anywhere else, the US cultural form of the youth generation, music, clothes, etc., was partly integrated by highly politicized forms of protest. This remarkable politicization, more deep-rooted and longer lasting than the only other comparable phenomenon in the rest of Europe, the French 1968 movement, concerned essentially the student population. Here we have two questions: why did students become so politicized in the period 1969–77, or at least why in Italy more so than in most other countries? Which forms did this politicization take?

There is no satisfactory answer to the first question although there have been many useful suggestions. So far we have only established the causes and the existence of a youth condition, but not why this cultural and sociological condition also gave rise to a political movement. One avenue for research which can be used on a comparative basis would investigate one essential aspect of the student condition: of all youth only students (but this is a majority of the age-group) actually have a structure within which to organize: the educational system.[48] Young workers in large plants can also do so, but not as young people (note, however, that the workers' revolt of 1969 was spearheaded by young workers). Another avenue for research would investigate the specificity of the history of Italian intellectuals in their relation with the State. Here we can only lay down the fundamental parameters.[49]

The fascist regime had successfully broken the critical independence which intellectuals had maintained *vis-à-vis* the Liberal State. Under fascism intellectuals could no longer maintain their position of being a separate stratum 'above politics'. They became essential to the fascist attempt to organize consent from above. The Fascist State intervened in cultural affairs and politicized intellectuals, it gave them a role and a political commitment. Their numbers expanded through the expansion of radio, the cinema and other popular forms of culture. By the end of the 1930s many of them had become disillusioned with fascism and particularly with fascist rhetoric, but they were not disillusioned with politics. Many transferred their allegiance to the Left, to the Socialist and Communist parties and many fought in the Resistance. After the war the bulk of the Italian intelligentsia did not return to the pre-fascist 'liberal' concept of intellectuals as being above politics. They joined political parties and maintained a high level of political participation.

By 1968 there was thus in Italy already a strong tradition of political activity among intellectuals. Until then students had followed more or less in the footsteps of their elders, that is, by joining political parties, although there had been a toning down of political participation in the period of the 'economic miracle'. The years of the Centre-Left revitalized political debates, but the developing 'generation gap' meant that the politicization of young people could not go through the main channels: the established political parties and the Church. They found themselves in a mass society which the much-heralded reformism of the Centre-Left had failed to reform and to modernize. They were faced with a strong and well-established labour movement within which they could not find a specific role. They were faced with a new sexual ethic coming from the country which their own establishment was presenting as the model of the good society, the USA, yet Italy was still bigoted and the influence of the clergy still strong.

The anti-authoritarianism characteristic of the young generation found a political outlet in the student movement which was against all forms of leadership and authoritarianism, at first within the universities against the excessive powers of the senior professors, then against the political parties (particularly those of the Left) and the trade unions which were accused of excessive bureaucracy. The essential themes of the student revolt were those common to leftist students in other countries: the Third World, the war in Vietnam, the democratization of the universities. Many of the most active students were not 'new' to politics. They had been active in the ranks of the Young Communist Federation or in various Catholic groups. The movement as such represented many things: the formation of new radical élites, the struggle for the modernization of university structures and also new youth demands culturally incompatible with authoritarian or technocratic models of development.[50] Here, too, a comparative analysis with other industrial countries would show the similarities. What is peculiar to Italy is that the birth of the student movement occurred at the same time as both the Church and the PCI, the two principal centres of political ideology, were in crisis. The PCI was, in the 1960s, rethinking its relations with the Soviet bloc, with Europe and the Third World, as well as with the Centre-Left's attempt to modernize Italian society. The Church, too, faced with the challenge of modernity, that is, the economic boom, urbanization, mass schooling, the media, consumerism, Americanism, etc. was changing course. With Pope John XXIII (1958–63) the Church had dropped its strident anti-communism and had begun to re-examine its relations with the Third World. Until then the organizations of young Catholics were politically very much like all Catholic organizations: they were instruments of the Church whose aim was to pressurize the DC to maintain its line of intransigent anti-communism.[51] After Pope John this changed and Third Worldism entered the organizations of young Catholics, also inspired by progressive Latin American priests such as Camillo Torres and Helder Camara.[52]

On the whole the student movement was decentralized. Many students, however, faced with what to them seemed the excessively moderate line of the PCI, attempted to rediscover the 'lost' heritage of the labour movement by forming Leninist groups. This was not simply a return to the past. It was an attempt on the part of the students to establish a direct relation with the labour movement without going through the established organizations of the labour movement: the PCI and the trade unions. Thus even when students were forming revolutionary organizations which were even more centralized than the PCI, they were rejecting one of the fundamental aspects of the Italian political system: the organization of society by the political parties.

The student events of 1968 forced both the PCI and the DC to react. Within the PCI there was an important debate. Although the initial reaction of the PCI was hostile to the student movement and although one of its main leaders, Giorgio Amendola, asserted that it was necessary to fight on two fronts, i.e. against the government and against the students, the party leader, Luigi Longo, was much more flexible.[53] Longo recognized that it was also the PCI's fault if there was such a wide gulf between the party and the students, that the party had become too sectarian and too bureaucratic and that the importance and political autonomy of the student movement had to be recognized. From the left of the party the self-criticism was even more pronounced: Rossana Rossanda, one of the leaders of the 'Manifesto' group within the PCI (which was expelled in 1969) declared that the PCI was mistaken not to accept that there could be a mass movement outside its control or that of other parties.[54] The entire strategy of the PCI was based on the assumption that the only sources of legitimate power in Italy were political parties. The growth of the youth question and of the student movement, like the growth of a feminist movement, would endanger this whole approach.

The reaction of the DC had different forms: an understandable hostility prevailed, but attempts were made to understand what the student movement represented and even to channel it. The fact that the movement's main target was so often the PCI meant that the DC could hope that its overall effect would be, if not a general weakening of the PCI, at least a temporary setback. Of its leaders, however, only Aldo Moro, who would be kidnapped and then killed by young terrorists of the Red Brigade group ten years later, tried to go beyond an instrumental understanding of the movement. In a speech in November 1968 he suggested that the revolt of the young was no mere anarchy, but represented a set of political demands which had to be answered by all Italian political parties, that it was a revolt against old ideas and an old system of power. 'The fact', he declared 'that young people do not accept the society in which they live and challenge it is a sign of the great changes and of the painful travails which generate a new humanity'.[55] Moro was then in a minority in his own party, the line which prevailed was to accept some of the general demands of the student movement such as making access to the universities easier without proceeding to a general reform. Masses of students entered the universities, causing a rapid growth of disciplines considered to be 'relevant' to the interests of the students, such as sociology and political science. By the 1970s the universities had acquired the economic characteristic of being a temporary refuge from unemployment.

It was evident that graduates expected to find jobs commensurate with their qualifications. These expectations could not be fulfilled and this caused much resentment. University studies had been considered by many to be the way out from manual labour and from monotonous and repetitive work. Distaste for manual and routine work was one of the causes of the growth in student numbers. This was an attitude which was not only particular to students but also to an increasing proportion of the younger generation. The old Catholic and communist rhetoric of work as a noble activity in which 'man' finds either his role in society or establishes his ability to master nature had little appeal for the new generations. Work was now seen as a sad necessity and it is perhaps because of this that often the young were readier to accept temporary or 'demeaning' work than their parents. Being a worker in a factory was no longer seen as a situation in which one could be inserted in a network of solidarity with one's peers. In rejecting the traditional conception of work the young were also rejecting the work their parents were engaged in, but often the parents themselves devalued their own work by insisting with their children that a good education would enable them to change their life-style and live differently.[56]

By the mid 1970s many small revolutionary organizations which had emerged out of the youth movement entered into a crisis. Organizations such as Avanguardia Operaia (The Workers' Vanguard), Potere Operaio (Workers' Power) and Lotta Continua (The Struggle Goes On) had not been able to establish a significant presence in the labour movement even though three of them had managed to produce daily newspapers and to establish some sort of influence, not only among young students but also among some young workers in large plants such as Fiat. The crisis of these organizations was in good part due to the fact that they had tried to subvert the system by using traditional instruments, political parties. Avanguardia Operaia and the Party of Proletarian Unity (PDUP) a left-wing party originating from the 'Manifesto' group of ex-PCI members – merged and established themselves as the critical conscience of the PCI, slightly to the left of it. Potere Operaio decided to become a clandestine organization in order to prepare for armed struggle, but in so doing it lost many of its supporters, some of whom turned to established politics, particularly to the PCI. Finally Lotta Continua which had always been the most anti-centralist of all the groups dissolved itself into the youth movement, retaining only its daily newspaper.

By the second half of the 1970s a clear majority of the young were voting for the parties of the Left (54% against 46% of those over 25) contributing to the successes of the PCI in the local elections of 1975 and the general election of 1976.[57] Many had become involved in the struggle to defend the divorce law in Italy and had begun to campaign in favour of abortion. This led them away from 'revolutionary' politics in the traditional sense towards single-issue campaigns more on the lines of the American experience, leading to an upsurge in campaigns for civil liberties: to reform the Italian prison system, to fight for a more humane treatment of psychiatric patients, to liberalize drugs, etc. Yet even these seemed destined to follow the party logic of the Italian political system: the campaigns were increasingly dominated by a new and small political party, the Radical Party.

By the late 1970s one of the most important developments among political youth was the movement known as Autonomia. It originated among some of the more active young workers. These had united in rank-and-file factory organizations outside the influence of the trade unions and whose fundamental demands were built around the themes of a reduction of the working week and a gradual levelling of wages.[58] When this movement expanded outside the factories and among students it assumed extreme anti-institutional forms. Its activities involved the refusal to pay fares on public transport, occupation of empty houses and even the looting of supermarkets (known as 'proletarian expropriation'). The Autonomia distinguished itself from the revolutionary groups by its distaste of conventional politics, its clear rejection of any form of organization and also by abandoning any attempt at a general change in society. If the revolutionary groups criticized the PCI for not being revolutionary, now Autonomia criticized it for defending only the organized working class and not the marginal groups. Autonomia expressed politically the marginalization of youth, redefined as some sort of subproletariat, a 'second society' of unprotected people ready to claim some of the existing economic resources by direct means. There was, in fact, a general deterioration in the condition of youth. In the course of the 1970s Italy became a European centre for the sale of hard drugs, and heroin consumption reached an alarming level. The presence of chronic violence, the development of criminality among youth, drugs and a general political disaffection with the system provided the opportunity not only for the development of connections with the Mafia (through the drug market) but also for the transformation of Autonomia into a recruiting terrain for terrorist groups such as the Red Brigades and the Nuclei Armati Proletari (NAP), the latter being particularly involved in the recruiting of the young from the prison system.

Autonomia, of course, never involved more than a small percentage of the young population. Its size cannot be estimated in a clear way, although its importance has been stressed by both leading political parties. In 1977 the year in which it was most active, Autonomia was able to mobilize in the streets – at times in violent confrontation with the police – tens of thousands of young people and had the sympathy and at times the solidarity of many more. The longer-term importance of Autonomia, however, would lay not so much in what it actually achieved (for this would only be of limited significance) but in the fact that it was an evident symptom of the disaffection of the young and of the development of yet another unresolved question in Italian political life.

REFERENCES AND NOTES

1. Filippini, G. (1978), p. 170. Proceedings of the conference held in Rome 7–9 October 1977.
2. Alberoni, F. (1979), vol. 1, p. 263.
3. Cutrufelli, M. R. (1980), p. 33.
4. Mancina, C. (1981), pp. 16–17.
5. Saraceno, C. (1979), p. 837.
6. ISTAT, calculations based on the 1981 Census.
7. Ibid., pp. 846–8.
8. Balbo, L. (1978), p. 4.
9. Ibid., pp. 4–5.
10. These data can be found in Accornero, A. and Carmignani, F. (1978b), p. 52.
11. Figures in Gasbarrone, M. (1984), p. 30.
12. Bianchi, M. (1979), p. 158.
13. Mannheimer, R. and Sebastiani, C. (1978), p. 24.
14. Weber, M. (1981), p. 191. Note the official data for female activity rates in the main industrial countries (1979):

	% of all ages	% rise since 1970	As % of male activity rates
US	38.4	8.3	69.4
Japan	36.7	1.3	60.9
UK	35.8	4.5	61.7
France	32.3	3.4	60.8
W. Germany	31.1	0.8	57.2
Italy	25.4	3.5	48.4

Source: EUROSTAT.

15. Occhionero, M. F. (1976), p. 129.
16. Ibid., pp. 139–40, 149.
17. Ibid., p. 150.
18. All data are from the *Rapporto sulla popolazione in Italia,* Istituto dell'Enciclopedia italiana, Rome 1980, quoted in Mancina (1981), pp. 17–19.
19. De Grand, A. (1976), p. 956.

20.   Mafai, M. (1979), pp. 50–1.
21.   Ibid., pp. 60–1.
22.   Weber (1981), p. 190.
23.   Balbo, L. (1976), p. 88.
24.   For these and the other data below see Weber (1981), pp. 193–6.
25.   Ibid., pp. 189–90.
26.   Menapace, L. (1974), p. 54.
27.   Caldwell, L. (1978), pp. 89–93. *Feminism and Materialism.*
28.   Weber (1981), p. 198.
29.   Ibid., p. 129.
30.   Menapace (1974), p. 63.
31.   Ibid., pp. 58–60.
32.   Mancina (1981), p. 10.
33.   For an analysis of feminist slogans see Rossi, R. (1978), esp. pp. 23–42.
34.   Boccia, M. L. (1980), p. 23.
35.   See figures in Fedele, M.
36.   Bassi, P. and Pilati, A. (1978), p. 77.
37.   Ibid., p. 79.
38.   Vacca, G. (1977), p. 168.
39.   Ibid., p. 170.
40.   These figures are based on a survey conducted by ENI–IRI reported in Accornero, A. and Carmignani, F., 'Laureati e diplomati nell'industria italiana', in Pinnarò, G. (1978), p. 186.
41.   Carmignani, F. (1980), p. 14.
42.   See Luigi Frey, L. (1981).
43.   Ministry of Labour figures cited in *Rinascita,* no. 16, 1980.
44.   Vacca (1977), p. 175.
45.   Bassi and Pilati (1978), pp. 68–73.
46.   The following considerations on the family are derived from Fedele (1975).
47.   This is the period when Italian sociologists begin to examine youth as a cultural subsystem, see: Ardigò, A. (1966); Livolsi, M. (1967); Alberoni, F. (1970).
48.   Cecchi, A. (1975), p. 42.
49.   There is a growing literature on the relation between fascism and intellectuals, see in particular: Mangoni, L. (1974); Isnenghi, M. (1979); Turi, G. (1980).
50.   Melucci, A. (1978), p. 16.
51.   Rodano, G. (1978), pp. 196–7.
52.   Occhetto, A. (1978), p. 80.
53.   See Amendola, G. (1968); Longo, L. (1968).
54.   See Rossa, R. (1968).
55.   Moro, A. (1979), p. 223.
56.   Accornero, A. (1978), pp. 218–23. On the general question of the rejection of work in Italy see Battaglia, F. (1980).
57.   Bassi and Pilati (1978), p. 8.
58.   Ibid., p. 17. The works of Antonio Negri represent a theoretical attempt to conceptualize the central themes of Autonomia, see in particular Negri, A. (1976).

Chapter 7

INSTRUMENTS OF POLITICAL MOBILIZATION

The most important instruments of political mobilization in Italy are undoubtedly political parties. In other countries political parties are often no more than electoral machines or parliamentary groups. In the USA political parties 'are not the centres of passion ... they are part-time organizations. ... parties do not appear to stand for anything very meaningful. Perhaps their most outstanding characteristic is their lack of ideology'.[1]

The specific role of political parties will be examined in Part III ('Politics'). In this chapter I want to examine instead the impact in Italy of instruments of political mobilization other than political parties.

The central importance of parties has meant that Italy has never been a 'growth area' for their traditional competitors: pressure groups. Where these existed they were either quickly absorbed by parties or became parties themselves (such as the Radical Party). I have chosen to focus on the interrelations between four specific 'instruments of political mobilization' and political parties: the trade unions, business, the Church and the media. Quite clearly the primary function of these four 'instruments' are not political but, respectively, the defence and improvement of the conditions of the working class, business profitability, religion and information. In the pursuit of these aims all four deal with politics and depend – to some extent – on some form of consensus and legitimacy. This is not necessarily, or not always, political, but it always has political *effects*. In all four cases there is, in the post-war period, a fairly close identification between each of these forces and political parties, but in the 1960s and 1970s there was a growing autonomy which contributed to the crisis of Italian political parties and hence of the political system itself. The kind of 'political mobilization' each of the four forces achieves is specific to its traditional role: trade unions organize at the point of production and mobilize workers through meetings, strikes and demonstrations, their strength depending on the degree of consensus achieved. The Church mobilizes the faithful through specific religious rituals and a range of activities in the home and the community. Industry and business organize economic activity, influence the shape of the market and the pattern of consumption, organize entrepreneurs and negotiate with the political system. The media contribute to the structuring of an increased proportion of leisure time, give shape to information, filter and condition political messages.

TRADE UNIONS

The reconstruction of the Italian trade-union movement began in the course of the Second World War. From its very inception the new Confederazione Generale Italiana del Lavoro (CGIL) was a creature of the three leading anti-fascist parties: the Socialist Party (PSI), the Communist Party (PCI) and the Christian Democrats (DC). In June 1944 representatives of these parties signed the so-called 'Pact of Rome' which was the basis of the reconstituted CGIL. Formally the CGIL declared itself to be 'independent of all political parties' and at the same time to be an expression of the common will of the three main parties.[2]

Traditionally, European trade unions have seen their functions as divided into two components: an economic function which seeks to defend and improve the wages of their members and their working conditions, and a political function which is connected with a wider aim of restructuring society usually, though not always, in a socialist direction. The implementation of the 'political function' is achieved either by connecting the trade union to a socialist or social democratic or communist party, or by acting as the collective representative of the working class and, in this guise, negotiating with or putting pressure on the government of the day in order to improve the political and social position of the working class. Not all unions are committed to socialism, but in virtually all major European countries the main trade union has a socialist orientation.

In the immediate post-war period the Italian case exhibited the peculiarity of having a highly 'political' trade union which was not connected to a single left-wing party but to at least three parties, the largest of which, the DC, was clearly outside the socialist tradition. The socialist and communist presence was by far the most weighty in the new CGIL, but they could not afford to dominate it for fear of driving out the Catholic minority. That being the case, it was established that, irrespective of the internal relation of forces, each of the three components of the union would have equal representation on the Executive Committee and each would be represented by a joint general secretary. Thus from the very beginning the actual structure of the union reflected the structure of the ruling coalition in the post-war period (i.e. DC, PCI, PSI). This also meant that the CGIL was not in any sense an 'opposition' force. It could hardly challenge the government of the day. Its leading personnel overlapped with the leadership of the three governing parties.

Given the Catholic presence the CGIL could not be classified as a socialist trade union. Nevertheless, it had an ideology: anti-fascism. These 'glued' together its three components in the same way as it held together the DC, the PCI and the PSI in the governments of 1945–47. As long as anti-fascism was the major issue in the political life of the country both government and trade union could be united. What of the 'economic' function of trade unions? For the DC component of the CGIL the economic role of the trade union in the immediate post-war period had essentially to be one of controlling any pressures which could endanger the possibility of economic reconstruction. As the policy of the DC was one of reconstruction on neo-liberal lines, i.e. giving private enterprises the leading role, it was necessary to guarantee an overall containment of wage levels. Thus the CGIL should accept a wage truce and convince its working-class base to enhance productivity without immediate monetary rewards.

For the Left, particularly the PCI which was already dominant within the industrial working class, a period of social peace was also necessary. The PCI had eliminated from its strategic options a socialist insurrection because, given the existing international relations of forces, it would have failed (the crushing of the left-wing insurrection in Greece loomed large), and because its leader, Palmiro Togliatti, was developing a new conception of the transition to socialism in an advanced capitalist country which precluded any resort to insurrectionary tactics. Given this framework a period of social peace was also necessary and for two reasons:

1. In order to implant itself in the Italian social system the PCI could not rely simply on the support of the working class. It needed to develop a system of alliances which would include the emergent middle classes. In order to obtain at least the passive consent of these groups it was necessary to guarantee some stability in their economic position.[3] This meant emphasizing the struggle against inflation, while at the same time improving the prospect of employment. In this context a wages struggle could not be given priority.

2. The improvement in the political position of the working class required a strongly interventionist state which would be committed to a policy of structural reforms. These reforms would reduce and perhaps eliminate the power of financial and industrial monopolies which, in the analysis of the PCI, constituted the terrain upon which fascism had emerged.

Given the policies and strategies of the two essential components of both CGIL and government (the Socialists were unable to demarcate themselves clearly from the Communists), it is not surprising if the Italian trade unions for the entire period 1944–48 behaved as if they had signed a form of social contract with the ruling coalition. However, it was not just a question of ideology. The fact of the matter is that there were fundamental structural reasons for the inability and unwillingness of the CGIL to lead a strong wages campaign, namely that the working class was weak. Its weakness was part and parcel of the general weakness of the Italian economy, the widespread misery and poverty, the homelessness, the extent of unemployment. Yet the working class was still able to extract one fundamental concession: the labour market was 'blocked', making it virtually impossible for entrepreneurs to make anyone redundant. However, when the ban on dismissals was abandoned in 1946 in exchange for the promise of maintaining existing employment levels, the CGIL lost effective control of the labour market. On the positive side the CGIL succeeded in negotiating price controls and an agreement on the indexation of wages in 1946 (for this, however, they had to accept a wage truce of seven months). By the winter of 1947 price controls could not be sustained and the indexation of wages never really protected the workers against inflation.[4] Nevertheless the very fact that the working-class parties shared in governmental power for the first time in the history of united Italy gave great psychological strength to factory workers and their trade-union representatives, even though this strength was not translated into wages militancy.

The unity of the trade-union movement thus depended on the unity of the anti-fascist coalition. In turn the unity of the latter depended on the international situation and the extent to which the Western Allies and the Soviet Union could find a *modus vivendi* in the post-war period. The Cold War destroyed this possibility and with it all the attempts in Europe to maintain in being coalition governments with communist participation.[5] As the post-fascist trade-union movement had been created in Italy on the basis of a strong party political unity, the break-up of the tripartite coalition in May 1947 led inevitably to the break-up of the CGIL. Thus party politics had an immediate effect on trade-union politics. Two years after the right wing of the PSI formed the Social Democratic Party (1947), their trade-union supporters left the CGIL and formed their own trade union which, in 1950, took the name of Unione Italiana del Lavoro (UIL).

In 1948 the DC group left the CGIL, establishing at first the so-called 'Free CGIL' which, a couple of years later, took the name of Confederazione Italiana dei Sindacati dei Lavoratori (CISL).

The break-up of the trade-union movement further aggravated the already weak position of organized labour. Throughout the 1950s hardly any gains were made. The influx of workers from the South had the effect of transforming the labour market into a highly flexible mechanism outside the control of the trade unions. Militant workers could be easily sacked, and the general threat of redundancy dampened the prospects of an economic struggle.[6] From an organizational point of view the structure of trade unions at the local level was weak and as a result the main form of bargaining was highly centralized.

Entrepreneurs had no interest in encouraging plant-level bargaining for this could only strengthen the trade union at the shop-floor level.[7] The most important workers' organization within the factories were the 'internal commissions'. These were not, strictly speaking, trade-union organizations. They were elected by all workers whether or not they belonged to a union. The internal commissions did not negotiate wages, but only some aspects of labour conditions. They could not rely on any backing external to the factories. In practice they were ineffective and at the mercy of the employers.

Elections to the internal commissions merely reflected national elections as the three trade-union federations tried to get their leading members elected to the commissions. Thus, even at the local level the organization of workers reflected party political divisions.[8] When in 1954 the CGIL lost control of the internal commissions at Fiat (which passed on to the DC-aligned CISL) this was a major defeat for the PCI.

Alessandro Pizzorno has described the 1950s as being dominated by a sort of social pact between the State and the entrepreneurs.[9] The entrepreneurs agreed to stop demanding protectionism in favour of international competition. In exchange (and in order to keep wages low) the State had to ensure 'social order'. This was done in two ways: the CGIL was repressed and there was an expansion of public spending. Thus the State intervened mainly in order to help private capital to increase productivity more rapidly than wages. From the point of view of the workers this had the same effect as an incomes policy: real wages hardly increased between 1948 and 1954. The CGIL was able to organize workers on the basis of an ideological commitment towards a 'better tomorrow', on the basis of future gains rather than concrete results. The Catholic CISL, on the other hand, was able to offer the workers something more concrete: an ambiguous future, but the prospect of the 'economic miracle'. The assumption on which the CISL was working was that the period of constant growth would last for a whole historical period and that the union movement would have to accommodate itself to it. The model offered was that of a non-political trade union which would leave the question of economic development to the private sector and seek in exchange a growing share of the cake (what was called the 'American' model of trade unionism).

The CISL tried to break with the Italian tradition of highly centralized collective agreements in favour of decentralized bargaining. Until 1955 the CGIL fought tooth and nail against this approach, arguing that decentralized bargaining would break up the unity and the organization of the workers.

As the leader of the CGIL, Luciano Lama, has admitted, it was the competition from the CISL and principally the defeat at Fiat in 1955 that forced the CGIL to review its position.[10]

Repression was facilitated by the fact that, thanks to the DC, in the post-war period there was no serious attempt to establish a new legal framework for industrial relations. If that had been done – given the prevailing anti-fascist climate – the unions would have obtained considerable advantages. The effect of not intervening was to keep on the statute books all the anti-strike regulations which were contained in the penal code established during fascism by Alfredo Rocco.[11] These were, of course, incompatible with the new Constitution, but as Italy did not have a Constitutional Court until the mid 1950s, they were not challenged. Thus offences such as 'to instigate class hatred', 'to organize a general strike', 'to hold a seditious demonstration', 'to insult the forces of law and order or the government' were all upheld with the help of a compliant and unreformed judiciary.

In fact trade-union legislation was further extended by Mario Scelba, the DC Minister for the Interior: in July 1947 it was decided that any assembly of workers within the factory gates required prior police permission. Later Scelba described the CGIL general strike after the attempt on Togliatti's life (1948) as 'insurrectionist acts' and proceeded – again with the help of the judiciary – to arrest and try hundreds of trade unionists.[12]

By 1960 the pattern of labour relations began to undergo a profound change. In structural terms the main causes were the growth of the working class in quantitative terms (see Ch. 5), its territorial concentration, the absorption of unemployment either directly or through emigration. This set the scene for the changes of the 1960s. At the international level the harshest years of the Cold War were over. International coexistence made the staunch anti-communism of the 1950s look outdated. The end of the post-war boom and of the Italian 'economic miracle' which led to the birth in Italy of the Centre-Left coalition and the massive expansion of the public sector meant that the State took upon itself not only to reform the economic system but also to become an economic power in its own right: it was no longer content to leave the economy to private capital. The trade unions felt stronger and the success of the wage offensive of the early 1960s made further economic development on the basis of low wages less likely.

The growing legitimation of trade unions depended only in part on the changing structure of the labour market. It was also the result of changes occurring in the balance of power at the political level. The CISL and the UIL who had privileged access to the government because their parties were in power had been putting pressures on the DC and the smaller centrist parties for a change in the role of the State in industrial relations. In the late 1950s and even more so in the early 1960s the State through the Istituto per la Ricostruzione Industriale (IRI) and the Ente Nazionale Idrocarburi (ENI) began to use the public sector as a laboratory for a more conciliatory pattern of negotiations with the trade unions.[13] By 1960–62 the State sector negotiated in practice also on behalf of the private sector because the kind of industrial relations system which developed in the IRI–ENI system could not be opposed by the increasingly divided employers' association, the Confindustria. Until then access of the trade unions to the political level had to be mediated through political parties. The unions could mobilize their own rank and file only on the basis of party alliance, their leaders owed their positions to parties and their styles of leadership, strategies and appeals were systematically borrowed from political parties.[14] Yet access to politics was limited because the CGIL parties (Socialists and Communists) were not in government and the CISL and the UIL could only work through those factions within the government parties which represented them. With the development of the centre-Left the status of the CGIL changed somewhat because the Socialists were part of the coalition. The CISL was considerably strengthened because the left-wing factions of the DC who had fought for a centre-left coalition had defeated the DC Right. The UIL too had become stronger because the elimination of the centre-right Liberal Party from the ruling coalition had strengthened the Republicans and the Social Democrats.

The trade unions were able to use their strength not only to impose better wage levels in the early 1960s but also to begin to distance themselves from the political parties. This took place because the new Centre-Left coalition, by giving a role to the three component parts of the trade-union movement, began to develop a system of direct negotiations with entrepreneurs and unions. The unions were promised social reforms and business was promised modernization. A system of triangular or tripartite consultation between government, employers and unions began to develop in Italy as it was developing in other European countries, notably the UK. The most important tripartite forum was the National Commission on Economic Planning which was set up in 1962. Since then a myriad of committees have sprung up which involved trade-union and employers' representatives.[15]

The development of trade-union involvement in politics brought about profound changes in the way in which trade unions perceived their role. Traditionally the CISL was not particularly interested in questions of institutional and political reform, which it considered best left to the political parties and in particular to the DC.[16] Moreover, it thought that the Centre-Left coalition could modernize the Italian economy without altering the institutional framework. As it became involved in consultations at the political level the CISL had to begin to re-examine its own tradition and to recognize the limitations of 'non-political' trade unionism. Until the Centre-Left coalition the UIL had been a fairly marginal force. It welcomed the new coalition because it assumed that the break-up of the alliance between the PSI and the PCI would have repercussions in the trade union field, i.e. that the CGIL socialists would join them. This would have established a perfect 'fit' between the three trade-union centres and the three leading political parties. It would also have facilitated the reunification of the PSI and the Social Democrats. But by 1964 it was evident that the CGIL socialists had been able to renegotiate their relations within the CGIL with the communists and obtain more power.

The tensions within the CGIL between communists and socialists were sufficient to convince the CGIL to become increasingly independent from the PCI. All unions now relied less on political parties.

In the course of the 1960s Italian unions came to realize that the government was not the centre of political power or, rather, that political power did not have a centre, but was diffuse throughout political and civil society.[17] This gave them an incentive to penetrate as much as possible into the various apparatuses of the State and at all levels. In so doing they modelled themselves on the DC system of power: establishing a 'presence' in social and political life. Thus at the same time as they were distancing themselves from political parties the three trade-union confederations were also developing some of the attributes of political parties.

In 1968–69 a third phase opened up in industrial relations. One of its main features was a new type of labour conflict: a high level of militancy, an active involvement of non-unionized workers, a dislike of bureaucracy expressed in rank-and-file slogans such as 'we are the union' and 'the work contract is just a piece of paper'.[18] They refused to accept any connection between an increase in wages and an increase in productivity: 'more money, less work'. Some of the conflicts escalated in violence: the police killed two agricultural labourers at Avola in November 1968, and two more working-class demonstrators at Battipaglia in the following year. Later that year a policeman was killed in Milan, and on 12 December 1969 a bomb in a Milan bank killed sixteen people. At first anarchists were suspected, then fascists; the trials dragged on for over a decade while political violence escalated. This did not prevent the growth of trade-union power in Italy. The decade after 1968 was characterized by a high level of sustained militancy and by an increase in workers' control over the conditions of work. If we compare 1968–78 with 1960–68 we note that in the earlier period wage differentials between skilled and unskilled workers had tended to increase, while in the second decade wage bargaining was directed towards reducing differentials. The ethics of equality pervaded labour relations and found a practical outlet in the new agreement with the Confindustria of 1975 over the indexation of wages. Furthermore, after 1968 collective bargaining was further decentralized towards firm- and plant-level bargaining.

The unrest of 1968 would not have occurred with that level of intensity if the Italian unions had been stronger. A strong and well-entrenched union movement would have exercised a measure of restraint and control, partly in order to protect vested interests, partly in order not to jeopardize the existing power relations. A weak trade-union movement had little interest in controlling rank-and-file unrest and, by definition, little strength with which to control it.

The new factory council system developed particularly, though not exclusively, where trade unions were weak. The growth of authentic grass-roots organizations (the factory councils) and of the factory delegates elected by the councils (i.e. by *all* workers in a factory) posed a problem for all unions. The unions could have tried to repress the councils by withholding any protection at the national level. Alternatively, they could have accepted the coexistence of two levels of organizations within the factory: a factory council open to all workers, and alongside it the formal trade-union organization (i.e. the British model). The third alternative, the one eventually adopted, was to declare that the factory council was the organ of the trade-union movement at the factory level. This had several effects, the most important of which was to unite the still nationally divided trade-union movement at the shop-floor level through the factory council. Perhaps one should not overstress this rank-and-file unity. It was only too obvious that the workers would choose delegates among the most active members of the trade unions and that the delegates' committee would still reflect, at least to some extent, the relations of forces within the trade-union movement. What the system did, however, was to involve all workers in the trade unions through the councils. This obviated the weakness of having a generally low level of formal membership and increased the credibility of the three confederations. Later, union leadership was reasserted when the three confederations established the principle that the delegates of the factory councils had to be members of the union.[19] Thus what had begun as a rank-and-file challenge to the trade unions became the basis for increased cooperation between the CGIL, UIL and CISL. Furthermore, the growth of the factory councils had enabled the unions to penetrate into hitherto non-unionized firms.

There is yet another aspect of the 1968–69 struggles which must be mentioned because it has a bearing on the relation betweeen unions and political parties. In the course of these struggles groups to the left of the PCI were able to have a remarkable effect on working-class struggles.[20] In some cases these were made up, at least in part, of 'new', i.e. migrant, workers in the large factories of the North where the unions were weak. In many cases workers responded positively to the students' unrest and adopted similar forms of struggle such as the open meeting as the central decision-making structure within the plant. The leftist groups were far more successful in Italy than in the UK or West Germany, or even than in France where they had a very strong impact only in May 1968. This was partly due to the weakness of the unions themselves, partly due to the crisis of the PCI in the 1960s, but also to the fact that the socialist language of the students, whether mediated by libertarian concepts or by orthodox 'Marxist-Leninist' ones, was not foreign to Italian workers. By 1968 various aspects of Marxist culture were so embedded in Italy that students propounding socialist and communist slogans at factory gates were given far more attention than their comrades in the rest of Western Europe, not to speak of North America where working-class culture is generally hostile to socialist ideas. However, any leftist notion that the factory council could be used in an anti-parliamentary function as the nucleus of future 'workers' soviets' met the strong and successful opposition of the CGIL.[21]

The struggles of 1968-69 also resulted in the adoption by Parliament in 1970 of the *Carta dei Lavoratori* (The Workers' Charter) which enshrined many rights which had been achieved in the course of the struggles, including the legal recognition of the factory councils. It made 'anti-trade-union' behaviour on the part of the employer an offence. It allowed paid time off from work for factory council delegates and the right to have an assembly of workers on the factory premises during working hours. It made it difficult to make workers redundant. One of the reasons why this law was passed was that the political establishment recognized that it was necessary to strengthen the trade-union leadership against its grass roots.[22]

The political role of the trade unions developed as they increasingly negotiated directly with the government. Political parties seemed to become less important and resented the growth of trade-union power. However, a system of permanent negotiations between unions and governments could not develop because (1) the trade-union movement did not achieve the goal of reunification because (2) governments were never able to produce concrete economic programmes and, finally, because (3) the trade unions were not able to become the centre of a new powerful social bloc which included the social movements which had emerged outside the traditional labour movement.

Let us examine each of these three elements:

1.   The debate on trade-union reunification could only develop on the basis of an increasing autonomy between each trade-union confederation and the political parties. By 1969 the CGIL accepted that trade-union autonomy required the adoption of the principle of 'incompatibility' between holding a union post and a post in a political party. The three confederations accepted the principle but disagreed on the extent to which it should be applied: did it apply only to the overlap in membership between the executive committees of the parties and those of the trade unions? Did it also imply that trade-union officials should not be elected to Parliament? Should the principle be extended to all levels? Extension to all levels would mean that the secretary of a trade-union branch would not be able to be elected to the executive committee of his party cell or branch.[23]

A compromise was reached and in 1972 it was decided to proceed towards a full merger by March 1973. What blocked this rapidly developing process was the collapse of the Centre-Left and the election of the right-wing DC leader Giovanni Leone as President of the Republic (with the help of neo-fascist votes) in spite of the combined opposition of the PCI and the PSI.[24]. Once more dissension within political parties affected the unity of the trade-union movement. The CGIL leader, Luciano Lama, suggested that in order to maintain the momentum towards unity the trade unions should enter into a 'federal pact' while maintaining their separate identities. This solution, initially seen as temporary became permanent.

The government of national unity of 1976–79 gave added impetus towards unification, but its break-up signalled the ever-increasing difficulty of trade-union unity. All hopes of reunification vanished in 1984 when – as we shall see – the dispute over the wages indexation system divided the communist trade unionists from all the others.

2. The lack of concrete government programmes became far more marked in the 1980s. Italian governments lived day to day, simply responding to a variety of pressures from interest groups. Trade unions, too, were forced to behave like pressure groups. Each union tried to apply pressure on a 'friendly' party or on a faction within a party in order to defend the gains of the past in a period of high unemployment. In this situation to maintain a united front became increasingly difficult.

3. Trade union difficulty in organizing and leading a vast social movement was due to both structural and ideological reasons.[25] Structural factors included the growth of sections of the Italian population which were outside the traditional reach of trade unions, such as the tertiary sector, white-collar workers in industry, small firms (while the number of those employed in large firms decreased), the unemployed, old-age pensioners. To these structural factors we should add:

   (a) the existence of the 'new' youth movement of 1977 known as the Autonomi which involved not only students but also young workers, many of whom sympathized with terrorism;
   (b) the growth of organizations of unemployed opposed to organized labour (in Naples there have even been attacks on trade-union offices);
   (c) the growth of the 'autonomous' unions, i.e. unions outside the 'Big Three';
   (d) the growing disaffection of white-collar workers with the trade unions' policy of reducing differentials;
   (e) the growth of different forms of work: part-time, overtime, two jobs and seasonal and casual work.

Two possible strategies could be envisaged: either the trade unions gave up any ambition of organizing the new social movements, thus becoming no more than the pressure group of a minority of the working class, or it attempted to form alliances with the new social groups. But it could not do the latter if it persisted in approaching all social groups on the basis of the traditional working class: the experience of the 40-hour-a-week male factory worker could not be generalized.[26] The feminist challenge could not be ignored by the unions without paying a price.

To these difficulties was added the fact that the unions found it increasingly hard to maintain their legitimacy among ordinary workers: there was a widening gap between union activists and the rest of the working class. The limitations of existing trade-union democracy were openly recognized even by prestigious communist leaders such as Giorgio Amendola (never a supporter of the factory council system) in a controversial article.[27]

On many traditional trade-union matters such as safety regulations and working conditions the factory council system worked reasonably well and strengthened the trade-union movement. However, it was also necessary to deal with economic and social life outside the factory gates by intervening in the formulation of economic policies at the regional or national level. This required the possession of a degree of expertise and knowledge the activists might have but not the mass of workers. Thus the gap between the two increased.[28] The factory council system worked effectively only within the factory. Outside the factory the support of the workers was obtained not on the basis of their concrete understanding of the issues but on an ideological support for the trade-union leadership. The way in which the unions approached bargaining was by putting on the table short-term economic demands (i.e. wages and working conditions) as well as more general ones, at times giving in on the short-term demands in exchange for vague and ill-specified long-term promises.[29] They were thus bargaining away the basis of their concrete support (short-term economic gains) in exchange for items of a political package which could not be delivered and on which working-class commitment was imprecise and ambiguous.

There is another reason for the growing crisis of trade-union legitimacy: traditional bargaining on wages and working conditions involved those affected by them, i.e. all or most factory workers. But issues concerned with local planning affected all the inhabitants of a particular area and implied that some form of popular participation was required outside the confines of the factory gates. This was not – and perhaps could not have been – achieved by the trade unions. It was tried by political parties on the basis of devolved power at the regional, city and neighbourhood level, but this often became little more than a reproduction of the traditional parliamentary relations between government and opposition.

As unemployment has risen throughout the industrialized world the strength of the trade unions has been decreasing. The ability of large firms, such as Fiat, to reduce its workforce was a blow to trade-union control over the labour market. The new wave of deflationary cuts did not enjoy in Italy the degree of political support that it had in the UK under the Thatcher government. Instead the Italian ruling coalition, under pressure from employers' organizations, tried to intervene by reducing labour costs (modifying wage indexation) and raising indirect taxes. The unions found themselves fighting an increasingly defensive battle precisely in a period in which their own credibility on the shop floor was under challenge. The effective end of trade-union unity occurred in February 1984 when the socialist Prime Minister, Bettino Craxi, issued a decree revising unilaterally the wages indexation system, reducing the amount of protection it offered against price rises by between 10 and 20 per cent. While the CISL and the UIL accepted the reduction the CGIL did not. The split went even deeper than that because the socialist component in the CGIL (a minority) was willing to accept the government's offer.

The CISL accepted the reduction of wages indexation for political reasons: by breaking with the CGIL in a period when trade unions were weak and under attack, the CISL could appear a reasonable and realistic trade union with which the government could negotiate. The government did not have many resources for a deal, but it could give the CISL that legitimacy which all trade unions find more and more difficult to obtain on the shop floor. With the CGIL 'out in the cold' and the UIL too small, the CISL hoped to become the main protagonist of future negotiations with the government.

The CGIL could not have accepted Craxi's proposals without a major *quid pro quo*. Its rank and file, mainly communists, would not accept an agreement which decreased their purchasing power *and* further isolated their own political party. The CGIL was in no position to alienate itself from its rank and file and there was a prompt response from the PCI and the CGIL: on 24 March 1984 a massive demonstration of around 1 million people converged on Rome to back up the parliamentary tactics of the PCI aimed at ensuring that the government decree would not become law within the statutory sixty days. The PCI was successful and, even though the government promptly introduced another, more limited, decree which was approved and upheld, by a referendum in June 1985, the point had been made: any long-term agreement on wages must be negotiated with the opposition.

The crisis of the trade-union movement affects the CGIL perhaps more deeply than the other union federations. In the first place the future of the CGIL is tied to the fact that it cannot assume that it will have a favourable government in the near future. Most European trade unions have or have had 'their party' in power and/or stand a reasonable chance to see it in power again. The CGIL is not in this position. The PCI may well one day be part of a government coalition, but the circumstances under which this would occur would be very special, it would be the 'unblocking' of the Italian political system. In the second place the CGIL suffers more than the other trade unions from the process of deindustrialization which affects all advanced countries: the bedrock of its strength, the engineering sector, is declining while the tertiary sector, which is in constant expansion is better organized by the CISL and the UIL. Furthermore, the advanced high-technology sectors have either no unions at all or have their own associations which are not part of any of the three trade-union federations. Finally, and as a consequence of the above, the age structure of the CGIL is getting dangerously lopsided towards the older age-groups. This is due to the fact that the CGIL has more old-age pensioners among its members than the UIL and the CISL (in Italy old-age pensioners can be union members), that unions on the whole are recruiting fewer young people because the growth of unemployment hits the young entrants, and because the expanding sectors recruit a higher proportion of the young than the declining ones.

PRIVATE ENTERPRISE

In Chapter 1 we pointed out that, in the absence of any strong alternative or opposition, the doctrine of economic liberalism prevailed and influenced the chief economic decisions of the post-war government and its immediate successors. This was one of the rare moments of Italian history since the Risorgimento when the entrepreneurial class could feel that it shared in political power, perhaps even that it was at the centre of it. Guido Carli who was for many years the Governor of the Bank of Italy and then led the Confindustria (Employers' Federation) has stated that since 1876 the Italian State has always been the State of the petty bourgeoisie and never that of the 'productive' classes: 'The State has never been the representative of the interests of the capitalists or of the workers. The ideals and the culture of the Italian State have been those of the petty bourgeoisie.'[30] Industrialists have also complained that there is no industrial culture in Italy.[31] The leaders of the DC were close to the Church and the countryside; in so far as they had a political philosophy it was the social doctrine of the Church. The anti-fascist political Right was against any form of state involvement akin to the New Deal or Keynesianism. The Left thought that Italian capitalism was backward and deprived of any internal capacity for growth. When the PCI–PSI trade union federation, the CGIL, put forward in 1949 a 'Labour Plan' which was essentially Keynesian, it encountered the indifference of the PCI. Even the Confindustria chose to subordinate itself to the DC and to Catholic values, assuming that the Church would work in favour of social control over Italy's recalcitrant working class. Only some politicians close to the leader of the Republican Party, Ugo La Malfa and the President of the powerful (state) bank, the Banca Commerciale, Raffaele Mattioli, propounded some version of that reformist capitalism which was based on the example of the UK's and Sweden's social democratic experiment. This ideology, commonly referred to as *Terza forza* or Third Force, was never dominant, except perhaps very briefly during the 1960s.[32]

As we have explained, this anti-industrial bias was no disadvantage. The Italian State removed as many obstacles as it could from the industrialists' path and added some strong incentives. During the late 1950s, the period of greatest expansion of Italian industry, there was a group of outstanding captains of industry, names such as Valletta (Fiat) Pirelli, Olivetti, Cenzato (Montecatini – chemical industry) and many others. By the end of the 1970s there were only two names left: Pirelli and Agnelli (Fiat).[33] The space for large private enterprises had considerably shrunk.

The dominant force in the 1950s was Fiat. It always worked closely with the political authorities and was able to influence the economic strategy of the DC and hence of the government. The Italian State helped Fiat by providing the infrastructure for the development of a large car market. This was done by building motorways, by keeping the price of petrol low, by running down public transport. Fiat maintained a privileged relation with the DC and particularly with its 'modernizing' wing led by Amintore Fanfani. It took bold initiatives abroad, the most important of which was the development of a large Fiat plant in Togliattigrad in the USSR.[34] Fiat maintained its distance from those large private companies such as the electrical and chemical industries which were leading a campaign against Fanfani and which fought tooth and nail against the emergence in the early 1960s of a Centre-Left government.[35] Fiat attempted successfully to project a progressive image distancing itself from the rest of the Confindustria which it considered too reactionary. Yet within its plants Fiat maintained a repressive regime against the trade unions, particularly the CGIL. Militant workers were isolated or expelled. In 1971 it was discovered that in the 1950s Fiat had collected thousands of files on its workers. This had been done with the help of the police, the carabinieri and the Italian secret service. The information thus collected was used to sack workers, blackmail them and threaten them.[36] There was a determined attempt to weaken the CGIL and to strengthen the Catholic trade union, CISL.

With the advent of the Centre-Left Fiat began to take some interest in the affairs of the Confindustria. As the Fiat–DC reformist line was being developed there emerged a rough division of labour between these two centres of power. The DC would split the Left by allying itself with the

PSI, adopt a policy of structural reforms and modernize the Italian economy. Fiat would attempt to rally the bulk of private enterprise around this strategy. The Fiat President, Valletta, succeeded in forcing the right-wing Alighiero De Micheli out of the presidency of Confindustria but was unable to prevent the election in 1962 of F. Cicogna, a conservative Catholic who fought against the Centre-Left. Valletta declared that the clock could not be put back, that not only the trade unions but also the Confindustria were to blame for the Italian crisis.[37]

When Agnelli succeeded Valletta, he began to gradually disengage Fiat from the DC. Agnelli attempted to build up a special relationship with the PSI and to support its reunification with the Social Democratic Party (PSDI). The Fiat-owned Turin daily *La Stampa* became rather pro-socialist. The DC too, however, was developing its own independence as its economic power grew. Until the early 1960s the DC had delegated economic policy to the private sector. With the development of the public sector the DC began to occupy an increasingly important economic role. The struggle between the DC and Fiat took various forms. For example, some 'anti-car' laws were passed and petrol prices increased.[38]

For Fiat the Centre-Left experiment had been a failure. It had not modernized the Italian economy in the way it had hoped, it had not created a large social democratic party and it had created a vast state sector. Furthermore, the workers' struggles of 1969 had challenged the entire assembly-line system of large firms[39] with the engineering workers (the bulk of Fiat's workforce) in the forefront of that militancy. Agnelli attempted to challenge the DC from the left and, in alliance with Pirelli, began to develop in the early 1970s a new, more progressive, political strategy. This was based on a formula which became known as 'the alliance of profits and wages against rent'. The meaning of this was that the 'productive classes', i.e. entrepreneurs and workers, should enter into an agreement against the backward features of the Italian economy exemplified in the 'parasitical' rent sector, presumably the abnormal profits deriving from trading, commercial and real-estate activities.[40] The economic implications of this formula have always been vague, particularly as the distinction between 'rent' and 'profit' is, in practical terms, fairly arbitrary. As in many other countries the industrial bourgeoisie is not purely industrial because its own interests are deeply intertwined with land and the entire banking and financial sector.[41] Politically the strategy was clearer: the 'rent' sector to be attacked was no other than the clientele system of the DC which had colonized the economy through the operation of the state sector.

This line was at first expressed in the Pirelli report to the Confindustria (1970). This document was fundamentally a pro-planning policy. The plan, however, would not be left to the State to elaborate, but would be the result of wide democratic consultation, with the private sector and the trade unions as the leading protagonists.[42] This was further developed by Agnelli in 1974 when he became President of the Confindustria. In his inaugural speech he called for a 'new pact' which, 'thirty years after the defeat of fascism would determine the national aim of the Italian people for the 1980s and 1990s.' He demanded a central role for industry, planning and a clear separation between the State and the private sector.[43] Agnelli had already made definite overtures to the trade-union movement and beyond that to the communist opposition, when he declared as early as 1972 that 'The reconstruction of a competitive and efficient industrial system and social reforms are not contradictory aims, on the contrary they complement one another.'[44]

In the early 1970s the clash between Fiat and the DC, or at least that section of the DC which was regrouped around the party leader Amintore Fanfani, took the form of a struggle within the Confindustria between the chemical giant Montedison and the Fiat–Pirelli group. The Montedison group had been formed in 1966 as a result of the merger between the chemical group Montecatini and Edison, a former electricity oligopoly (the electricity industry had been nationalized and the huge compensation paid enabled the Edison shareholders to use the vast liquid resources thus acquired for the merger). Montedison was a private firm even though the government had acquired enough stock to control it.[45] In 1970 Eugenio Cefis, former boss of ENI, the state oil company, became President of Montedison which by then had managed to accumulate amazing losses and was in debt to the banks (in turn controlled by the State, i.e. the DC). Cefis further expanded the company and diversified its holdings into fibres and textiles, finance companies and newspapers[46] (at a certain stage it acquired the *Corriere della Sera,* Italy's most prestigious newspaper). Cefis could expand Montedison because he enjoyed the support of Fanfani and hence of the vast financial resources of the State. The aim was to place the chemical industry at the centre of the entire industrial system.[47] This was a direct challenge to the centrality of Fiat (and Pirelli). The clash took the form of a dispute within the Confindustria about its organization. Cefis was able to impose his version of the reform, but the main issue soon became the election of the President of the Confindustria who would have had the key task of implementing the reform.[48] Cefis was able to assemble a broad coalition of interests: chemical and oil interests, the financial system, small Catholic entrepreneurs as well as the support of Fanfani and the bulk of the DC, but, given the power still in the hands of Agnelli, a compromise was reached whereby Agnelli became President of the Confindustria with four vice-presidents including Cefis and Pirelli.

The fortunes of Cefis took a turn for the worse when the 1974 divorce referendum resulted in a dismal defeat for the Fanfani line of strong anti-communist opposition. Now the initiative was in the hands of Agnelli who put forward his strategy of a 'social contract' negotiated with the Left, i.e. both the PCI and the trade unions. The basis of this contract (which coincides in timing with a similar policy in the UK) would be[49]:

1. The acceptance of the principle that economic efficiency be the main criterion for firms.
2. The enterprise would not have any special relationship to any political party.
3. The PCI and the trade unions would be involved in a policy of modernization, productivity and efficiency.
4. Real wages would be defended while differentials would be reduced. In fact in 1975 the Confindustria signed a new, more egalitarian, agreement on the indexation of wages.

Even though the PCI and the trade unions did not deny that there could be a temporary coincidence of interests between the labour movement and the private sector, the importance of Agnelli's proposal was that it represented an attempt by Italy's main private industrialist to gain a leading political role on behalf of the private sector. The period in which the private sector delegated the management of the political system to the DC in exchange for dominance in the economic field was over. If the DC was going to intervene in the economy, then big business had to do the same in politics. Agnelli's proposal was the first attempt by the big bourgeoisie in Italian history to recognize the legitimacy of some trade-union demands, even when these entailed economic sacrifices by the private sector.[50]

The 1970s heralded the growth of Fiat independence from the DC. Not only did Fiat challenge the DC on the political terrain but it also attempted to reform it from within. Taking advantage of the internal divisions within the DC, Umberto Agnelli, younger brother of the Fiat chairman, was able to become a DC-supported candidate in Turin in 1976. Unconnected to any of the main DC factions, Umberto Agnelli tried to become a rallying point among dissatisfied DC backbenchers. The experiment was a total fiasco: Agnelli was humiliated and ostracized by the leadership and abandoned active politics after only three years.[51]

The 'productivist' and modernizing line adopted by Fiat never had a chance of being implemented. It implied the assumption that economic growth was impeded by the existence of a backward sector whose chief representative was the DC (or at least some important sectors within this party). In reality 'backwardness' was functional to the kind of economic growth Italy had enjoyed and even enabled the country to survive the crises of the 1960s and 1970s. There would have been no cheap labour for Fiat without the existence of a depressed South. There would have been no cheap energy and steel without the role of the State. There would have been no southern market without the existence of southern clienteles based on the DC control over the public purse. The only modernizing line which could exist as an *alternative* to the DC was an alternative to the *system of power* of the DC. Such an alternative would have entailed a leading role for the main opposition, the PCI, but this was not acceptable to Fiat. Later in the 1970s Italian large private enterprises – like those of other countries – suffered a major profit squeeze leading to a further decrease in their possibility of self-financing, an increase in their indebtedness and in their recourse to state help.[52] This was far from being an Italian peculiarity due to its unique blend of 'backwardness' and 'modern industry'. The automobile sector from Detroit (Chrysler) to the UK (British Leyland) was hit by the crisis. The only strategy open to big Italian firms was either to expand on a multinational level or to decentralize through a network of small firms. Fiat chose the first path (together with Pirelli, which had merged with Dunlop, and Montedison) becoming a large financial holding in which the car division accounted for no more than half of total turnover.

What was and is particular to Italy is the traditional weakness of large private enterprise and the fact that there are very few large firms. If we look at *Fortune's* list of the top non-USA 500 companies for 1980 we find that Italy has only 11 firms in the list, the same as Spain and the Netherlands (a much smaller country), and comes after Switzerland (13), Sweden (26), Canada (31), France (42), West Germany (62), the UK (88) and Japan (121). It is true that if we take the top 30 firms in the world (including US companies) we find 3 Italian ones, but there are also 3 Italian firms among the top 5 loss-makers (and 8 among the top 75 loss-makers).[53] Finally, it is also an Italian peculiarity that the top three firms for volume of production are either owned or part-owned by the State: IRI (third largest firm in Europe in 1976), ENI (seventh) and Montedison (twentieth).[54]

The chief reasons why there are so few large private firms in Italy are that it is difficult to raise capital on the Italian stock exchange, that very few competent technical cadres are able to emerge within small and medium firms which are usually dominated by the founder and his heirs, and that as soon as a small or medium firm is in some difficulty it is 'saved' by a larger firm which is often a public sector company.[55]

Small firms have grown in importance throughout the 1970s. They have been able to enjoy lower labour costs, taking advantage of the decentralization of production which has occurred after the 'hot autumn' of 1969, and thanks to the spread of the hidden economy, many of them can ignore safety legislation and evade taxation. But there are also positive reasons for their growth. Small firms have been able to specialize, to use available entrepreneurial skills, albeit of a traditional kind, cooperate with local government and operate in a relatively safe local Italian market. They have also been good at exporting local products which depend for their success abroad on a recognizable 'Italian style': wine, shoes, clothes, jewellery, furniture.[56] As a result of this small firms produce 25 per cent of the nation's wealth, account for 20 per cent of imports and between 25 and 35 per cent of exports and 50 per cent of the workforce.[57] Those operating in sectors such as glass, clothing, shoes, etc. are independent firms, but the bulk of the others, operating in the engineering, steel and mechanical sector are in fact dependent on large firms. Small firms have been increasingly located in the north-east of the country as well as in the central regions of Emilia and Tuscany, thus further diversifying the industrial structure of Italy to the extent that recent literature on the subject tends to talk of 'three Italys': the depressed South, the industrial triangle of the North-west, and the central and north-eastern sector.[58]

The great weight of the public sector makes it difficult for private industry to emerge as a political protagonist. This partly explains the eventual defeat of the Agnelli line. The end of the old DC–Fiat alliance of the 1950s and 1960s has certainly weakened the DC, but it has also left the private sector with limited options. This may explain Agnelli's enthusiasm for the 'modernizing' line of the socialist leader, Bettino Craxi, in 1983.

In the late 1970s and early 1980s the objective of the Confindustria seems to have been a return to a period of confrontation with the trade-union movement. In 1982 it broke the agreement on the wages indexation system which it had signed in 1975. In October 1979 Fiat sacked sixty-one workers suggesting that they were connected with terrorism. A long series of court cases ensued and even though the courts ruled that the majority of the sixty-one workers had been unfairly dismissed they also established that Fiat was not contravening the 1970 Workers' Statute.[59] Fiat returned to the offensive in 1980, achieving mass redundancies after defeating a five-week strike thanks to a demonstration by 40,000 middle managers and foremen in defence of the 'right to work' and against the trade union. This was the signal for other companies to make massive lay-offs.[60]

The Fiat counter-offensive (which saw its counterpart in the UK in the series of victories reported by the management of British Leyland against its workforce) further reinforced its independence from the DC and the other political parties. It constituted an attempt to impose on the government a monetarist policy which the coalition parties themselves did not have the strength to pursue in a consistent manner.

In this more recent period the Confindustria further developed its independent role. It became readier than in the past to confront the unions directly without the mediation of the DC. In 1984, however, the battle for modifying the index-linked scale of wages seemed to have been entirely delegated to the government. The temporary success of the CGIL and of the communist opposition contributed to strengthen the more militant sections of the Confindustria. The engineering employers' association (the Federmeccanica) produced a document (approved by its Executive Council on 30 November 1984) in which it envisaged a thorough 'recasting of the entire system of industrial relations', taking advantage of what it saw as the end of the traditional working class.

Collective bargaining – it said – will have to be considerably reduced in scope and limited to the traditional unskilled or semi-skilled sector. Elsewhere negotiations will have to bypass the unions completely, while managerial prerogatives, the rules of the market and entrepreneurial freedoms will have to be re-established.[61]

Alongside this attempt to introduce in Italy some of the economic concepts of the 'New Right' (propagandized in the USA and in the UK by supporters of the Reagan and Thatcher administrations), a quite different tendency was emerging in the public sector. An agreement signed on 18 December 1984 between the three trade unions and the IRI established that the introduction of new technologies and investment plans in the IRI system would be negotiated between the two parties concerned. This would not only take place at the top but also in each IRI sector through newly created consultative committees in which employers and unions would be represented. These committees would be given all necessary written information on future plans including investments and the introduction of new technologies.[62]

Thus we can surmise that what might develop in Italian industry is an accentuated political gap between a militantly anti-union private sector and a public sector based on union–employer cooperation. In both cases, however, mediation by the government would have a decreasing importance.

THE CHURCH

The Church in Italy emerged from the war and the fascist period considerably strengthened. With the Lateran Treaty and the Concordat it had signed with the fascist regime it obtained sovereign status (the 'City of the Vatican'), virtual control over marriages, important financial concessions as well as a monopoly in religious education in state schools.[63] Its basic strategy of coexistence with the regime enabled it to expand its ecclesiastical structures through numerous parallel organizations among the laity (of which by far the most important was the Azione Cattolica (AC)). For nearly twenty years the Church has been the only official alternative to fascism and provided an organizational home for political and intellectual cadres who would become the leaders of the post-war DC.[64]

By the end of the war the Italian middle classes had shed some of their traditional anti-clericalism which dated from the period of the Risorgimento. Unlike the political parties the Church had a powerful centralized organization and an obedient following. It had also developed a political ideology, known as the 'social doctrine'; this was a fairly vague set of principles which could be used for social and political activity and which could be constantly reinterpreted by the Church.[65] Its central tenet was class reconciliation.

There were three forces which posed a threat to the Church.[66] The first was anti-clericalism. This was not a serious threat because its main political expression, the Action Party, was electorally a small force and because the PCI, having voted in favour of the inclusion of the Concordat in the new Italian Constitution, demonstrated that it had no wish to engage in a religious civil war.

The second threat was modernity. In the long run this would prove to be the most formidable, particularly as the development of the Italian economy and the growth of the consumer society, urbanization and emigration loosened the traditional ties which had been the strength of the Church. However, in the immediate post-war period, modernity was not considered by the Vatican to be as threatening as 'atheistic Marxism'.

The post-war strategy of the Church was to compete with this threat (embodied in the PCI) by becoming more like a political party. It organized new forms of mass devotion and large processions. These had once been religious and local. They now became national and semi-political. The Church used the media through a popular radio slot called 'God's microphone' and organized mass rallies and mass preaching.[67] Azione Cattolica, led by Luigi Gedda, became increasingly political. As Giancarlo Poggi has written: 'The impression was given that for the Head of the Universal Church himself the solution about to be offered to the problems of how to form an administration in a little town somewhere in Southern Italy was a more momentous matter than what was happening or about to happen in the Catholic communities of Africa or Asia'.[68]

Although it behaved more and more like a political party, the Church was necessarily dependent on the existence of one or more political parties which would seek to guarantee its power in Italian society. Some Church exponents believed that the Church would have had more influence if it did not tie its own fortunes too closely to a single party.[69]

The emergence of a single Catholic party and the principle of the 'political unity' of Catholics had to be fought for by the DC leader, Alcide De Gasperi. He tried to prevent the reconstruction of a Catholic movement opposed to liberal culture and at the same time the emergence of a left-wing Catholic party. The strength of the DC, the international recognition they received from the USA and their success in obtaining from the Church the suppression of the tiny Partito della Sinistra Cristiana (Party of the Christian Left) meant that by 1947–48 the Vatican had no other option in the political field apart from the DC.[70]

It has often been suggested that the DC was no more than the long arm of the Church, at least in the immediate post-war period. It is true that the DC used the influence of the Church and its organizations in order to gain electoral popularity in Italy and that, to some extent, it became its political guarantor, but it was always able to maintain an effective autonomy. The relation between the party and the Church was thus a relatively complex one, even in the early years and just as the DC sought to maintain some independence, the Church never officially accepted the doctrine of a single party for the Catholics and the Pope never *explicitly* told the faithful to vote for the DC: thus the Pope intervened in the 1948 elections instructing Catholics to vote for 'candidates prepared to defend God's law and Christian doctrine'. The Church's political role was not directly promoted by its own hierarchy but by the large lay organization, AC.[71]

Soon, however, De Gasperi was strong enough to use the support of the Church not only to prevent the formation of an alternative Catholic party but also to win his internal battles against his rivals, particularly the left-wing Dossetti. The Church was not always happy with De Gasperi's independence and in turn tried to use its influence within the DC by playing one faction against the other. At times in the early 1950s it also tried to use the threat of favouring a second more right-wing Catholic party in order to control the DC. In general political matters, however, the Church could do little else than to follow the lead of the DC. To illustrate this we shall take two examples: the Church attitude to the PCI and the Church attitude to the 'Southern Question'.

The anti-communism of the Church had been evident throughout its modern history. However, it had not been able to stop DC–PCI cooperation in the period 1945–47 in government, in the Constituent Assembly and in the trade-union movement. The diaries of De Gasperi tell the story that on 12 November 1946 he received the visit of 'an important member of the Vatican hierarchy' who told him that any cooperation with the 'anti-clerical parties' (i.e. the Communists and the Socialists) could no longer be tolerated.[72] His attitude changed somewhat when De Gasperi mentioned the words 'Constituent Assembly', thus implying that it was necessary to be on good terms with the PCI in order to obtain the inclusion of the Concordat in the Constitution. Giulio Andreotti, then a close aide of De Gasperi's, later many times Prime Minister, recently revealed that the 'Vatican personality' was none other than the Assistant Secretary of State (or 'Deputy Foreign Minister') of the Vatican G. B. Montini who became Pope Paul VI in 1963.[73]

It was only after the expulsion of the PCI from the government (at a time of De Gasperi's choosing) and after the victory of the DC in the 1948 elections that Pope Pius XII made his most important statement on the PCI. On 13 July 1949 a papal decree was published which prohibited Catholics from joining the PCI, from writing or reading or publishing or distributing any communist literature. Those infringing any of these prohibitions would be *ipso facto* excommunicated and would not receive any of the sacraments. Two weeks later the Holy See explained that excommunication would apply not only to those who joined or supported the PCI but also any of its associated organizations or allies including the trade union CGIL and the PSI.[74]

From a political point of view this move was a mistake as it did not stop the growth of communist electoral support over the next thirty years nor did it stop the *rapprochement* between the DC and the PSI in the 1960s. Furthermore, it seriously weakened the Church's freedom of action as it tied its fortunes to the most intransigent anti-communist factions of the DC which were precisely those factions which, in the long run, would prove to be the weaker.

If we examine Church policy towards the peasantry and the South and we compare it to government policy (see Part I) we can detect a similarly 'tailist' attitude. When peasant struggles for the land began in 1944 the initial attitude of the Vatican was to depict them as instances of criminal behaviour, mindless violence and class hatred. The peasantry was seen as an ignorant mass easily manipulated by communist agitators.[75] The expression 'Southern Question' was never mentioned in Vatican documents and there was no admission that the *latifondo* had to be eliminated. As the DC began to establish its roots in the South by formulating a series of proposals for an agrarian reform the attitude of the Church began to change. This is, of course, not entirely due to the influence of the DC. The Holy See had been made more aware of the misery of the South by its own clergy as well as by those active in the charitable programmes for the South instituted by the Vatican. In November 1946 the Pope described small peasant property as a genuine rural civilization which he set against the city, the 'expression of the domination of big capital not only over economic life but over man himself'.[76] The association of small peasants, the Coldiretti, was considered a representative of the Church in the countryside as well as being a vote-gatherer for the DC. By 1948 the Church had joined the DC in supporting the principle of the agrarian reform.[77]

The populist defence of small peasant property with its anti-modernist undertones was modified in the late 1950s when the Church began to move from exclusive support for smallholdings to accepting the need for greater efficiency in modern farming and for larger capitalist farms – just as the DC had done. In the encyclical letter *Mater et Magistra* (1961) Pope John XXIII implied that small peasant holdings were no longer the best form of economic life in the countryside. Christians had to consider developing the whole infrastructure of transport, water, the health system, etc.[78]

The *Mater et Magistra* signalled the desire of the Church and particularly of the new Pope, John XXIII, who had been elected in 1958 to move with the times. The encyclical no longer harked back to medieval corporatism but looked favourably on scientific and technical advances. It coincided not only with the debate on the modernization of the Italian economy but also with the debate on the constitution of a centre-left government of the DC in alliance with the PSI. The PSI welcomed the *Mater et Magistra* which it interpreted as a papal blessing for the Centre-Left government.[79] With this encyclical the Pope was probably trying to force through a new course for the Church because the bulk of the hierarchy was clearly opposed to political as well as religious modernization.

The debate on the Centre-Left had begun in the late 1950s and seriously divided both DC and PSI. The Church hierarchy intervened clearly on the side of the opponents of the Centre-Left. In April 1959 the Holy See reminded Catholics that it was forbidden to vote for Marxist parties and asserted that it was similarly forbidden to vote for parties which might call themselves Christian, but in fact helped the communists or cooperated with them. The Jesuit journal *Civiltà cattolica* suggested that Christians should not support those who still cooperated with the PCI (i.e. the PSI) or those who called themselves Marxist (as the PSI did). The problem was that even the pro-American centrist Social Democratic Party still called itself Marxist and that it had been a close ally of the DC since it split from the PSI in 1947. Taken literally the *Civiltà cattolica* article was a clear sign of support for a centre-right coalition.[80] This was in fact the policy of the right wing of the DC.

Again in May 1960 the Church hierarchy attempted to establish its supremacy in Italian affairs. A leading article in the *Osservatore romano,* the official Vatican daily, established the following *punti fermi* or 'basic points'[81]:
1. The Church must guide the faithful in both ideas and practice.
2. The Church cannot be politically neutral.
3. The Church must be the judge of whether political cooperation between the faithful and the non-believers was permissible.
4. The Church cannot allow believers to cooperate with Marxists.

A few days later, however, Montini, the future Pope Paul VI, by then Cardinal of Milan, specifically declared that the 'opening to the left' (as the Centre-Left operation was called) was not permissible 'in the manner and form now being contemplated'. This could be read as meaning that there was no objection in principle: it was just the 'manner and form' which was wrong.[82]

The divisions within the Church enabled the DC to circumvent any opposition from the Vatican. At the Eighth Congress of the DC, on 27 January 1962, Aldo Moro formally proposed support for a Centre-Left coalition. To the Vatican he declared: 'Our independence means that we must take risks on our own and this is our way of being of service to the Church.'[83] In this way Moro virtually said that the framework of DC strategy was to be determined by political considerations and not by religious ones. True, the DC was still a Christian-inspired party, but it had to be the sole judge of how it could maintain its central role as the sole political representative of the Catholics.

It was in the course of the 1960s that the Church began to follow its own political path and to develop, at one and the same time, its political independence from the DC and a new international outlook.

The first steps along this road were taken by Pope John XXIII. At first he distanced himself from Italian political affairs which he delegated to the Italian bishops.[84] The immediate results were that in fact the Church intervened more rather than less in national politics, particularly, as we have seen, in the hope of preventing the Centre-Left government.

Pope John's political strategy was to revise Church relations in three directions: (1) towards Eastern Europe; (2) towards non-Catholics including Marxists; (3) towards capitalism.

The process of *détente* with Eastern Europe was initiated through a series of symbolic acts, the most important of which were the welcome he gave to the Polish Cardinal Wyszinski, who had been considered by Pius XII as a collaborator of the communists,[85] and the private audience he granted to Nikita Khrushchev's son-in-law Alexei Adzubei, editor of the Soviet newspaper *Izvestia*. This was achieved in spite of the opposition of his own Secretary of State who refused to make public a transcript of the audience.[86]

The 1961 encyclical *Mater et Magistra* began to question the support given by the Church to capitalism.

The important 1963 encyclical *Pacem in terris* opened up the possibility for a dialogue with communism. It makes a distinction between 'false ideologies' (e.g. Communism and Marxism) and the political movements they inspire (e.g. the actual communist movement). It argued that political and social movements, unlike doctrines and ideologies, are never static, they change with history and may produce just and worthy demands. A dialogue between believers and non-believers can produce the truth, and non-believers too must be allowed to keep their dignity as human beings.

The repercussions in Italy of the *Pacem in terris* were very far reaching. In practice the Pope had given his effective blessing to the new coalition.

The changes in the Church were also underlined by the papal decision to convene an ecumenical council (the twenty-first in the history of the Church and the first since 1870). The Council, known as Vatican II, was to modernize the Church as an organization, develop better relations with other religions and face the problems of modern society.[87] Vatican II opened in October 1962 and closed under Pope Paul VI (John XXIII had died in 1963) in December 1965. It did not modernize the Church, but produced sufficient material for the reformists within the Church to build on.

The position of the bishops was considerably strengthened by instituting the synods of bishops to be elected by the national Churches. The distinctive contribution that the laity could make to the Church was recognized and encouraged: the Church was no longer to be the exclusive prerogative of the clergy. An important aspect of the tradition established by St Thomas Aquinas was thus abandoned together with its rigid conceptual framework in favour of a return to more flexible biblical concepts. The abolition of Latin for most rituals permitted more freedom of interpretation: translations allowed for a multiplicity of views.[88]

Relations with the other Christian Churches, particularly the Eastern Orthodox Church were improved; clerical anti-Semitism came under attack as Jews were 'acquitted' of the ancient accusation of deicide (the murder of Christ).

The new Pope, Paul VI, had at first to contain the zeal of the reformists in order to avoid a split in the Church. He continued the policy of detente with the East and pursued vigorously a policy of dialogue with the Third World. As the Vatican became a more international body, it also became less of a 'Christian Democrat' supporting system. The important encyclical *Populorum progressio* (26 March 1967) declared as incompatible with Christian principles a system which puts at the centre of everything the pursuit of private profit and competition and the absolute right to private property. The encyclical also asserted that even though revolutionary insurrections can be evil they may be necessary in exceptional circumstances such as the struggle against a permanent and cruel form of despotism.[89] In the *Octogesima adveniens* (14 May 1971) Paul VI asserted in the strongest terms his belief that no social system could be derived from the 'social doctrine' of the Church. If there was no 'Christian political thought' then it followed that there could be no 'Christian political party'.[90] The same man who, when working in the Vatican Secretariat had accepted the principle of the political unity of the Catholics in the DC now suggested that Catholics could be active in various political parties.[91]

The *Octogesima adveniens* marked a decisive turning-point in the history of the modern Church and constitutes – in the Italian context – the parting of the ways between the Vatican, as an international organization whose seat is in Italy out of historical accident, and the DC.

The DC, while it had been able to establish its independence from clerical influence was not prepared to allow the Church to have an autonomous role. Church autonomy might endanger its monopoly of Catholic support and contract its electoral and social basis. Already organizations such as the Association of Italian Christian Workers (ACLI), and even AC had rescinded all official links with the DC, and in the case of ACLI even those with the Church hierarchy. The DC still needed the help of the Church particularly as it had suffered a major defeat when in 1970 the parties of the Centre and the Left had legalized divorce.

The Church strategy was to seek a modification of the law and had expected that the DC would act as a mediating force with the pro-divorce parties. But the DC, by taking a more intransigent anti-divorce stand than the Church, obliged it to tail once again behind the DC. The Vatican was unhappy about the DC leader Fanfani's strategy to use a popular referendum to abolish the divorce law; it was worried that a referendum would cause a major religious split in Italian society. Fanfani was more worried that a compromise over divorce would cause a split within the DC.[92] The Vatican attitude was in keeping with the new tendencies within the Church, and in particular with the strengthening of the power of the national bishops which had been sanctioned by Vatican II: the entire conduct of the anti-divorce campaign was delegated to the Italian bishops with little backing from the Vatican hierarchy. The attitude of the Vatican could not but encourage Catholic dissent in Italy. The youth branches of ACLI came out in favour of divorce, ACLI itself refused to take a position and so did a number of leading bishops and some important cardinals, such as Cardinal Pellegrino of Turin. Many leading Catholic intellectuals fought openly on the side of the divorce parties and during the course of this campaign loosened their ties with the DC and forged new links with the parties of the Left, particularly the PCI. In 1976, two years after the divorce referendum, many of these Catholic intellectuals would be elected to Parliament on the PCI lists.

The referendum was to be held on 12 May 1974. On 5 May, speaking in St Peter's the Pope did not condemn divorce, preferring instead to invoke religious peace. Two days later even the Italian bishops in their final meeting before the poll did not condemn the growing pro-divorce Catholic lobby.[93] The opponents of divorce were able to muster only 41 per cent of the vote. Clearly a large number of Catholic voters supported the lay position. It has been estimated that 16 per cent of DC supporters voted in favour of divorce and a defeated Fanfani did not hesitate to blame divisions within the Church for the setback, and in particular the more advanced interpretations of Vatican II.[94]

The Vatican disengagement from Italian politics had also taken the form of toning down the political involvement of its main lay organization, AC. In 1962 AC was still a very large organization, in fact the largest in Italy with 3.6 million members. In 1964 Paul VI named Vittorio Bachelet as head of the association. Under Bachelet AC was considerably democratized, became more autonomous from the clergy and stressed its religious nature as opposed to political involvement. It ceased in fact to be a 'transmission belt' for DC politics at the cost of a massive decrease in membership (down to 800,000 in 1973). Under the leadership of Livio Labor in 1961 ACLI began to cut all ties with the DC. By 1975–76 the DC feared that it had lost its monopoly over Catholic representation. The 1970s were in fact a traumatic period for the Catholic world in Italy and elsewhere.

As a result of the tension of the 1960s, the end of the 'economic miracle', the growth of political dissent, the student movement, the workers' unrest, the birth of feminism as well as the changes within the Church itself, young Catholics became interested in and attracted to new forms of internationalism and particularly by the 'new theology' emanating from Latin America as well as by new anti-authoritarian forms of organizations. The development of an anti-institutional Catholic culture meant not only that many young Catholics voted in favour of divorce or against the DC, but that they began to construct for themselves new organizations outside the control of the Church and the established political parties.[95]

The new Catholic groupings now constitute one of the main elements of the Catholic world in Italy. It has been estimated that there are some 8,000 communities involving several hundred thousand people. Some are deeply religious groups committed to a mystical and ascetic personal religiosity; others are community-based and active in organizing 'marginal' groups in society, like the handicapped or drug-addicts; others still are deeply committed to a Third World form of politics or to the anti-nuclear and peace movement.[96] But these groups are only one element, albeit the most modern, of the Catholic world. One should not discount the traditional lay organizations such as ACLI and AC as well as new lay organizations such as Comunione e liberazione. This is a 70,000-strong movement of young people based in the North and the Centre against modern capitalism and technical progress. This seems to signal a return to the anti-modernist tradition of the Church. Yet Comunione e liberazione is organized like a modern political lobby, sponsoring DC candidates and seeking to condition DC politics without giving up its freedom of action. Finally, there is still the formidable apparatus of the formal Catholic Church with its 28,000 parishes performing every Sunday 160,000 services attended by 16 million people. Its cultural machine is responsible for the production of 660 new books every year as well as a daily paper, 63 weeklies (one of these *Famiglia Cristiana* is the largest circulation weekly in Italy with over 1.7 million copies sold), 249 monthlies and 792 parish bulletins.[97]

There has also been a transformation in the real functions of the Church in Italian society.[98] Its social functions, i.e. its hospitals, charities and educational establishments, have contracted remarkably as the growth of the Welfare State has enabled the State and local authorities to intervene in territory which had been for centuries the prerogative of the Church. Its spiritual functions, i.e. its ritualized intervention in some of the fundamental moments in people's lives such as birth, marriage and death have also contracted, although not as much as it is commonly suggested. The lay State cannot provide any appropriate substitute for these functions which are still demanded even by people whose commitment to religion is very limited. Finally, the

Church used to provide a focus for social life through the local parish and various Church-based associations. Political parties, clubs, social circles, sporting associations can now provide a lay outlet for these social needs.

In the immediate post-war period the Italian Catholic world was still enclosed in a traditional Church. By the 1980s it was faced by a bewildering pluralism of great complexity. The processes which had begun to develop in the early 1960s had come to fruition. All attempts by the DC to 'colonize' the Church and vice versa had come to naught. The most significant development has undoubtedly been the gradual transformation of the Church from a Eurocentric body for whom Italy was the leading country, to an international body whose centre of interests has spread far more to the rest of Europe and to the Third World, particularly Latin America.

When Pius XII died in October 1958 the College of Cardinals had 55 members of whom 36 were European (18 Italian). Europe had the highest number of baptized Catholics. When John Paul II was elected twenty years later in October 1978 the College of Cardinals had doubled in number with 56 non-European cardinals, 44 of whom came from the Third World, and Latin America had the highest number of Catholics (40%).[99] The leader of this Church was no longer an Italian but a Pole, a citizen of a non-capitalist country. John Paul II had no need of a specific power basis in Italy and no wish to grant leading Christian Democrats privileged access or special support. The difference with his predecessor but one, Paul VI, is striking. Paul VI had been a powerful member of the Vatican Secretariat and then Cardinal of Milan, and in these roles had followed all the vicissitudes of DC politics from the very beginning and was in close contact with its leaders.[100]

When Karol Wojtyla became Pope he was heading a Church which had become more self-confident. Having detached itself from the politics of the West the Church could project itself far more than ever before as a non-aligned force working against the hegemony of the two superpowers and the nuclear balance of terror. In his first encyclical *Redemptor hominis* (4 March 1979) the Pope announced that the post-Vatican II period was now over and so was the period of intense self-criticism.[101] Now freed from any commitment towards any given economic system, capitalist or otherwise, the Church would try to give *religious* and not political answers to the problems of modern society.

The charismatic figure of the Polish Pope and his overt use of the media, exemplified in his constant travels, all suggest that the Church feels it can re-establish a direct relation with the masses without the help of political parties.

In the Italian context this meant not only that the DC could no longer rely on the Church, but that not even those Catholic groups which had emerged in Italy in the later 1960s and throughout the 1970s would look to the DC as the 'party of the Catholics' or the 'party of the Church' but as an instrument which is more or less likely than others to implement their wishes and aspirations.

MASS MEDIA

The mass media form part of an information system which involves messages sent to receivers, an entire electronic industry, a telecommunications system, education, marketing, etc. The main surveys which have recently investigated this question all stress the need for a global approach.[102] The growth of data banks, television satellites, computers, information technology, teletext, video-recorders, etc. give support to the view that we are at the beginning of a transition from an industrial society based on the factory system to an information society based on microprocessors.

While actual changes may not occur with the rapidity some of the commentators suggest, there is little doubt that mass communication is one of the central terrains of a radical restructuring of the world economy. This restructuring has two essential characteristics: a very pronounced centralization of production in the hands of a few – mainly American – multinational companies and a widespread decentralization of distribution.[103] This process is particularly evident in the most important of the mass media, television. [104]

That production is increasingly centralized is not in question: the Japanese are acquiring a virtual monopoly in the manufacturing of television and video-related equipment, while the Americans have control over the manufacture of television programmes (80% of telefilms for instance, are made in the USA) and their relay via satellite.[105]

The centralization of the world market is already causing difficulties for national governments, for it has been the general rule in Europe that television broadcasting systems are publicly owned or closely regulated.

In most cases public broadcasting is increasingly challenged by private television.[106] The advent of satellite broadcasting which would enable the owners of a special aerial to watch hundreds of programmes will further weaken public broadcasting and the control of the nation-state over television.

In Italy the monopoly of public broadcasting was decisively broken by a decision of the Constitutional Court in July 1976. The Court upheld the monopoly of RAI (the public network), for *national* broadcasting, but decided to permit private broadcasting as long as it was not on a national scale. Since then there has been a formidable growth of local private radio and television stations whose output is totally unregulated

– the only case in Europe, perhaps in the world (even in the USA a licence is required). It has been estimated that in 1983 there were more than 700 private television stations in Italy.[107] Of course, most of these transmit very little and were created by local or national groups purely in order to occupy a transmission band. What is perhaps more significant is that the RAI audience had crumbled to 50 per cent by the end of 1983, that private television and radio stations employ directly or indirectly 20,000 against 13,500 employed in the public sector, and that the RAI's total share of advertising revenue was down from 25 per cent in 1977 to 20 per cent in 1981.

Private television stations are vertically integrated with advertising agencies and the main publishing groups. In the absence of regulation two or three television groups have emerged which will eventually control the entire private sector. These oligopolies are Italian, but they transmit programmes they have purchased from abroad, mainly films, telefilms and cartoons from the USA and Japan. They thus act, *de facto*, as agents for the distribution of products manufactured by the great multinational companies.

The international structure of the information system and the subordinate role Italy plays within it are mirrored within Italy itself in the unevenness between North and South. If we look at 'traditional' or written information we will notice a persistent gap: The South has 34 per cent of the total population but publishes only 400 out of 12,000 book titles a year (1975 figures), prints only 16 out of 87 daily papers and of these not one sells more than 100,000 copies (in a country where there is no real national press), buys only 10 per cent of daily papers and 17 per cent of periodicals. If we examine the figures for television we see that there is virtually no 'consumption' gap between North and South: 94 per cent of the southern population own a television set against a national average of 96 per cent. The closing of this particular gap is relatively recent.[108] In all cases, however, there is a production gap: most of the programmes broadcast come from abroad, but most of the Italian programmes broadcast come from the North or the Centre. Southern culture has no outlet. The role of the South in this domain is, even more than that of the rest of Italy, its traditional one: a market for goods made elsewhere.

The growth of private television stations – an essential part of the 'unification' of North and South at the level of the market – has been facilitated by the ruling political parties not only because there has been no serious attempt at regulation, but also because state aid for the newspaper industry has freed resources for investment in the far more profitable television sector[109] and because there are numerous links between the DC political élite and the publishing groups. As parliamentary control has increased over public broadcasting the DC has had to share some of its influence in RAI with its main allies in government. This has made it all the more urgent for the DC to be able to influence the private sector. The connection between the political authorities and the media also extends to the film industry which relies on state aid, and whose only way out of its present crisis is in close integration with television production following the Hollywood pattern.

Turning to the press, let us now briefly examine state involvement in the newspaper industry which dates back to fascism. Italian journalists belong to a 'registered' profession with restricted entry and high salaries; the price of newsprint is regulated by a state commission on paper; the price of newspapers is part of the basket of goods which is used to calculate the cost-of-living index which in turn affects the indexation of wages (it is thus in the government's interest to keep the price of newspapers down); there are various forms of direct aid and subsidies and now newspapers are virtually exempt from most taxes.[110] Newspapers as such are an increasingly unprofitable industry,[111] but integrated with radio, television and advertising they represent a state-subsidized loss-making sector which indirectly contributes to the profitability of the rest of the industry: radio and television, the newsprint industry, advertising, etc. State support for newspapers provides an outlet for advertising, a demand for newsprint and an information network for radio and television. The main newspapers are owned by banks (these are under DC influence), or by big firms such as Fiat (owners of *La Stampa*), or by state companies such as ENI (owners of *Il Giorno*) or by the Confindustria (owners of the leading financial paper *Il Sole-24 ore*). Italy is also the only liberal-democratic country with a large circulation political party daily paper: *L'Unità*, organ of the PCI. However, there is no mass circulation popular press as in West Germany or the UK. The highest circulation is reached by Italy's most prestigious newspaper, the *Corriere della Sera,* but this hovers around 470,000 copies. In Europe Italy has a newspaper readership which exceeds only countries such as Spain, Portugal and Turkey. Furthermore, the number of readers has been around 5 million for nearly fifty years. The most obvious explanation for this low level of readership is that Italy is a latecomer in the field of mass literacy and mass education. When this was achieved the age of television had already come. One should consider the newspaper as a fairly obsolete means of information destined to survive only for the benefit of political, cultural and economic élites (which is the present case in Italy) or by becoming an entertainment sheet (e.g. the *Sun* in the UK) where there is an already existing mass habit of buying newspapers. Here it is interesting to note that in the last ten years three newspapers have been created in Italy; two of these, *Il Giornale Nuovo* (1974) and *La Repubblica* (1976) deliberately set themselves out to appeal respectively to a right-wing and a left-wing élite. The third attempt was *L'Occhio* which set out to be the Italian equivalent of the *Daily Mirror*. While the first two papers succeeded, particularly *La Repubblica* which also contained technical novelties in layout and style, *L'Occhio* was a dismal failure and had to close down.[112]

The only mass press readership is in the field of weekly news magazines. While the daily press remained stagnant the weeklies went from 12.6 million sold each week in 1952 to 21 million in 1972.[113]

In spite of the connections between the press and the governing party, DC, much of the Italian press, particularly since the mid 1960s is not pro-DC but tends rather to favour the smaller parties of the Centre and the socialists. Ideologically the press tends to espouse various aspects of the liberal tradition whether in its radical (*La Repubblica*) or centrist form (*Corriere della Sera*). Clearly, as in many other countries, its power in terms of shaping electoral opinion is quite negligible as the PCI and DC together are able to obtain nearly 70 per cent of the popular vote.

The DC, as the dominant government party for the whole post-war period, has concentrated its efforts upon the control of broadcasting. Until the early 1970s the DC had a virtual monopoly of television. What form did this control take? In the 1950s and early 1960s this consisted in control over the news section of the RAI. This was done in a blatantly propagandistic manner. The voice of the opposition, particularly that of the communist opposition was virtually ignored. The rest of broadcasting was in the hands of cautious producers who were left fairly free provided their output did not offend Catholic values (which caused problems with variety shows).[114] In the 1960s this changed because of: (1) the development of a second channel which introduced an element of competition among broadcasters (2) an increased ferment among the intellectual élites (in turn a reflection of the student and labour struggles of the period); (3) the growth of the whole information system. Thanks to the increased availability of and the demand for US programmes, Italian television had acquired the production structure of the modern media.[115]

Media messages must be produced following particular techniques and these determine their form of presentation. This rule is valid not only for 'sit-coms' or soap operas or variety shows but also for news and current affairs. Increasingly, politicians must be prepared to accept that the information they want to broadcast be processed through the media whose structure is that of a market. What they say must be properly packaged and properly presented; political discourse must change and politicians must at least in part, adapt themselves to media techniques.[116] Political discourse must become more like a 'show', a spectacle. It becomes more uniform because *all* politicians are subjected to the same rule. Politics becomes more 'Americanized'. This creates difficulties not only for the governing party but also for the communist opposition whose entire outlook on communication had been based on the development of 'alternative' information such as their own newspapers, magazines, live entertainments, rallies, etc. – all increasingly obsolete forms of communication.[117]

The 'Americanization' of politics in terms of media presentation is only one aspect of the 'Americanization' of the rest of Italian society.

By the 1960s the model of social behaviour and the consumption habits described in American situation comedies was something which was no longer seen as the image of a distant society characterized by great wealth, but as one which could be attained by many Italians through the expansion of the market. Furthermore, the very class structures of Italian society became 'Americanized', as traditional industry entered a period of continuous decline, as the tertiary sector expanded and an increased part of production was directed towards the communication system.[118]

The 'Americanization' of the media signalled a growing autonomy on the part of the information system as a whole from politicians. These had to accept the 'form' of the media, but sought to retain control over its contents in the mistaken belief that the 'message' could be isolated from the apparatus which produces it.

In opposition to the DC the other political parties also sought to intervene at the level of the 'message'. By the mid 1970s a greatly weakened DC was no longer able to aspire to the exclusive monopoly over the RAI and had to compromise with those who wanted reforms. This compromise was embodied in Law 103 which was enacted in April 1975. With this law, control over the RAI shifted from the government to Parliament, which established a parliamentary committee of forty members in proportion to the strength of the political parties in Parliament. The committee's task was to ensure that the RAI was a pluralistic organization which represented all shades of opinion. The committee, however, necessarily had a majority corresponding to the government parties. The law also required that the governing body of the RAI, the Consiglio d'amministrazione or Board of Governors be composed of 16 governors, 10 nominated by the committee (i.e. the political parties) and 6 nominated by the RAI's shareholders (these are in fact IRI, the state holding company). In other words the board, too, establishes a majority which reflects the governing majority. Control of the RAI had passed to an oligopoly of political parties. In practice both the board and the committee do not intervene on resources (except on the level of advertising permitted) or on planning or on the licence fee (which remains under the control of the Minister of Posts and Telecommunications). However, the board is responsible for all senior and middle-level appointments.

The personnel thus must be made up almost entirely by people politically trusted by the ruling majority. These people, however, also possess all the technical skills with which to run a modern media. This knowledge enables them to play a significant role in the elaboration of a media policy.[119] Thus, even though the Board of Governors is on paper an all-powerful body, in practice it tries to obtain 'correct' political messages by appointing the 'right' personnel. Party political control is thus limited by the fact that the apparatus of the RAI, like all apparatuses, has a life of its own. There is also another important limitation: mass behaviour is not much influenced by the degree of bias in news programmes, otherwise one would be unable to understand how the PCI has managed to obtain one-third of the vote when having only a minute percentage of 'favourable' television time. Mass behaviour, however, may well be influenced by the whole range of *television* messages, by what these messages define as being 'normal' and 'acceptable' or 'reasonable', as well as by the totality of messages they receive. Political control cannot be established over the totality of television output because this depends on the entire cultural industry, that is, on the cinema, on the theatre, on the press, on the educational system and on all producers of information within and without the nation-state. Thus the colonization of the RAI by the governing political parties could not prevent the growing autonomy of the media while increasingly subordinating it to the world (i.e. American) communications and culture industry.

The blatant nature of this colonization was formalized by an agreement made by the DC and the PSI soon after Law 103 was passed. This stated that the DC would be the dominant voice in Channel 1 (television) and Radio 2, while the PSI would get Channel 2 and Radios 1 and 3.[120] This agreement also at first completely excluded the PCI from any representation on the Board of Governors of the RAI (after 1977 four PCI representatives took their seats on the board). The significance of this carve-up lay in the control established over the news programmes of the two channels because the evening news has the highest rating on Italian television. The DC-dominated evening news programme (TG1) was organized in direct competition with the PSI-run TG2 in a successful attempt to maximize the audience. The news programmes partly overlap, but TG1 achieves a far greater rating than its socialist rival. Journalists could choose which channel they wanted to work for. The results show not only the political colour of the two news and current affairs sections but also that political affiliation is virtually universal among journalists: of the 95 journalists opting for TG1 4 were communists, 1 socialist, (most of the other socialists having opted for TG2), 2 social democrats, 1 republican, 2 Liberal Party members, 5 'independent' of left-wing orientation and the remaining 80 were all DC or DC-leaning. As for the senior executive positions such as head of channel or departmental heads there were 8 DC, 4 PSI, 2 PSDI, 1 PRI and 1 left-wing independent.[121]

Control over the message generally took the form of giving far more time to the ruling parties than to the opposition (only the news programme of Radio 2 was unashamedly the mouthpiece of one of the factions of the DC). According to the Radical Party, from 1 March 1981 to 31 January 1982 the leaders of the five government parties were interviewed for a total of over ten hours, while all opposition leaders together were interviewed for two hours.[122]

Again it should be stressed that there is no evidence that, in electoral terms the media are able to influence the results to any significant degree. However, there may be some influence over a small percentage of the population which thus contributes to the small electoral swings. With a system of proportional representation these small swings do not affect the overall result, but they have a great symbolic value and do affect the composition of the ruling majorities and the strength of the opposition.[123]

In the long run, however, this system of carving up the RAI apparatus reveals the growing crisis of legitimacy of the political parties. The ability to control the output of television news is necessarily very limited, first of all because – as previously stated – political messages must be transformed by the media and this means that the political parties are less and less an independent source of information, they tend to become mere items in an information system dominated by television. Secondly, overall mass behaviour is affected by the entire information system and not just by television. This information system, being transnational, goes against the very logic of the nation-state and of national politics. Finally, the very carve-up of RAI reflects a conception of politics based on the idea of the markets – i.e. so many votes, so many political resources – while trying to exclude the opposition.[124]

REFERENCES AND NOTES

1. Apter, D. and Eckstein, H. (1963), p. 327.
2. Romagnoli, U. and Treu, T. (1977), pp. 11–12.
3. Pizzorno, A. (1980), p. 108.
4. Salvati, B. (1972), pp. 196–7.
5. Pizzorno (1980), p. 103.
6. See Triola, A. (1971), pp. 617–87.
7. Pizzorno (1980), p. 105.
8. Ibid., p. 106.
9. Ibid., pp. 106–7.
10. Lama, L. (1976), pp. 33–4.
11. Romagnoli and Treu (1977), p. 24.
12. Ibid., pp. 28–9.
13. Ibid., pp. 56–9.
14. Farneti, P. (1978a), p. 417.
15. Romagnoli and Treu (1977), pp. 62–3.
16. Ibid., p. 76.
17. Ibid., p. 81.
18. Ibid., pp. 83–4.
19. Farneti (1978a), p. 430.
20. Pizzorno (1980), p. 141.
21. Lama (1976), p. 53.

22. Romagnoli and Treu (1977), p. 87.
23. Turone, S. (1976), p. 86.
24. Ibid., p. 93.
25. Rieser, V. (1981), pp. 62–3.
26. Ibid., p. 68.
27. Amendola, G. (1979).
28. For a critique of the factory council system see Trentin, B. (1982). Bruno Trentin, a former leader of the engineering workers' union, was one of the principal architects of the factory council system; see his *Da sfruttati a produttori* (Trentin, 1977) and *Il sindacato dei consigli* (Trentin, 1980).
29. Pennacchi, L. (1982).
30. Carli, G. (1977), p. 75.
31. See Castronovo, V. (1981), p. 1261.
32. Ibid., pp. 1278–80.
33. Colajanni, N. (1976), p. 31.
34. Comito, V. (1982), pp. 133–7.
35. Cassano, F. (1979), p. 71.
36. Comito (1982), p. 142. However, apart from the stick there was also the carrot in the shape of higher-than-average wages and some company-based benefits, see Castronovo (1981), p. 1282.
37. See the account in Turone, S. (1974), pp. 349–50.
38. See Comito (1982), pp. 137–9 who also asserts that the price of petrol could be taken as the main index of the relation between Fiat and the State.
39. Castronovo (1981), p. 1290.
40. Sylos Labini, P. (1974), p. 149.
41. Ibid., pp. 85–6.
42. See text in Villari, L. (1975), vol. II, pp. 692–3. A pro-planning attitude was becoming diffuse among Italian entrepreneurs. Even Olivetti, the most intransigent defender of the freedom of enterprise lamented the fact that there was 'no national plan for electronics', see Forcellini, P. (1978), p. 117.
43. See text in Villari (1975), pp. 717–23.
44. Quoted in Comito (1982), p. 139.
45. Libertini, L. (1976), p. 30.
46. Castronovo, V. (1980), pp. 322–3.
47. The plan eventually failed. See Addario, N. (1982), p. 106.
48. Ibid., pp. 107–9.
49. Ibid.
50. Ibid., pp. 108–10.
51. Comito (1982), pp. 141–7.
52. Garavini, S. (1977), p. 30.
53. See the issues of *Fortune* of 13 Aug. 1979 and 10 Aug. 1981, also cited in Comito (1982), pp. 14–15.
54. This listing is in *Mondo Economico* of 24 January 1976 cited in Saraceno, P. (1977), p. 185. Fiat ranked twenty-ninth in Europe for volume of production but second to IRI in Italy for the size of the workforce, see Amoroso, B. and Olsen, O. J. (1978), p. 137.
55. Forte, F. (1974), pp. 350–1.
56. Castronovo (1980), pp. 326–7.

57. Ibid., p. 328.
58. See Bagnasco, A. (1977).
59. An account of this can be found in Ghezzi, G. (1981).
60. See Revelli, M. (1982).
61. See Federmeccanica (1984).
62. See 'Protocollo d'intesa tra IRI e sindacato. Roma, 18 dicembre 1984', in *Rassegna sindacale,* vol. XXXI, nos. 1–2, 4–11 January 1985.
63. Poggi, G. (1972), pp. 136–7.
64. Carlo Cardia in Baget-Bozzo, G. (1979), p. 83 (interview by Cardia).
65. Poggi (1972), pp. 144–5.
66. Ibid., pp. 140–1.
67. Ibid., p. 147.
68. Ibid., p. 153.
69. Magister, S. (1979), p. 49.
70. Ibid., pp. 41–7.
71. Baget-Bozzo, G. (1974), pp. 220–3.
72. See extract from the diaries in Scoppola, P. (1977), p. 293.
73. Andreotti, G. (1977), p. 73.
74. Magister (1979), pp. 132–3.
75. Casmiri, S. (1980), p. 208.
76. Quoted in Casmiri (1980), p. 219.
77. Ibid., p. 235.
78. Ibid., p. 289.
79. Pierini, M. N. (1965), pp. 309–10.
80. Baget-Bozzo (1977), pp. 190–2.
81. Ibid., p. 270.
82. Ibid., p. 272.
83. Moro, A. (1979), pp. 64–5.
84. Magister (1979), pp. 237–8.
85. Pierini (1965), p. 309.
86. Magister (1979), pp. 286–7.
87. Jerkov, A. (1966), pp. 57–61.
88. Baget-Bozzo (1979), pp. 128–9.
89. See the contributions by Lucio Lombardo Radice and Luigi Pestalozza to the debate on the *Populorum progressio* in Lombardo Radice, L. (1967). and Pestalozza (1967).
90. Baget-Bozzo (1977), pp. 41–3.
91. Chiarante, G. (1979), p. 48.
92. Magister (1979), pp. 416–22.
93. Ibid., p. 432.
94. Ibid., pp. 447–9.
95. Note the birth in 1973 of Cristiani per il Socialismo, a political group which accepted Marxism as a methodology while criticising the Church, the DC as well as the PCI for being too institutionalized. See Milanesi, G. (1976).
96. Cardia, C. (1979), pp. 48–50.
97. Ibid., pp. 51–2.
98. Garelli, F. (1977), pp. 165–7.
99. Chiarante (1979), pp. 43–4.
100. Ibid., pp. 57–9.

101. John Paul II, *Redemptor Hominis,* 4 Mar. 1979.
102. See in particular *Les activitiés d'information de l'électronique et des technologies des télecommunications sur l'emploi, la croissance et le commerce* (OECD) and the Unesco report of the International Commission for the Study of Communication Problems (chaired by Sean McBride) (Unesco, 1980).
103. On multinational companies and the communications industry see Mattelard, A. (1979).
104. In Italy as in the rest of Europe television is the main protagonist of the information system even though the number of television sets per 1,000 inhabitants (232) is slightly below the European average (264) (238 in the USSR and 604 in the USA).
105. On US dominance in the information system see Tunstall, J. (1981).
106. See Doglio, D. (1981), pp. 26–9.
107. Data obtained from the RAI's Centro di Documentazione e Studi. A more extensive examination of the development of Italy's private television broadcasting system and its effects on the public sector can be found in Sassoon, D. (1985), pp. 119–57.
108. All data in Vacca, G. (1984), pp. 25–30.
109. Ibid., p. 72.
110. Smith, A. (1978), p. 170.
111. No one is quite sure how much newspapers have lost. William Porter, writing in 1976 stated that in that year total losses were 45 million and that they were expected to double by 1980, see Porter, W. (1977), p. 268.
112. Asor Rosa, A. (1981), p. 1235. In the last few years the increase in the number of dailies has pushed circulation to just over 5 million copies.
113. Ibid., p. 1236; these figures come from Ajello, N. (1980), p. 208.
114. Cesareo. G. (1981), pp. 22–3.
115. Ibid., pp. 24–5.
116. Ibid., pp. 28–9.
117. Ibid., p. 29. Francesco Pinto (Pinto 1977) points out that in the 1950s the PCI leadership in trying to uphold the principle of freedom of information concentrated its attention exclusively on the news programmes while communist intellectuals had a distinct old-fashioned disregard for the whole phenomenon of mass communications. This situation did not change in the 1960s.
118. Vacca, G. (1982), p. 5.
119. Gentiloni, G. (1980), p. 149.
120. Ibid., p. 149.
121. Fracassi, C. (1982), p. 17.
122. Ibid.
123. Rositi, F. (1981), p. 88.
124. Vacca (1982), p. 21.

Chapter 8

ELECTIONS

In June 1946 the Italian people elected a Constituent Assembly and, at the same time, decided, by referendum, that Italy should become a republic. The republican majority was decisive but not overwhelming: 54.3 per cent. The referendum results also revealed how divided was Italy on this question. In northern and central Italy the pro-republican vote was, respectively, 64.8 and 63.3 per cent, while in the southern mainland it was 32.6 per cent, in Sicily 35.1 per cent and in Sardinia 39.1 per cent. Most of the pro-monarchist votes came from the ranks of the Christian Democratic Party (DC) and reflected more a general conservative attitude rather than an outright commitment to the monarchy. In fact the Monarchist Party in post-war Italy was never a strong force, obtained only 2.7 per cent of the votes in the elections for the Constituent Assembly and disappeared completely after 1968, its few remaining followers merging with the neo-fascists.

The Constituent Assembly was elected by universal suffrage and with a system of proportional representation (PR). The adoption of this system for all future elections was debated in the Constituent Assembly. It was, however, decided that it should not be incorporated in the Constitution. Article 56 says only that the Chamber of Deputies should be elected by universal direct suffrage. In deference to the wishes of the Italian Communist Party (PCI) that some mention should be made of proportional representation a motion was passed by members of the Assembly in favour of PR.[1] There are, of course, different types of PR and we shall briefly examine the one adopted in Italy. It should be pointed out, however, that even though there is no necessary link between an electoral system and the numbers of political parties represented in Parliament, it is clear that the more an electoral system is proportional the greater the tendency for all political forces to be represented. In June 1946 56 political parties fought the election, 11 of which presented a national list. These 11 parties collected 96.5 per cent of the votes and all obtained seats.[2] Thus from the very beginning a fairly wide array of political forces were represented.

If we examine Italian electoral history in the period to 1983 we can make the following observations concerning the degree of stability of Italian political parties (see Table 8.1):

1. The DC remained the largest party and never had to face a significant split, and, after 1948 and until 1979 it was always around or just below the 40 per cent level.

2. The PCI increased its vote regularly until the 1979 elections.[3]

3. The Italian Left (i.e. PCI, PSI and other smaller left-wing parties) had in 1946 nearly 40 per cent of the vote. In the three subsequent elections (1948, 1953 and 1958) it obtained respectively 31.03, 35.35 and 36.99 per cent. Since 1963 the PCI and PSI were no longer allied but their joint vote, if added to that of the smaller left-wing parties, went beyond the 40 per cent level. In 1976 (if we include the Radical Party but exclude the social democrats of the PSDI) the total vote of the left reached its highest level: 46.70 per cent.

4. The centrist vote (PSDI + PRI + PLI) oscillated more radically, reaching a peak of 14.47 per cent in 1963 and its lowest point (7.8%) in 1976.

5. The right-wing vote (neo-fascist plus monarchist) also followed an oscillating course, obtaining the following percentages in the nine elections we are examining: 8, 4.8, 12.7, 9.64, 6.88, 5.77, 8.67, 6.1, 5.3.

6. The joint vote of the two largest parties hovered just below the two-thirds mark throughout the 1950s and 1960s. In 1976 the joint vote reached 73.20 per cent, then went down to 68.7 per cent in 1979 and 62.8 per cent in 1983.

7. The joint vote of the three largest parties (DC + PCI + PSI) has usually been well over 75 per cent, reaching a peak of 82.9 per cent in 1976 and falling to 74.2 per cent in 1983.

At least until the 1976 election the Italian electorate has behaved with remarkable stability. However, it we consider all post-1948 elections we note that the electorate has eliminated one political party (the Monarchist Party) and created two small left-wing parties, it has added 10 per cent to the PCI vote and reduced considerably the electoral strength of the PLI. This would suggest that the DC has maintained its total vote by decreasing the strength of the parties to its right (Liberals, neo-fascists and monarchists) while losing some votes to the left. Over a thirty-year period this fluctuation would indicate that a greater proportion of the new generations tend to vote for the Left. Giacomo Sani, in a number of studies on the youth vote, had come to the provisional conclusion that this is indeed the case.[4] A survey he conducted in 1975 showed that irrespective of other cleavages such as North–South, sex, town–country, class and level of schooling the generation born between 1948 and 1958 was well to the left of the other two generational groups with which it was being compared (the group born between 1933 and 1947 and those born before 1933). A vote for the

TABLE 8.1 Election results of national parties 1946–83 (1946: Constituent Assembly. 1948–83 Chamber of Deputies); percentages and seats

	1946	1948	1953	1958	1963	1968	1972	1976	1979	1983
PCI	18.96 (104)	31.03 (183)	22.64 (143)	22.73 (140)	25.31 (166)	26.96 (177)	27.21 (179)	34.4 (227)	30.4 (201)	29.9 (198)
PSI	20.72 (115)		12.73 (75)	14.26 (84)	13.87 (87)	14.51 (91)	9.63 (61)	9.7 (57)	9.8 (62)	11.4 (73)
PSDI	—	7.09 (33)	4.52 (19)	4.56 (22)	6.11 (33)		5.15 (29)	3.4 (15)	3.8 (20)	4.1 (23)
PRI	4.37 (23)	2.49 (9)	1.62 (5)	1.38 (6)	1.37 (6)	1.97 (9)	2.86 (15)	3.1 (14)	3.0 (16)	5.1 (29)
DC	35.18 (207)	48.48 (304)	40.08 (262)	42.35 (273)	38.27 (260)	39.09 (265)	38.74 (266)	38.8 (263)	38.3 (262)	32.9 (225)
PLI	6.79 (41)	3.38 (19)	3.02 (13)	3.55 (17)	6.99 (39)	5.83 (31)	3.89 (20)	1.3 (5)	1.9 (9)	2.9 (16)
Monarchist	2.7 (16)	2.78 (14)	6.86 (40)	4.87 (25)	1.77 (8)	1.31 (6)	—	—	—	—
MSI	[5.3] (30)	2.01 (6)	5.85 (29)	4.77 (24)	5.11 (27)	4.46 (24)	8.67 (56)	6.1 (35)	5.3 (30)	6.8 (42)
PR	—	—	—	—	—	—	—	1.1 (4)	3.4 (18)	2.2 (11)
Leftists	—	—	—	—	—	—	1.33 (0)	1.5 (6)	2.2 (6)	1.5 (7)
PSIUP	—	—	—	—	—	4.46 (23)	1.95 (0)	—	—	—
Others	5.9	2.74	2.68	1.53	1.2	1.41	0.57	0.6	1.9	3.2
Turnout	89.1%	92.2%	93.8%	93.8%	92.9%	92.8%	93.1%	93.1%	90.1%	88.3%

Notes: PCI: Partito Comunista Italiano; PSI: Partito Socialista Italiano; PSDI: Partito Social Democratico Italiano; PRI: Partito Repubblicano Italiano; DC: Democrazia Cristiana; PLI: Partito Liberale Italiano; MSI: Movimento Sociale Italiano (neo-fascist); PR: Partito Radicale. In 1946 the far-right vote shown [5.3%] is that of a short-lived party called the Uomo Qualunque. In 1948 PCI and PSI fought the elections jointly. In 1968 the PSI and the PSDI merged and fought the elections as the Partito Socialisti Unificato (PSU). They split again shortly after. Socialists who split from the PSI in the 1960s formed the PSIUP (Partito Socialista di Unità Proletaria) and fought the 1968 and 1972 elections; having failed to obtain any seats in 1972 they joined the PCI. In 1976 three leftist groups joined into an electoral agreement and won six seats. In 1979 the Partito di Unità Proletaria (PDUP) stood on its own and won six seats, but the Nuova Sinistra Unita failed to gain any (although they obtained one seat in the European Parliament during the elections which were held a week after the national elections).

Left can mean a vote for the PCI, one of the leftist parties or the Italian socialists. It is relatively easy to compute the youth vote in Italy because while all over 18 can vote for the Chamber of Deputies, only those over 25 can vote for the Senate. Traditionally, the PCI has always obtained more votes for the Chamber than for the Senate. This was reversed in 1979 when the PCI obtained 31.5 per cent in the Senate but only 30.4 per cent in the Chamber, however, the total vote of the Left (including the Radical Party) was bigger in the Chamber.

It is more difficult to ascertain party political support in terms of sex, occupation and educational level because this has to depend on surveys. These are not very reliable in Italy because of the multiplicity of political parties and because too many people decline to answer. A survey conducted in 1980 by Demoscopea, one of the leading polling agencies, provides at least an indication.[5]

1. *Women.* According to the survey the DC is by far the favoured party of Italian women. Out of 100 DC voters 60.5 are women.[6] The DC is followed by the small centre-right party, the PLI (50%) and the far Left (47.6%). Of the communist electorate 45 per cent is made up of women, but only 35.7 per cent of the MSI votes.

2. *Education.* Over 50 per cent of the PLI electorate and 45.2 per cent of that of far Left groups have a university education. The lowest education level is reached by DC voters, 59.9 per cent of whom have had no schooling at all or left school at the age of 10 and only 17.5 per cent of whom have had some form of university education. The equivalent percentages for the PCI are, respectively, 54.1 and 20.2.

3. *Occupation.* Nearly one-quarter of DC voters are old-age pensioners, 15.8 per cent are blue-collar workers, 29.2 per cent are housewives, 4.2 per cent are in agriculture. The PSDI (social democrats), which has long sought to become the old-age pensioners' party, does less well in this sector (23%) than the DC, the MSI (27.4%), the PLI (28%). Over one-third of communist voters (35.3%) are blue-collar workers (23.4% of the PSI voters, 23.8% of the Far Left and 19% of the MSI). Ten per cent of the voters of most parties are teachers and students except for the Far Left: nearly half of their voters (45.2%) come from these two groups.

The PR system adopted by Italy is one of the most representative. Basically it is a list system, that is, voters must choose a party, then they can also indicate three or four candidates of the party for which they have voted by using what is called the preference vote. In the elections for the Senate a modified system operates in which each party presents only one candidate per constituency.[7]

The Chamber of Deputies is made up of 630 members on the basis of 32 constituencies or electoral districts, each of which returns more than one deputy (except Val D'Aosta region). To win a seat it is necessary to achieve a quota of votes. This is calculated by dividing the total number of votes cast by the sum of the seats allocated to that particular constituency plus two.[8] A party which gets twice the quota will have two deputies and so on. For example, if the quota is 50,000 votes and a party obtains 325,000 votes it will return six deputies and its 'surplus' 25,000 votes will be added to a national pool where all the 'rests' are added on. Usually about one in ten seats ends up being allocated through the national pool. To obtain seats through the national pool a party must obtain at least one quota of the votes in one constituency *and* 300,000 votes in the whole country. In 1976 the Radical Party exceeded the quota in the Rome constituency by only 351 votes and, having polled 392,419 votes nationwide, qualified for the national pool and obtained another three deputies (in addition to the one elected outright in Rome). Thus thanks to 351 voters the Radical Party was able to send four deputies to the Chamber. In 1972 none of the smaller leftist parties obtained a quota in a constituency and, as a result, nearly 1 million votes were 'wasted'.

Having calculated the number of seats each party has won, the preference votes are then counted to ascertain which candidates from the list have been elected. Many voters will simply vote for a party and will not bother to indicate a preference, but some will do so. They can favour three or four candidates according to the constituency. These personal votes are counted and the candidates of each party are ranked accordingly. If a party wins, say, six seats in a particular constituency these will be given to the six candidates with the most preference votes. A candidate can stand for election in more than one constituency (and many leaders do) and, should he/she win in more than one, can decide for which constituency to opt. In this case the first of the non-elected will obtain the seat thus left vacant. The first of the non-elected can also 'succeed' a deceased deputy or one who retires in the life of a Parliament.

Let us use as an example the 1979 elections in the largest constituency for the Chamber: the Rome–Viterbo–Latina–Frosinone constituency to which 53 seats are allocated. The total number of votes cast was 3,173,556. To find the quota we divide this number by 53+2 which gives 57,701. Thus in order to win a seat outright a party must have polled at least this amount. All national parties except the PDUP (a leftist party) obtained at least one quota. The DC polled 1,163,820. If we divide this by the quota we get 20 (the number of seats allocated to the DC), the remaining 9,800 votes going to the DC vote in the national pool. To find out who, among the 53 DC candidates, will win a seat we look at the preference vote. As was to be expected the most prestigious candidate topped the preference vote: Giulio Andreotti, the then Prime Minister (for the fifth time). Andreotti had obtained over 300,000 preference votes which means that nearly one DC voter in four had voted for him. The runner-up had over 100,000 votes and the twentieth had just over 38,000.

In practical terms the system means that in order to be elected a candidate must ensure that his/her party obtains as many votes as possible *and also* that his/her party's supporters will 'prefer' him or her. In most parties, particularly in the DC, this leads to highly personal electoral campaigns. The PCI, however, can count on such a degree of discipline from its supporters that it can ensure that all or most of those the leadership wish to see elected will be successful without a personal campaign. Supporters of the PCI will enquire at the local party branch and obtain a list of preferred candidates.

Each party will have presented beforehand its list of candidates, usually naming as many candidates as there are seats in the constituency. The effect of the system is to give a remarkable importance to political parties. In the first place the electoral system as a whole favours a multi-party system (as opposed to the two-party system as it exists in the UK and the USA); it then puts before the electorate a range of parties rather than personalities by subordinating the casting of the preference vote to the all-important choice of a particular party; unlike the single transferable vote system it is not possible to vote across parties (i.e. the voter cannot write in the names of candidates from different parties); it makes it quite impossible to be elected to the Chamber without the support of a party, i.e. without being on a party list. However, once the parties have chosen their candidates they have no formal control over who among them will actually be elected. The PCI relies on a discipline based on ideology and not on possible sanctions while the struggle for the preference vote is an important aspect of internal factional strife within the DC.

The elections to the Italian Senate (which has exactly the same powers as the Chamber of Deputies but only 315 seats) proceed in a different manner. The system used is the so-called *D'Hondt Highest Average Formula* (while the one used for the Chamber is a modification of the *Imperiali* system). Each region is divided into various senatorial districts according to population size (except the Val d'Aosta which has only one district). Each party nominates one candidate per district. Any candidate which gets more than 65 per cent of the votes in a district is elected outright (this hardly ever happens). All party votes are added up in each region. The number of seats to be allocated to each party in a given region is determined in the following manner.

The 'average' of each party is calculated. This is given by dividing its total regional vote by the number of seats won outright in that region. If no party has yet gained a seat because none of its candidates has obtained 65 per cent in a district then the first seat is allocated to the party with the highest regional vote. Then that party's average is recalculated by dividing its regional vote by two (i.e. the number of seats it has gained so far plus one). If its average is still higher than anyone else's total vote, it will also get the second seat (which leads to the recalculation of the average total vote divided now *by three* and so on ...). An example may clarify.

Let us take the Abruzzi region and the senatorial elections of 1979.

Seven seats were to be allocated and none of the candidates got 65 per cent in any of the districts. The results are as given in Table 8.2. The DC has the highest number of votes and hence gets the *first* seat. Its average is now 311,872/2 = 155,936. The highest 'average' is now that of the PCI (213,556) who gets the *second* seat. This lowers the PCI's average to 106,778 (i.e. its total vote divided by two) and gives the *third* seat to the DC. The DC's new average is now 103,957 (total vote divided by three) which is lower than the PCI's last average, hence the PCI gets the *fourth* seat. Now the PCI's average has fallen to 71,185 (total vote divided by three). This means that the DC gets the *fifth* seat. The DC's new average is 77,968 and, as this is still higher than the PCI's last, gets the *sixth* seat as well. Now the DC's average is down to 62,374 and the *seventh* and last seat goes to the PCI. The PCI has won three seats and the DC four. None of the other parties had a total vote higher than the last average of the DC or PCI and, consequently, they were not able to obtain any seats. Had the PSI obtained an extra 15,000 votes or so it would have gained one seat at the expense of the PCI.

TABLE 8.2 Results of the
senatorial elections for the
Abruzzi region, 1979

DC	311,872
PCI	213,556
PSI	56,553
MSI	39,756
PSDI	15,649
PRI	13,558
PR	11,181
PLI	6,571

This procedure determines the number of Senate seats which must go to each party in every region. Now it is necessary to allocate the seats to particular candidates. Within each party all regional candidates are ranked according to the proportion of votes each has collected in each district. Then the seats are distributed to the party's candidates beginning with the one which tops the ranking. In our example the PCI candidates for the seven seats would be ranked accordingly and only the top three would gain a Senate seat.

The method used for the Senate elections is less proportionate than the one used for the Chamber elections and is more favourable to the two largest parties. This is shown in Table 8.3.

It is important to bear in mind that the number of political parties represented in a parliament is not directly related to a particular electoral system. The British first-past-the-post system cannot be said to make the two-party system inevitable even though it undoubtedly

TABLE 8.3 Proportion of votes to seats in the Chamber of Deputies and Senate, 1979

| | *Chamber Deputies (1979)* | | *Senate (1979)* | |
	% votes	*% seats*	*% votes*	*% seats*
DC	38.5	41.6	38.4	44.1
PCI	30.5	31.9	31.5	34.6
PSI	9.8	9.9	10.4	10.2
MSI	5.3	4.8	5.7	4.1

penalizes any small party whose votes are fairly well distributed throughout the country. The dominance of the two-party system in the UK is due to a number of factors of which the electoral system is only one. All one can say is that a British-type system would probably eliminate all national Italian parties except the DC and the PCI. However, it would probably not eliminate the South Tyrol People's Party which represents the German-speaking population of the Trentino (and which obtained 206,264 votes and 4 seats in 1979).

Italian political parties are, on the whole, well represented throughout the country, as can be seen in Table 8.4. As can be seen the PCI is strongest in the Centre and weakest in the North-east, while the DC is strongest in the North-east and weakest in the Centre. However, both parties are always the top parties in all Italian regions (except in the Trentino where the largest party is the South Tyrol People's Party, STVP). In all regions (again excluding the Trentino) the PSI is third and the MSI is fourth. This distribution has enabled political scientists to use the available data in order to determine what would be the outcome should the present electoral system be changed.[9] Would it be easier to form governments in Italy if this were to happen? This is doubtful as a study by Fulco Lanchester demonstrates. He has calculated that should the *British system* be adopted in Italy and should voting be exactly as it was in 1979, the results would be to eliminate completely from Parliament all national political parties except the DC and the PCI.[10] The DC in alliance with the South Tyrol People's Party would collect 72.2 per cent of parliamentary seats, the PCI 27.4 per cent and the remaining seats would be given to the minorities in Val D'Aosta and Trieste. This is due to the fact that the PCI would be first past the post mainly in some of the urban areas and in the 'red' regions of the Centre. If, however, the parties of the Left (including the Radicals and excluding the PSDI) were to enter into an electoral pact their 44.6 per cent of the votes would become a parliamentary majority of 57 per cent.

Obviously the results would be further modified according to the kind of electoral alliances entered and the degree of voters' support for the parties they voted for in 1979. This would be true for virtually any other

electoral system adopted. Thus if the *German system* were to be adopted we would face the following possibilities[11]:

1. If all parties refuse any electoral agreement then only five would survive: the PCI, the PSI, the DC, the STVP and the MSI. None of them, however, would be able to win an outright majority. The PCI and PSI together would not be able to form a government. The DC and MSI would be able to do so but it would be politically difficult if not impossible for the DC to depend on neo-fascist votes. The only possible coalition would be either a grand coalition of PCI, PSI and DC or a Centre-Left coalition (DC + PSI). The latter would be the most likely outcome and would not present a radical difference with the centre-left coalitions which have ruled Italy for most years since 1963. It is of course possible that eventually the voters of the 'defunct' parties would realign themselves towards the DC and the PSI, altering the results in such a way as to permit either an outright win for the DC or the possibility of a PCI–PSI coalition.[12]

2. Should there be an electoral agreement of the Left of such breadth as to include not only the leftist parties, the PCI, the PSI and the Radicals but also the PRI and the PSDI, then this coalition would gain an absolute majority irrespective of the kind of agreements reached by DC, PLI and MSI and STVP.

3. An electoral agreement between the parties of the traditional Left (PCI + PSI) plus Radicals and leftist groups would not win a parliamentary majority but would prevent the formation of any other government except one which included the DC *and* the MSI.

The *Spanish system* would give the DC a tiny majority of seats (50.3%) which in the present state of internal factionalism would not guarantee any greater stability than that achieved by Italian governments so far. It is very difficult to predict the outcome of the adoption of the *French system* because we would have to know how voters would vote in the second round once their first choice candidate had dropped out or been eliminated.[13]

Only the adoption of the British system would reduce the numbers of Italian political parties to two (plus the inevitable STVP). The adoption of this system, however, is not being suggested by anyone in Italy concerned with electoral reform.[14] It cannot be suggested by the party which would benefit the most out of it, the DC, because it would involve the drastic elimination of practically all the parties with which it has shared political power at one time or the other since the end of the Second World War. Furthermore, it would effectively and drastically reduce the political pluralism existing in Italy.

Since the war there has been only one serious attempt to modify the electoral system precisely in order to ensure that there could be stable majorities. The law of 15 March 1953 established that if a party or an alliance of parties succeeded in obtaining 50 per cent plus 1 per cent of the national vote that party or that alliance of parties would obtain 64 per cent of the seats. There was an outcry against this legislation not only by the PCI (which promptly dubbed it the *Legge Truffa* – the fraudulent law) and the PSI but also by dissidents in the centrist parties. As it turned out the alliance of DC–PLI–PRI–PSDI obtained only (with the STVP and the Sardinian Action Party) 49.8 per cent of the votes, while in the previous elections (1948) they had obtained 62.61 per cent.[15] Thus by slightly more than 50,000 votes the PR system was kept and subsequently the law was repealed.

The objections which have been levelled in Italy against the existing PR system is that it produces too many political parties, makes decision-making more difficult and does not offer the electorate a clear-cut alternative between potential governments. *De facto,* the Italian electorate does not vote for a future government but to strengthen a particular party's parliamentary representation. At most the Italian electorate is able to rule out a possible coalition government. For example the centrist coalition governments which dominated Italy after 1948 were no longer possible after 1976 because they no longer had a majority, while governments of national unity (i.e. including both PCI and DC) and centre-left governments (i.e. including both PSI and DC) have always been possible.

In spite of the ongoing debate on electoral reform there is very little evidence that the population is dissatisfied with the electoral system (even though, according to opinion polls, they are dissatisfied with the existing parties). The percentage of abstention is extremely low, with a 12 per cent peak in 1983. The proportion of voters is much higher than in the UK and tends to be higher than in most European elections. There is a high level of electoral participation even in local elections and referendums. Voting is not compulsory but it is regarded as a 'civic duty'.

REFERENCES AND NOTES

1. See Falzone, V., Palermo, F and Cosentino, F. (1976), p. 181.
2. Of the nine national parties represented in the 1983 Parliament six belong to this original group of eleven (although some names have been changed). The total percentage of votes of the original six in 1946 was 91.32, in 1983 it was 89.
3. The best quantitiative analysis of the decrease in PCI votes in 1979 is by Mannheimer, R. (1979), pp. 694–714.
4. Sani, G. (1979), vol. 1. See also Sani, G. (1976).
5. The results were published in *Panorama*, no. 740, 23 June 1980, shortly after the regional elections. Similar results also emerge from a survey undertaken by Renato Mannheimer and Roberto Biorcio on behalf of the

PCI, see *Rinascita*, no. 10, 23 Mar. 1985 ('Autoritratto dell'elettore comunista').

6.   A clear majority of women, however, had voted in favour of divorce and abortion in the referendums of 1974 and 1981 against the wishes of the DC.

7.   A good explanation of the voting system for both Chamber of Deputies and Senate can also be found in Wertman, D. (1977), pp. 44–51. This volume contains interesting analyses of various aspects of the 1976 elections.

8.   The addition of two to the denominator lowers the quota and thus makes it easier for a small party to gain representation in the Chamber of Deputies.

9.   Obviously any simulation of this kind depends on the debatable assumption that voters will vote for the same parties irrespective of the electoral system. While this simulation has little predictive value, particularly in the long run, it provides indispensable material for any discussion of electoral reform.

10.   Lanchester, F. (1981), pp. 256–61.

11.   Similar results would be arrived at if the Swedish system is adopted. The following discussion relies on Lanchester's simulation (1981), pp. 264–73.

12.   The German electoral system combines a single-member plurality system and a list system. Each person votes twice, once for the local representative in one of the 248 constituencies which uses the UK-type single-member plurality system. The second vote is for a party list which is compiled for the *Land* (State) in which the voter's constituency is found (there are ten *Länder* and 248 seats to be allocated on the basis of the list system). The number of party seats in each *Land* is determined by using the d'Hondt rule (as for the Italian Senate) with the significant difference that parties obtaining less than 5 per cent of the votes cast are eliminated outright.

13.   The French electoral system is based on the single-member preferential method with a double ballot. People vote for one particular candidate in a single-member constituency (as in the UK and the USA). If no candidate wins more than half the votes a second ballot is held a week later. Some of the candidates may withdraw and any candidate with less than 12.5 per cent of the total electorate (not of the votes cast) must withdraw. In the second ballot the candidate who has a plurality of the votes wins the seat. In practice the outcome of the elections will be heavily determined by the agreements entered into by the candidates' parties over who will withdraw in favour of whom.

14.   Maranini, G. (1967) seems to have been the only advocate of the UK system in Italy and has no real followers. Traditionally, Italian critics of the existing system have tended to be conservative, see, in particular Sartori, G. (1973), and Fisichella, D. (1975). Even though most communist political scientists are still opposed to any change in the existing system, some would like to abolish the preference vote and some have tentatively suggested the adoption of a modified version of the French system, see Cotturri, G. (1983). More recently proposals for reforms have come from the PSI and intellectuals close to the PSI such as Guiliano Amato (Amato, G. 1980, pp. 173–95) and close to the PCI such

as G. Pasquino (Pasquino, G. 1980); however, for these authors the problem of governability entails not only an electoral reform but also a strengthening of the power of the executive.

15. Ghini, C. (1975), p. 113.

Chapter 9

GOVERNMENTS

Since 1945 Italy has had well over 40 governments. This constitutes one of the highest rates of government instability in Western Europe. Changes in governments have been due to any one of the following factors:

1. Internal dissent within the leading Christian Democratic Party (DC) facilitated by the secret ballot system which allows DC parliamentarians to vote against their own party or abstain without being detected and disciplined.
2. Internal dissent within the coalition parties.
3. The dissolution of Parliament.
4. The decision of the Prime Minister to resign because of his inability to hold his coalition together.
5. The decision to establish a different coalition system as when, in 1962–63, it was decided to 'open to the left', bringing the Italian Socialist Party (PSI) into the coalition.
6. The establishment and subsequent resignation of a 'temporary' government (often called a 'summer' government) which had been put into office with the sole purpose of filling the gap between major coalition realignments.

Between 1944 and 1983 there have been forty-four governments. The longest-lasting was the third Moro government (1966–68) which lasted 833 days followed by the seventh De Gasperi government (1951–53) which lasted 704 days.[1] Some governments have lasted only a couple of weeks. The average has been less than twelve months. Between each government there is a period of intense negotiations known as a 'government crisis'. The President of the Republic proceeds to a series of consultative rounds with a whole range of politicians. There is a ritualized element: first he consults former Presidents of the Republic, then former Prime Ministers, then party leaders and other politicians. He can then designate a potential Prime Minister either because he has reasons to believe that a relatively stable coalition can be formed, or because he hopes that the very fact of designating someone will lead to the resolution of the crisis. In most cases the designation of the Prime Minister occurs because party leaders have agreed on a particular coalition. In practice the powers of the President (constitutionally empowered to designate the Prime Minister) are limited by the decision of party leaders. Thus political parties have a decisive role not only in bringing about the collapse of a government, but also in creating a new one.

Formally it is the Prime Minister who then decides on the make-up of the government, distributing ministerial positions. In practice the actual composition of the government, that is, not only which parties will be in the coalition but who will get which job, is decided by the leaders of political parties. Party leaders themselves hardly ever sit in the government, but as they make and unmake governments, decide who is to be Prime Minister and who is to be a minister and as their period of tenure is considerably longer than that of the average Prime Minister, their power is considerable.

The length of a government crisis is very often determined by the length of the negotiations to distribute ministerial jobs and seldom by controversies surrounding the government programme.

There are different formulae for forming a government, as follows:

1. A government can be made up of a coalition of parties all of whom vote for it in Parliament and all of whom obtain some cabinet posts. This is the most common type of government.
2. A government can be made up of only one party, the DC, with the support or abstention of other parties not holding cabinet posts. This is called a *governo monocolore*: there have been fourteen of these between 1945 and 1978.
3. There can be a coalition of parties within the government relying on the support or abstention of other parties in Parliament.

In the entire history of the Italian Republic there has never been a case of a government made up of a single party relying exclusively on its own votes in Parliament. In 1948 the DC obtained a clear majority in the Chamber of Deputies (though not in the Senate). However, it chose to govern in coalition with other parties because it was aware how impermanent its success was and realized that it had to avoid being isolated from other potential allies.

The rapid succession of Prime Ministers has obviously contributed to the erosion of their powers of government-making. The process of ministerial appointments has become a rather precise art in which the electronic calculator has had a role to play. Massimiliano Cencelli, the private secretary of a DC notable, Adolfo Sarti, has become famous for having perfected a mathematical system for the distribution of ministerial jobs according to the relative strength of coalition partners and the relative strength of the DC factions (as established at the preceding DC party congress).[2] Within the DC power depends not so much on the size of the faction, but rather on the preference votes obtained by faction leaders in general elections. There is thus a constant link between elections, governments and ministerial appointments. The proportional system is, in a sense, applied to the distribution of government positions and these in turn depend to a large extent on the preference system. As the preference vote is the main avenue for political promotion, it is not surprising that there has been a constant tendency for this to increase over the years as DC notables devoted a considerable part of their energies to preserving and increasing their personal vote. Given the clientelistic nature of the system, the size of the preference vote depends in turn on the power of patronage wielded by DC notables. This introduces an element of stability: a good preference vote opens the door to a ministerial position, a ministerial position enables the holder to exercise patronage, this in turn increases the size of his personal vote. Two Italian political scientists, Mauro Calise and Renato Mannheimer, have even been able to quantify this process and isolate the variables which enable a junior minister to become a minister.[3]

The preference vote, when sufficiently high, opens the door to the continuous holding of ministerial power. This, and the fact that the Italian electorate, like most West European electorates, is fairly stable, results in great stability and continuity in Italian governments. We are thus faced with a paradox: the Italian political system, if measured in terms of numbers of governments, is one of the most unstable in Europe; but if the yardstick is the continuity of government personnel it is the most stable.

The most remarkable element of stability derives from the dominance of the DC throughout the post-war period. This party not only has been the keystone around which over forty coalitions have been formed, but has also had the post of Prime Minister in all governments with the following exceptions: a few months in 1945 when the Prime Minister was the Action Party leader Ferruccio Parri; about eighteen months in 1981–82 when Spadolini, the Republican leader became Prime Minister; and the government created in August 1983 which saw, for the first time in Italian history, a socialist Prime Minister (Bettino Craxi, leader of the PSI). Thus the DC has led all governments from 1945 to 1981. No political party in any democratic country in Western Europe and North America has been able to control the chief political position without interruption for thirty-six years and to be present in *all* governments since 1944 (even if we include Eastern Europe we find that this record is held only by the Communist Party of the Soviet Union). Continuity of government and political stability can also be calculated in terms of the continuity of government personnel. Calise and Mannheimer have examined the percentages of government ministers who were also present in the previous government and have discovered that the average rate of stability/continuity between 1946 and 1978 has been 58.6 per cent. This means that, on average, well over half of the ministers of each government are ministers again in the next government.[4]

Government stability under DC hegemony has led a number of political scientists to define the specificity of the 'Italian case' as one of 'limited democracy' (*democrazia bloccata*), i.e. where an alternative government cannot emerge. The communist opposition was excluded from government after 1948 by its lack of international and national legitimacy. Non-communist Italian political parties have repeatedly asserted either that the presence of communists in the government would be a threat to Italian democracy or that it would not be acceptable to Italy's international allies (i.e. the USA) or that it would destabilize the political system because powerful political and economic interests would sabotage any coalition which includes the communists. Thus the DC, according to this view, is virtually forced to rule and the only 'alternative' to a DC-led coalition government is another DC-led coalition government. The choice of possible coalitions is fairly limited. The following are those which are technically possible:

1. A coalition of 'national unity'. This includes the DC, the Italian Communist Party (PCI) and the PSI (and, but not necessarily, the other smaller parties of the Centre).
2. A 'centrist' coalition. This is made up of the DC and the other smaller parties of the Centre: the Italian Social Democratic Party (PSDI), the Italian Republican Party (PRI) and the Italian Liberal Party (PLI).
3. A Centre-Left coalition. This is made up of the DC and the PSI. It will also include the PSDI and the PRI and, at times, the PLI (e.g. after 1979).
4. A Centre-Right coalition. This is any DC-led coalition which relies on the support of the neo-fascists (MSI).

Of these four coalitions only that of national unity and of the Centre-Left have always had sufficient parliamentary backing throughout the post-war period. Centrist and Centre-Right coalitions had a technical majority only until 1976. The elections of that year were an authentic electoral turning-point because they narrowed the options facing the DC to two: national unity and the Centre-Left.

A left-wing alternative defined as a coalition of communists and socialists in alliance with the Radical Party and the far Left group has never been possible. A wider left and centre alternative which would also include the PRI and the PSDI has been possible since 1976. The chances of this sort of coalition are, however, fairly remote.

At this stage the only coalitions which are both technically (in terms of votes) and politically feasible are those of the Centre-Left and of national unity. Thus the choice is fairly stark: either the PCI and the DC are in coalition together or the DC and the PSI join forces to exclude the PCI.[5]

The range of possibilities and the actual governments are illustrated in Table 9.1. As can be seen, there have been only two periods of coalition governments in which the votes of the neo-fascists have had a determinant effect (1957–58 and 1960). These represented an attempt of the right wing of the DC to block the advance towards the formation of a Centre-Left coalition.

After the 1960 Tambroni government which was supported by the neo-fascists had to resign because of a wave of popular discontent it had sparked in a number of Italian cities, it was seen that such a coalition had virtually no chance. After 1976 it could not have a majority in Parliament. The centre-left governments of 1960–62 did not include the PSI. We have called them 'Centre-Left' in Table 9.1 because they enjoyed the abstention of the PSI and were governments which were meant to pave the way to what was called the 'organic' Centre-Left, i.e. governments with socialist ministers. Disregarding these specific variables we can therefore describe the succession of Italian coalitions in these terms:

1. 1944–47: governments of national unity.
2. 1947–62: centrist governments.
3. 1963–68: 'organic' Centre-Left governments.
4. 1968–76: crisis governments: succession of centrist and Centre-Left coalitions.
5. 1976–79: governments of national unity (in reality three years of *monocolore* DC backed by the abstention and then the supporting votes of all other parties including the PCI and excluding the neo-fascists).
6. Since 1979: Centre-Left governments (but, unlike those of 1963–68, these have no coherent programmes of reform, they exist simply because, given the difficulty of having a coalition with the PCI, they are the only way in which Italy can have a government).

We can use these six phases and three types of coalitions (Centre, Centre-Left and national unity) to compare Italy with some other European countries and underline the extent to which for a considerable period and in spite of the specificity of DC monopoly the Italian political system followed a cycle not dissimilar to that of countries which do have some form of alternance in governments.[6] For example, the governments of national unity 1944–47 correspond to the various governments with communist participation which ruled France, Belgium and many other countries in the immediate aftermath of the war as well as the Labour government which ruled the UK between 1945 and 1951. From the late 1940s to the early 1960s Italy was ruled by centrist governments which corresponded to the conservative governments of the UK and West Germany in a similar period. The birth of the Centre-Left coalition corresponds to the victory of the Labour Party in Britain after thirteen years of Conservative rule (1964) and the German grand coalition of the Christian Democratic Union (CDU) and the Social Democrats (SPD) of 1966. The programme of modernization adopted by the Centre-Left corresponds to the modernization plans of the Wilson government of 1964–70 and of the

TABLE 9.1 Possible coalition and actual coalition governments 1946–83
(NU – National Unity; CL – Centre Left; C – Centrist; CR – Centre-Right;
LA – Left Alternative)

Legislature	Posible coalitions	Actual coalitions
1946/1948 (Constituent Assembly)	NU CL C CR LA	NU (1947–48)
1948/1953	NU CL C CR	C
1953/1958	NU CL C CR	C CR (1957–58)
1958/1963	NU CL CR C	C CR (1960) CL (1960–62)
1963/1968	NU CL C CR	C (1963) CL (1963–68)
1968/1972	NU CL C CR	C (1968 and 1972) CL
1972/1976	NU CL C CR	C CL
1976/1979	NU CL (LA + small centre parties)	NU CL (1979)
1979/1983	NU CL (LA + small centre parties)	CL
1983 +	NU CL (LA + small centre parties)	CL (1983–

SPD in West Germany and De Gaulle in France. The 1970s represent a period of reassessment and crises for most European states.

In Britain there was a rapid succession of policies: Edward Heath's Conservative attempt to cut down on state intervention (1970–72) followed by incomes policies and confrontation with the trade unions (1972–74), followed by a Labour government committed to a 'social contract' with the trade unions (1974–76), followed by a drastic Labour deflation paving the way for a Conservative victory (1979). In both France and West Germany we have a long period of rule by the same coalition; a social democratic one in West Germany and a conservative one in France, but in both cases by the end of the decade these governments were in difficulty and had to surrender power in the course of the early 1980s.

In practice these political cycles correspond to specific economic cycles: the period of immediate post-war reconstruction, the long period of economic growth (to the mid 1960s) leading to attempted modernization, further interventionism and development of welfare policies in the 1960s and the 1970s. Since 1970 we have witnessed the breakdown of the international monetary system (the Bretton Woods arrangements), the tenfold increase in oil prices, the crisis of Keynesian economic policies and the re-emergence of unemployment and inflation in capitalist countries.[7]

How each country coped with the transition from one cycle to the next has obviously been determined by a complex interaction of traditions, institutions and external constraints. Changes in policies are always necessary to cope with changed circumstances, but changes in policies do not always require changes in governments. Given the *de facto* exclusion of the PCI from political power, Italy has had to resort to changes in *the type of coalition* government, changes which, in turn, have been subjected to the constraint of DC dominance. The changes in governments within each coalition phase correspond very often to no more than government reshuffles. The establishment of political parameters which have assigned to the PCI the role of permanent opposition and to the DC the role of permanent ruling party are a far more significant and important phenomenon than the succession of forty-odd governments. Seen in this light the main special feature of the Italian government system has been an extraordinary stability.

REFERENCES AND NOTES

1. Calise, M. and Mannheimer, R. (1979), p. 49.
2. Venditti, R. (1981).
3. Calise, M. and Mannheimer, R. (1982)

4. Calise and Mannheimer (1979), p. 60.
5. For a similar definition of the 1976 turning-point see Chiarante, G. (1979), p. 6.
6. The idea of a comparison of 'political cycles' in Europe has been suggested by Somaini, E. (1979), pp. 17–47.
7. Maddison, A. (1982), esp. pp. 136ff.

Chapter 10

PARLIAMENT

' In parliamentary democracies based on the two-party system it is often the case that the powers of Parliament are seriously limited by the ability of the government of the day to use its majority to set the agenda of debates and to enact legislation. In a multi-party system – such as the Italian one – there is no pre-given majority. A majority must be constructed.

In the United Kingdom a majority is 'constructed', i.e. is determined by the workings of a particular electoral system, the existence of particular cleavages in the electorate, the geographical distribution of these cleavages and the internal cohesion of the parliamentary groups. In most British elections since the inter-war period the electoral system has produced a governmental majority. In Italy the effect of the elections is to produce not a majority but rather a particular distribution of forces within Parliament. The construction of a majority is something which occurs *after* an election. This is not a necessary effect of the electoral system, just as the creation of a pre-given majority is not a necessary effect of the British system. In the Italian case it would be perfectly possible to imagine a coalition of parties entering into a pre-electoral agreement around a given programme. This, however, has never happened, and one of the consequences of this has been the succession of governments described in Chapter 9.

The existence of weak and unstable governments might suggest that the real powers of Parliament are much greater in Italy than in the UK. If majorities must be constructed, then deputies and senators may be able to exercise considerable power as governments attempt to mediate and aggregate interests on the floor of the two assemblies. In fact this work of mediation and interest aggregation is not conducted in this way. The real protagonists of the construction of majorities are the political parties, particularly those which are 'legitimized' to form a coalition government. The legitimation of parties is only in part due to the electorate. This has given the Italian Communist Party (PCI) up to one-third of the vote in parliamentary elections and has never given the

Italian Social Democratic Party (PSDI) more than $7\frac{1}{2}$ per cent of the vote. Yet the PCI has never held government seats after 1947 while the PSDI has always been a part of the ruling coalition. The main source of legitimation has therefore not been the electorate as such, but rather the ruling Christian Democratic Party (DC). It is this party which, until the early 1960s, had defined the centrist parties as being the sole legitimate parties, exclusive tenants – with the DC – of the so-called 'democratic area'. The 'opening to the left' and the creation of the centre-left government had been defined by the DC as the 'enlargement of the democratic area', so as to include the Italian Socialist Party (PSI) in the coalition. After the 1976 elections the DC was forced to ask the PCI to abstain in Parliament. This was the result of the PCI's gain and the PSI's refusal to support the DC government should the PCI oppose it. The DC, however, was still able to define the limits of PCI involvement in policy-making: there could be no question of the PCI becoming a member of the government. The PCI accepted this, i.e. accepted that it was not yet legitimized to enter the government.

If we were to put in a nutshell the essential differences between the British and the Italian systems in so far as parliamentary decision-making powers are concerned, we would say that while in the UK the powers of Parliament have been taken over by the Cabinet (and perhaps by the Prime Minister), in Italy these powers are firmly in the hands of the leadership of the 'legitimized' political parties. Formally, of course, the British Parliament is completely sovereign as it is not even hampered by a written Constitution. At the formal level, however, the Italian Parliament, too, has considerable powers. Unlike the USA the government cannot veto bills. Unlike the UK the government does not decide on the parliamentary agenda. The government cannot impose a 'guillotine' motion to curtail obstructionism. Members of the Italian assemblies can use a secret ballot and thus can escape party discipline; they can also initiate any legislation except budgetary laws. Government bills do not have priority (as in the UK). Unlike the American President, the Prime Minister or the President of the Republic are not directly elected by the people. The government depends on a majority in both assemblies. The President of the Republic is elected by both houses in joint sessions. Both houses also elect one-third of the members of the Constitutional Court.

All these are, however, formal powers. In practice – as in many other countries – there are numerous important centres of political power: political parties, the Civil Service, the trade unions and the private and public sectors of the economy and various pressure groups. Parliament has then served as the place where the political parties establish their ideological differences.[1] Legislation has tended to be concentrated in the protection of relative small corporate interests through so-called 'mini-laws' or *leggine*, i.e. laws devised specifically for the protection of small groups.

Before 1971 the presidents of the two assemblies had considerable powers. They could determine the agenda of their respective chambers, they could assign bills to the standing committees and decide whether a bill could be enacted by a committee or whether final approval should be referred to the assemblies. In turn the presidents of the standing committees also had considerable powers and could even decide whether a bill could be 'killed' in committee thus preventing legislation. Up to 1968 most presidents of the Chamber and of the Senate were members of the DC. The DC had also the lion's share of the presidencies of the standing committees. These, however, had limited powers. They could not, for example, subpoena officials of the state bureaucracy or employees of state agencies.[2] These limitations were not very important as long as the DC controlled the standing committees as well as the Civil Service and the state agencies.

In 1971, as a direct consequence of the weakness of the governing coalition after the crisis of the Centre-Left coalition, the rules were changed. The powers of the presidents of the assemblies to set the agenda were transferred to the 'standing conference of the leaders of the parliamentary groups' (including the leader of the PCI group). These *capigruppo* would meet and decide unanimously the agenda for the subsequent three months. Furthermore, it was decided that Parliament could set up its own investigative committee and could subpoena state officials.[3] The decrease in the powers of the presidents of the Senate and of the Chamber of Deputies made it easier for the PCI to obtain the presidency of the Chamber in 1976–79 (after the biggest pro-communist swing in post-war elections) and again after the 1979 and 1983 elections. Furthermore, during the 1976–79 legislature when the PCI was in the parliamentary majority (though not in the government), the communists were able to obtain the presidencies of many important standing committees.

The 1971 changes in parliamentary procedure did not signal a transfer of power from the DC to Parliament, but rather a fairer distribution of power among the political parties, with the lion's share still firmly in the hands of the DC. This confirms that it is in fact unusual for Parliament to have much power in a modern 'parliamentary' democracy. In the first place, there are other major centres of power. In the second place, parliamentary power depends on the weakness of political parties and on that of the executive branch of government. Most European countries have very strong executives (e.g. the UK and France) that can discipline their parliamentary groups *and* strong political parties. The USA which has a very loose party discipline in Congress has a strong executive: the President. Italy has a weak executive but very entrenched political parties. Thus what is peculiar about the Italian system is not the lack of effective parliamentary power, but the fact that this power is concentrated in political parties and particularly in one party – the DC – which has always been able to maintain its hegemony. The changes in parliamentary procedure of 1971 are an expression of the weakening of this hegemony and at the same time of the inability of the Italian political system to express an alternative to this hegemony.

At the beginning of this chapter we suggested that the construction of a parliamentary majority is a task which is entrusted to the potential partners of a coalition government and that the central role is in the hands of the DC. The DC, however, is not a monolithic bloc. Taken as a whole it is undoubtedly a strong political party, but in order to be 'taken as a whole' it must first become a 'whole'. Its own unity must be achieved and maintained at the same time as it establishes parliamentary alliances. Its leadership is itself the product of intense negotiations. What the leadership must accept as more or less 'given' is its internal distribution of power which, in turn, is established in the final analysis by the electorate through the preference vote. Thus the DC leadership cannot easily choose who will be elected to Parliament. In the PCI, parliamentary work is simply a task which is given to leading party members or activists. This is – at least partly – because the communist electorate can be relied on to use its preference vote according to the wishes of the local and national leadership. Maurizio Cotta's research on Italian Members of Parliament (MPs) for the period 1946–72 provides evidence for the different approaches of the PCI and the DC to the selection of the parliamentary élites.[4]

The first feature of the post-war Italian Parliament which emerged is that it had little continuity with its predecessor, the last pre-fascist Parliament. Only 15 per cent of those elected in the Constituent Assembly in 1946 had previously been MPs.[5] This slumps to 3 per cent for the Parliament elected in 1948. Thus in terms of personnel there is an entirely new generation of politicians which emerges after the war. Comparing the turnover of parliamentarians in subsequent Italian Parliaments with the turnover in the British House of Commons, the US House of Representatives, the German Bundestag and the Austrian Nationalrat, Cotta is able to establish that Italian turnover is consistently higher: each new Parliament between 1946 and 1972 consists of at least one-third newly elected members. This figure is mainly due to the extremely high turnover of PCI deputies and senators, because the percentage of newly elected DC parliamentarians is similar to that of other countries.[6] The chief reason for this is that DC parliamentarians leave parliamentary life either because of electoral defeat or because they retire (or die), while communist parliamentarians are out of Parliament because they are not reselected by their own party.[7] This is programmed by the PCI leadership. In general only the party leadership and some of the experts are regularly reselected. Other deputies and senators usually last for no more than the life of two Parliaments.

To become a senator or a deputy is for many communist cadres no more than one of the many aspects of party work; for some it is the prelude to retirement. A long period of parliamentary activity is not, for a communist, the necessary prerequisite for a political career. The leader of the PCI, Enrico Berlinguer, became a member of the Central Committee in 1945, a member of the Executive Committee in 1948, leader of the PCI youth organization in 1949, member of the PCI Secretariat in 1958, in charge of party organization in 1960 and entered Parliament for the first time only in 1968. A year later he was elected deputy leader of the party and in 1972 became party leader. Thus his advancement in the party did not depend on a long parliamentary career, and when he became party leader he had but a limited parliamentary experience. For the communist MP the party remains the main focus of his/her loyalty, whereas Christian Democrats have the parliamentary group, the government, the party, the faction they belong to, a particular leader, local and/or national interest groups.[8] Research has shown that communist MPs give far more importance to party cohesiveness than do DC MPs, that they are far less likely to introduce bills without party approval and that they tend to use information which comes from their own party to a greater extent than do Christian Democratic MPs.[9] In recent years, as the PCI jettisoned more and more features of its Leninist past, the communist parliamentary group has acquired greater independence from the party. Should the PCI ever enter government it is likely that the power of its parliamentary group would increase at the expense of the party machine.

What do communist MPs do in Parliament? As the PCI has been forced into the role of permanent opposition it could be expected that its sphere of action would be rather limited and that it would use the parliamentary platform essentially to express its ideological differences with the DC. On the whole this is not the case. What tends to happen in a parliamentary system in which the opposition can become government (as in the UK) is that the minority follows the principle that 'the duty of the opposition is to oppose' in order to demarcate itself in the sharpest possible manner from the government and offer the electorate a clear-cut choice (even though its actual behaviour in government may not be so dramatically different from that of its opponents). In Italy, however, the communist opposition needs to gain legitimacy and be able to modify and amend legislation to establish that a vote for the PCI is not wasted. The important role standing committees play also enables the PCI to use the floor of the Houses of Parliament to make the more general ideological and political points while using the standing committees for participating in legislative decision-making. A sample survey of 326 laws (out of a total of 7,781) passed between 1948 and 1968 shows that a very large proportion of laws are passed in committees (over 80%) and not by the whole House.[10] The same research reveals that three-quarters of all legislation in the twenty years after 1948 was passed with PCI approval.[11] In the period 1968–72 when the Centre-Left coalition was in shreds the PCI was able to contribute decisively to major pieces of legislation. These were the reform of the penal and civil codes, the law instituting divorce, the so-called Workers' Charter on trade union and individual workers' rights, a new family law, the establishment of the regional system, reforms of the education, health and fiscal systems, as well as the 1971 parliamentary code.[12]

Thus even though the distance between the political traditions of the DC and the PCI may appear to be vast the actual functioning of the Italian Parliament has been far less conflict-oriented than that of the British House of Commons. Even though one party has always had a relative majority, it has had to negotiate not only with its potential partners but also with the opposition while maintaining its unity.

The crucial question which has been at the centre of many political debates in Italy throughout the 1970s is whether the weakness of the executive is due largely to the strength of Parliament or, rather, of the parties in Parliament. The PSI, in particular, has insisted that the most important reason why it is so difficult to govern Italy is that the executive is too weak. The government is faced with massive problems: it must attempt to resolve some of the basic economic contradictions of Italian development while facing the constant pressures that interest groups are able to advance. Political parties use Parliament to satisfy the corporate, localistic and selfish interests of these groups. Politics has become a market where votes are swopped for pieces of legislation. In these circumstances no government can offer a coherent programme. The PSI sees Parliament as an arena where interest groups can find satisfaction for their demands. Demands, however, have increased at a much faster rate than political and economic resources. Thus the Italian political system suffers from an excess of demands: it is 'overloaded'. Only a strong executive with greater legitimacy can tackle the situation. The PSI has therefore suggested that votes in Parliament should no longer be secret to strengthen party discipline. Christian Democratic MPs (who are the least disciplined) would become forced either to bring down a government openly and suffer the political consequences for their action, or to support it even when legislation threatens some of their favoured interest groups. The PSI has also suggested some more fundamental political reforms such as the direct election of the President of the Republic or of the Prime Minister.[13]

The DC, too, seeks to strengthen the executive and accepts the PSI's view that Italy's chief problem is one of 'governability'. The DC has suggested that ways should be found to give greater legitimacy to the executive by presenting a stable coalition to the electorate instead of forming a coalition after the elections, and that the Prime Minister be elected by Parliament at the beginning of a new legislature for the whole duration of that legislature.

Both the DC and PSI seem to want to insulate the executive from Parliament as much as possible, the DC by giving the executive more electoral legitimacy, the PSI by giving it more decision-making powers.

In both cases, however, the powers of party leaders increase at the expense of individual MPs. The reforms advocated by the DC and the PSI seem to be aimed essentially at resolving their internal problems of discipline.

The PCI has few if any problems of discipline. Its MPs accept the decisions of their groups and vote in a fairly united fashion as MPs do in the British Parliament (where, however, there is no secret ballot) and the indiscipline of other parties works to its advantage. It is therefore little wonder if it objects to the abolition of the secret ballot. However, its fundamental difference from the PSI and the DC is based on a different assessment of the decision-making process in the Italian political system. The PCI does not accept that its basic problems can be reduced to the rather technical question of 'governability'. It argues that 'governability', is not a technical problem. If it means that governments and parliaments find it increasingly more difficult to rule, then it is a political problem which affects virtually all other countries in Western Europe. All these countries' governments are subjected to the constraints of an increased dependence on the international economy, are faced by the ever-growing complexity of their societies and the rise of new cleavages and by the growth of bureaucracy and pressure groups. Furthermore, new technologies in surveillance and social control and the increase in political violence have increased the powers of the military and police establishment, powers which are seldom subjected to public scrutiny and accountability and which, in some cases, cannot be made public precisely because they depend on secrecy for their efficacy. The PCI, however, points out that the question of institutional reforms cannot be reduced to a question of the relations between Parliament and government, but that it is fundamentally a question of political power and asserts that the reason why decision-making is more difficult in Italy than in other West European countries is that it is only in Italy that the opposition cannot become government, that the permanent majority party, its factions and its allies have colonized the bureaucracy, the media and the public sector of the economy.[14]

The PCI accuses the other political parties of having usurped the functions of Parliament by carving up among each other control over the apparatuses of the State. Far from having too much power, Parliament has virtually no control over who really makes economic policy, who controls the military and police establishment and who controls the information system. Thus all communist institutional proposals tend to strengthen the powers of Parliament by cutting down on the number of government decrees, increasing parliamentary control and the coordination between Parliament and the regions.[15] The PCI does not deny that the executive must be strengthened, but seeks to achieve this by enabling the Prime Minister to form his/her own cabinet (as the Constitution requires) rather than allowing the task of Cabinet formation to be monopolized by the leadership of the coalition parties.

The PCI as well as many socialists also want to abolish the Senate. Giuliano Amato has pointed out that the Italian two-chamber system is virtually unique in the world because both chambers have identical powers and have the same kind of representation, even though the Constitution says that the Senate should be elected 'on a regional basis'.[16] Support for the abolition of one of the two chambers is usually based on grounds of efficiency. A communist political scientist, Giuseppe Cotturri, has pointed out that there are other reasons for the abolition of one of the two chambers: the incessant negotiations which occur between the Chamber and the Senate over every piece of legislation works to the advantage of the DC. The time it takes for a bill to go from one chamber to the other enables the DC to make deals between its various factions and lobbies. He points out that the number of DC amendments to DC legislation always tends to be much higher than that of the PCI. Legislation is thus a process which occurs 'within' the DC. It is a process which enables it to achieve and maintain its unity.[17] The extent to which this is true must still be demonstrated by more empirically based research.

Any future reform must consider seriously what the real functions of Parliament are:

1. Legislation.
2. Legitimating political parties.
3. Providing the governing parties and the factions of the DC with a structure within which they can unite, albeit temporarily.
4. Providing the PCI, otherwise excluded from so many positions of power, with a national platform where its influence is commensurate to its electoral strength.

To the extent that Parliament and other elected bodies, such as regional assemblies, have been stripped of their powers, the PCI can claim, with some justification, that it has been given access to empty shells.

REFERENCES AND NOTES

1. Cazzola, F. (1972), pp. 71–96, see p. 80.
2. Leonardi, R., Nanetti, R. and Pasquino, G. (1978), p. 165.
3. Ibid., pp. 167–9.
4. Cotta, M. (1976). Cotta uses his data for other purposes, namely to demonstrate that the PCI has not accepted the basic principles of parliamentary practice.
5. Ibid., p. 80.
6. Ibid., p. 82.
7. Ibid., pp. 84–94.
8. Leonardi *et al.* (1978), p. 177.

Chapter 11

THE CONSTITUTION

The Constituent Assembly (CA) which drafted the Italian Constitution was elected on 2 June 1946. On the same day a national referendum was held to decide whether Italy was to be a monarchy or a republic. The victory of the republican cause meant that the first words of the Constitution ('Italy is a democratic republic . . . ') had been enshrined by the means of direct democracy rather than by the decisions of a representative assembly. The CA designated seventy-five of its members to form a committee which presented a draft at the end of January 1947. Between March and December of that year the CA discussed the draft. The Constitution took effect on 1 January 1948. It was signed by the Liberal provisional President of the Republic and representative of the pre-fascist political élite, Enrico De Nicola, the Christian Democratic (DC) leader and Prime Minister, Alcide De Gasperi, and the communist President of the CA (who had spent most of the inter-war years as a political prisoner) Umberto Terracini. The three signatories symbolized the compromise between liberalism, socialism and the DC which the Constitution embodied.

By the standards of Italian parliamentary proceedings, or indeed by any standards, the drafting and approval of the Constitution was a speedy affair. Yet the works of the CA took place in a rapidly changing political climate. When it first met, in June 1946, the Cold War had not begun and the Italian Communist Party (PCI) was still in the government. By the time the Constitution was approved the Left had been expelled from the government and Europe was divided into two spheres of influence. Inevitably, the political situation had an influence on the proceedings, but the government did not try to influence the debates directly and did not use ongoing political controversies as a bargaining tool in the CA.[1]

The Constitution was approved by 453 votes against 62. The three main parties, the DC, the PCI and the Italian Socialist Party (PSI) (including the social democrats which by then had split away) resulting in the creation of a social democratic party) voted in favour. Only the extreme Right voted against. The fact that the Italian communists had taken an active part in the proceedings, had initiated or approved most of the main articles and had had one of their most distinguished leaders as President of the CA has given it considerable constitutional legitimacy. It would be difficult to maintain, as some have, that the PCI is a straightforward 'anti-system' party since it helped to create and continues to endorse the charter which gives institutional form to the Italian State. In the years that followed the PCI was, in words and deeds, an upholder of the Italian Constitution. It will not be difficult to understand why, once we have examined the fundamental features of this document.

THE ROLE OF THE WORKING CLASS

The very first article of the Constitution gave a particular role to the working class: 'Italy is a democratic republic founded on labour. Sovereignty belongs to the people, who exercise it within the forms and limits of the Constitution.' Lelio Basso (PSI) and Giorgio Amendola (PCI) had wanted the wording 'Italy is a workers' republic', but the majority felt that this would seem to give a position of superiority to a particular class (even though Basso and Amendola denied that this was their intention). It was, however, accepted that it was important to give recognition to human labour as a fundamental value of the Italian State. The 'workers' republic' option was rejected by only twelve votes and Fanfani's wording prevailed: ' ... a democratic republic founded on labour'.[2]

Non-Marxist constitutional lawyers, such as Massimo Severo Giannini and Costantino Mortati (the latter was one of the members of CA), have maintained that the insertion of this article has signalled the acceptance within the Constitution of the Marxist principle of the emancipation of the proletariat.[3] On the other hand, Leftist critics of the Constitution such as Antonio Negri postulated that the first paragraph seeks to protect productive labour, i.e. exploited labour thus subsuming all values to those of production and capitalist organization.[4]

A special recognition of the working class appears elsewhere. Article 4 enshrines a 'right to work' in the Constitution, which at the time was widely considered to entail a demand for full employment.[5] It is an example of the way the Constitution dealt not only with an existing state of affairs but also with a desirable one, a future society which was still to come. In 1965 the Constitutional Court decided that Article 4 meant that the State must try to increase jobs and that no one can interfere in the people's choice of work or how they go about performing it. This gave rise to interpretations asserting the rights of strike-breakers.[6] The right to strike is enshrined in Article 40 (even though the same article specifies that it must be exercised 'within the sphere of laws which regulate it'). The DC had argued that Civil Servants should not have the right to strike while the PCI trade-union leader Di Vittorio had insisted that there would be no legal restriction. The compromise reached established a right, but refused to make it an absolute one.[7]

Article 46, which has been read by some as establishing a right for industrial democracy and workers' control,[8] and by others as establishing the principle of class collaboration, is another instance of ambiguous compromise. It states: 'With a view to the economic and social advancement of labour and in harmony with the needs of production, the Republic recognizes the right of workers to collaborate, in ways and within limits established by law, in the management of enterprises.' This article was in part inspired by the experience of the workers' councils which had taken over the management of many Italian factories immediately after the war. The legal owners, many of whom had collaborated with the fascist regime, gradually returned to exercise control, but in 1946 the situation was still fluid. A communist proposal stated simply that the article should read: 'The workers have the right to participate in the management of the enterprise.' The DC was split because its left wing (especially Fanfani) agreed with the PCI. The drafting committee accepted a wording which retained the expression 'participation' (October 1946), but on 12 May 1947 the tripartite coalition government fell and the Left was expelled from the government. The following day the CA had to vote on the article. To save its substance the left wing of the DC accepted the word 'collaboration' instead of 'participation'. The communist trade-union leader Di Vittorio accepted, while explaining that for him 'collaboration' means 'active participation'.[9]

Clearly the Constitution, like any legal document, offers ample scope for conflicting interpretations. The clauses dissussed here show that this is a document which, though ambiguous, is open to a 'pro-working class interpretation' particularly when one looks, as it is legitimate to do in Italian legal practice, at the 'intentions of the legislators'.

The radical nature of the Italian Constitution was particularly enhanced by Article 3, one of the most important and controversial. This article has two sections. The first paragraph is a declaration of formal equality for all: 'All citizens have equal social dignity and are equal before the law, without distinction of sex, of race, of language, of religion, of political opinion, of personal and social condition.' The second paragraph reads:

> It is the task of the Republic to remove the obstacles of an economic and social nature which, limiting in fact the liberty and equality of citizens,

prevent the full development of the human personality and the effective
participation by all workers in the political, economic and social
organization of the country.

The first aspect represents the classical 'liberal' aspect of the
Constitution: everyone is equal before the law, no one must be
discriminated against. The second aspect enlarges and, according to
some, even negates the first: people are not in fact equal; there are
obstacles to their being equal; these obstacles are of a social and
economic nature; the new republican State is not indifferent to this; it
neither accepts that these inequalities are inevitable or natural nor does
it assume that they will wither away on their own; it must actively
intervene to eliminate these social and economic obstacles. Umberto
Romagnoli has gone as far as saying that the intention of Article 3,
paragraph 2, is to reject the existing social order and the model of formal
equality in favour of 'real' equality.[10] Others warn that the wording and
intentions of Article 3, paragraph 2, are also open to a reformist
interpretation: the second paragraph does not say that a new social
order should be created, it merely says that there are still some
inequalities and that these should be removed. An enlightened upholder
of capitalism would readily agree that capitalism has an 'unacceptable
face' which can and should be eliminated.[11]

There is strong evidence that the 'intentions of the legislators' were
radical. Piero Calamandrei, a noted jurist and veteran anti-fascist who
was neither a socialist nor a revolutionary, had no doubt as to the
revolutionary nature of Article 3 when he declared in the CA on 4 March
1947, that this was ' ... the prelude, the introduction, the announcement
of a revolution, in the juridical and legal sense, which has yet to come'.
The author of the second paragraph was Lelio Basso, a socialist leader
who represented the most radical wing of the non-communist socialist
tradition in Italy. Basso wrote: 'The reason why I was keen to insert this
article is precisely that it negates all the statements in the Constitution
which assume as existing that which is yet to come (democracy, equality,
etc.); ... '[12]

Article 3 probably constitutes one of the most visible instances of the
departure from a strict observance of the principles of classical
liberalism. It is by no means the only one. Liberal principles are
modified or 'enriched' even in Article 2 which is, at first sight, an
orthodox declaration of human rights because it begins with the words:
'The Republic recognizes and guarantees the inviolable rights of
man ... ', but it then continues ' ... whether as an individual *or in
associations* through which his personality develops ... ' (my
emphasis). The Republic is not a mere conglomeration of individual
citizens whose political participation is embodied in individual acts such
as the vote. The individual has rights not only as an individual but also
as a member of an association. Here there was a clear convergence

between the PCI and the DC, even though their ideological starting-point was quite different. The PCI was worried that a mere declaration of individual rights could be used to block social and economic reforms. The DC wanted to limit the powers of the State by enhancing not only individual rights but also those of voluntary associations.[13] The attempt to give constitutional force to collective rights as well as individual rights is another illustration of the ideological strength of the non-liberal traditions in the CA, 75 per cent of which was made up of Catholics and Marxists, neither of whom were rooted in an individualistic ideology.

PRIVATE PROPERTY

To counterbalance the collective rights for independent working-class action there were guarantees for property-owners. The nature of the constitutional compromise which would protect private property was explained by the communist leader, Togliatti, when the communists abstained on a socialist proposal to give constitutional protection only to some forms of private property, namely cooperatives and small firms. Togliatti argued that the Italian Constitution should not be a socialist one, that it should lead to a state in which different forms of property would coexist and that the struggle ahead should not be directed against private property in general but only against monopolies and vast concentrations of wealth and power.[14] The protection of private property was eventually upheld by Articles 41 and 42. Article 41 establishes that 'private economic initiative is free', but limits this by adding that it must not develop 'in conflict with social utility or develop in such a manner as to damage security, liberty and human dignity'. It is therefore a limited right. The article goes on to specify that legislation can try to coordinate the public and private sectors of the economy towards social ends, thus giving constitutional legitimacy to economic planning. Article 42 recognizes private property but also different forms of property: that owned by the State, that owned by groups and that owned by individuals. It also gives constitutional validity to nationalization by asserting that 'private property may be expropriated with compensation for reasons of general interest'.

Therefore the right to private property and the principles of free enterprise are not absolute and 'inviolable', as are the rights of man in Article 2, and are not even enshrined in the 'Fundamental principles' of the Constitution.[15]

DEMOCRACY

The election of representatives to a national assembly is only one of the forms in which popular sovereignty is exercised.

Article 75 specifies a non-representative form, that is, a *direct* form, in which popular sovereignty can be exercised: a referendum. A referendum can be held if 500,000 citizens (or five regional councils) sign a petition. However, a referendum cannot legislate. It can only repeal, partially or totally, a piece of legislation (except international treaties, taxation or budgetary laws and laws dealing with amnesty). In practice this power could not be used until after 1970. The final section of Article 75 required Parliament to determine the procedures for a referendum, but this was not done until a law was finally passed in 1970.[16]

The other main form in which sovereignty is exercised is through political parties as established in Article 49: 'All citizens have the right to associate freely in political parties in order to compete by democratic methods to determine national policy.' The Constitution thus established political parties as legal entities (a similar clause was rejected by the French CA in the same period), even though it refrained from establishing any form of legal control over them.

Popular sovereignty is not unlimited. In the first place it can only be exercised according to the 'democratic method' meaning 'without recourse to violence or the threat of violence' (i.e., the interpretation of the Constitutional Court, July 1967).[17] Secondly, Article 139 states: 'The republican form is not subject to constitutional amendment.' Thus there is no constitutional way in which the people or its elected representatives can abolish the republic. Thirdly, Article XII of the section on transitional and final arrangements states: 'The reorganization under any form whatsoever of the dissolved Fascist Party is prohibited.' This article symbolizes both the anti-fascist unity which prevailed in the CA and the desire to give the Constitution a clearly anti-fascist character. It has a value which is more symbolic than practical. There is little possibility of banning a fascist or quasi-fascist party as long as it avoids an overt use of fascist symbols or ideology as the Italian Social Movement (MSI), the obvious candidate for the title of 'reconstructed fascist party', has been careful to do.

Finally, the Constitution attempted to establish alongside Parliament other forms of representative democracy in order to devolve political power.

Article 5 requires the widest administrative decentralization in the services which depend on the State. Having established this general principle the Constitution offers a detailed series of rules on local government: Article 114–33. Article 5 and the rules on local government are important because they seek to break the centralist tradition of the Italian State, a tradition which had been established after the

Risorgimento and which had been most stringently enforced by Italian governments at the end of the nineteenth century and by the fascist regime. The most explicit exponents of the principle of decentralization were the DC. In the first place they did not identify with the principles of the Risorgimento. In their view this had been led by anti-clerical forces who had forced the unity of Italy on the Roman Catholic Church and had disregarded the religious feelings of the population. Secondly, the main preoccupation of the DC in the CA was to promote the development of as many as possible intermediate layers between the State and the individual.[18] They did not seek simply to protect the individual against the State but to promote collective organizations within civil society and to protect *these* against the State. This aim coincided in part with that of the PCI, who sought the maximum guarantees for organizations such as political parties and trade unions. Finally, the promotion of local government had a long history in the Catholic movement. In the 'Catholic–rural' conception of Luigi Sturzo, founder of the Partito popolare (the first fully-fledged Catholic party in Italy, established in 1919 and suppressed in the 1920s), local government would promote local rights particularly in the countryside.[19]

This regionalist and decentralizing tradition was foreign to Italian communism as it emerged from the war. The communists had sought to present themselves as the authentic heirs of the Risorgimento whose principles they alleged, had been 'betrayed' by the bourgeoisie. The socialists adopted the same standpoint. Both PCI and PSI were thus reluctant to follow the DC in the direction of decentralization. The PCI accepted the principle of devolution of power to the regions, but purely for tactical reasons. It then fought tooth and nail in the CA to modify the DC proposals on the powers to be given to the regions and succeeded in reducing considerably the scope of regional power. Only then did it vote in favour of the regions, leaving only the traditional Right to oppose them.[20]

One of the paradoxes of post-war Italian history is that these roles were soon reversed. The DC, in full control of the State after 1948, did not implement the articles of the Constitution which dealt with the regions until the late 1960s. Until 1970 only five regions had been formed: namely those which the Constitution had given a special status, i.e. by giving them more powers than the remaining fifteen 'ordinary status regions'. These five regions had all special characteristics: either a deep-rooted tradition of autonomy and resistance to excessive centralization as in the case of Sardinia and Sicily, or the presence of linguistic minorities, the Slovenes in the Friuli–Venezia–Giulia region, the French in the Val d'Aosta and the Germans in the Trentino–Alto–Adige region (South Tyrol). The fifteen 'ordinary' regions did not receive the appropriate legislation until the 1970s. As for the PCI, it soon became the most vociferous exponent of decentralization and devolution of powers at all levels including the regional level. This change occurred as it gradually abandoned the centralist tradition which had been part of the communism of the Third International and as it sought to use its power in the three regions of central Italy to experiment with new forms of local democracy.

As has been seen so far the relation between the DC and the PCI dominated the workings of the CA. From the very beginning the PCI, recognizing that the DC, as the 'party of the Catholics', would have a dominant role in the Italian political system for a long time, was prepared to downgrade its alliance with the PSI in order to be recognized as legitimate by the DC. This attitude did not even change after the Left was expelled from the government.

THE CHURCH

One of the more delicate issues which the CA had to decide upon was the constitutional position of the Roman Catholic Church. For the PCI the DC had a fundamental historical task: to convince the Catholic and peasant masses of Italy to accept the new democratic republic and hence the major role that the PCI would be playing in it. For this reason the PCI did not want to reopen the issue of the relations between the Italian State and the Roman Catholic Church. In a sense this had already been settled by the Concordat signed by the Vatican and the fascist regime in 1929: the Lateran Treaties.

The PCI leader, Palmiro Togliatti, proposed at the outset a compromise: the Lateran Treaties would not be enshrined in the Constitution but the Italian State would promise not to revise the Concordat unilaterally. The communist text was thus formulated: 'The State recognizes the sovereignty of the Catholic Church within the juridical order of the Church itself. The relations between State and Church are determined by both (*in termini concordatari*).'

This did not satisfy the DC who wanted a specific mention of the Lateran Treaties. The lay forces, including the PCI, were worried that if the treaties were incorporated in the Constitution then each and every article of the Constitution itself would have to avoid contradicting each and every article of the Lateran Pacts. They were, of course, right to worry. Article 1 of the treaty stated that 'Roman Catholicism is the sole religion of the State'. Article 1 of the Concordat (the Lateran Pacts were made up of a treaty and a 'Concordat') asserted the 'sacred' character of Rome, defined as the 'Eternal City'. Other articles maintained that ordained priests were exempt from military service and jury service, that marriage was the foundation of the family, that it was indissoluble and could only be annulled by an ecclesiastical tribunal and that 'Italy considered the Catholic doctrine as the foundation of public education'.[21]

The DC text of Article 7 of the Constitution read: 'The State and the Catholic Church are, each in its own order, independent and sovereign. Their relationships are regulated by the Lateran Pacts. Modifications of the pacts, which have been accepted by the two parties, do not require the procedure of constitutional amendment.' Giuseppe Dossetti, who was the DC drafter and proponent of Article 7, explained that it was not his intention that this should be read as an attempt to incorporate into the Constitution every single article of the treaties. Those who opposed him did so on the grounds that they thought that the article did precisely that. Thus the intentions of all the legislators, both the proponents and the opponents, was that it was undesirable that each article of the treaties would have constitutional validity.[22] The more intransigent defenders of the secular State, mostly PSI members, were not satisfied. The article was adopted by 350 votes to 207. In addition to the DC, the extreme Right, the Italian Liberal Party (PLI) and the PCI voted for it. Had the PCI voted against, the DC would have been defeated. Article 7 was seen for years to come as the most vivid instance of communist subservience to Catholic ideology.

The constitutionalist Francesco Finocchiaro has written that Article 7 represents no more than a declaration of 'religious peace' and that it could not stop a future government from passing legislation against the wishes of the Church.[23] Thus, in spite of marriage being declared 'indissoluble' by the treaties the Italian Parliament could – in spite of DC and neo-fascist opposition – legalize divorce in 1970.

The communist leadership had even been prepared to compromise on the indissolubility of marriage. The original text of Article 29 stated that it recognizes 'the rights of the family as a natural society based on the indissoluble marriage'. Togliatti as well as two leading communist women members of the CA (Nilde Jotti and Maria Maddalena Rossi) declared that they did not think the word 'indissoluble' should be inserted, but they refrained from trying to delete it, fearing to offend the DC. It was a humble communist backbencher, Grilli, who put forward an amendment deleting the offending word. The PSI and the PCI felt obliged to support the Grilli amendment which passed by only three votes, but only because 170 members (including a large number of Christian Democrats) were absent.[24] The revised Article 29 now also included not only the definition of the family as a 'natural society' but also the assertion that marriage is based on the 'moral and legal equality of the [two] parties'.

Notwithstanding this declaration of equality the CA's view of women was distinctly traditional. Thus even though a monarchist amendment which specified that only men could serve in the armed forces was not passed, the commission in charge of the draft suggested that the armed forces should themselves examine which tasks of a 'caring nature' would be particularly suited to the 'disposition and gentle nature of women'.[25] Nor was it just the Catholic contingent of that overwhelmingly male CA which sustained a traditional view of women's role. Pietro Calamandrei, a representative of Italian radical culture and a veteran anti-fascist, objected to sex equality (Article 3) on the grounds that in civil law the husband was defined as the 'head of the household'. It was a communist woman, Maria Maddalena Rossi, who answered him, 'Women will change civil law!'[26] But changes in legislation would not be achieved easily. The Constitutional Court defended, in November 1961, Article 559 of the penal code which said that adultery of the woman could be punished with a prison sentence, whereas that of the man was not a criminal offence. The court maintained that this did not contravene the sex equality article of the Constitution because a woman's adultery is an act of 'different and greater entity' than that of a man. The court changed its mind only in December 1968.[27] Many of the discriminatory features of Italian laws were finally abolished in the 1970s.

THE CONSTITUTIONAL COMPROMISE

As we have repeatedly pointed out, the Constitution bears the mark of the compromise between Italian communism and Christian Democracy which was a feature of the Resistance and of the first post-war governments. Both the PCI and the DC wanted to establish certain principles which could be accepted by the other side while allowing for an interpretation which would favour, or at least not contradict, their own political line.[28] The PSI was decisive in putting forward a number of propositions, in particular Article 3, paragraph 2 (by Basso, see p. 198), but it could never impose its will on a matter of major importance against the other two main parties. It was the PCI which systematically sought to be the compromiser, siding with the DC on certain matters, such as Article 7, against the other secular parties and joining them when it felt that it had to oppose the DC.

On some questions the DC–PCI convergence was due to tactical considerations. The PCI wanted a strong Parliament and a weak executive because they had realized that their electoral weight would guarantee them a major role in Parliament, but that the gathering Cold War would preclude them access to government.[29] The DC, at that stage, was still suspicious of the State and sought to keep executive powers at the minimum. It was concerned to maximize the guarantees to be given to all intermediate groups in civil society. Only the PLI was in favour of a strong executive. But the old PLI was now no more than a rump. Its real strength did not lay in votes, but in the very weight of its economic ideas and political tradition. It could be argued that this tradition was so strong that it produced a 'liberal' Constitution in spite of the dominance of the CA of two political ideologies hostile to this tradition: Marxism and catholicism. A socialist jurist like Giuseppe Mancini can thus write that while it is true that left-wing ideas contributed important innovations such as Article 3 and the principle of the self-organization of the working class (Articles 39 and 40), this does not alter the fact that the Constitution is a 'neo-capitalist' document.[30] In other words, it expressed positions which are those of enlightened and progressive capitalism. It is not a *laissez-faire* but a 'technocratic' and 'modern' Constitution precisely because it recognizes the role of the State in intervening to redress injustices, to create equality, to control private industry in order not to destroy it but to make it 'useful'.

The Italian Liberals were all opponents of the interventionist state. There was, it is true, a 'Catholic neo-Keynesian' interventionist position, but it was still relatively dormant in the commodious entrails of Italian catholicism. It could not yet worry the old liberals because – as Romagnoli has wryly written – the members of the CA could spend all day long saying to each other that the Liberal State was dead and buried, yet the Bank of Italy and the Treasury were in the hands of great liberal economists such as Luigi Einaudi.[31] It was there that the liberals fought their battle, and with great success, in defence of what they called the comparative advantages of the Italian economy, that is, a reserve army of 2 million unemployed which would ensure the best defence of the old liberal principles: low wages. As for the Catholic interventionists, in economic matters their chief representative was Amintore Fanfani who sought to introduce the principles of Catholic corporatism into the Constitution. At that stage Fanfani and his followers were still orthodox Catholic corporatist and not Keynesian. They did not seek state intervention in the economy but other forms of collective controls. They were inspired by the Church teachings on the social question as originally defined by Leo XIII in the encyclical *Rerum Novarum* (1891) and further refined by Pius XI in *Quadragesimo Anno* (1931). In the latter we find a reaffirmation of the necessity of class collaboration as an instrument against socialism but also a denunciation of monopolies, of 'economic imperialism' and the trends towards 'economic hegemony', resulting in an economy which is 'horribly harsh, inexorable and cruel'.[32]

As put forward by Fanfani, Catholic corporatism entailed the control of economic activity not by the State and even less so by the 'invisible hand' but by economic councils made up of the representatives of professional associations, trade unions, employers. Political society would be organized around the State, Parliament, political parties, etc. The economy did not belong to this sphere, but to that of civil society, to 'non-political' organs based on the people's role in the production process. These propositions had also inspired fascism which had promoted corporatism as the answer to the twin evils of capitalism and socialism, and Fanfani had been an upholder of fascist economic policies. Now freed from the embarrassment of a compromise with fascism the Catholic corporatists continued their battle against the Liberal State. Their attempt to establish a leading role for their particular ideology in the Constitution failed and the architects of this defeat were the communists. Against the Fanfani proposals the PCI proposed a formula which would be incorporated, after some modifications, in Article 41: not economic councils made up of representatives of professional and occupational categories but the principle of democratic control over production.[33] The only 'corporatist' principle which was introduced in the Constitution was in Article 99: 'The National Council of Economy and Labour is composed ... of experts and of representatives of the productive categories ... ', this is, however, a purely *consultative* organ which remains to this day subordinated to Parliament and to the political parties. It was not even used when there developed – in Italy as in most Western countries – a tripartite system of consultations between government, employers and trade unions.

CONCLUSION

A constitution gives us the *formal* ground rules within which political activity takes place. Formal rules are not unimportant because they establish a consensus within which differing political forces can pursue their objectives. The Constitution thus constitutes a terrain of struggle and political debate, but not the only terrain. Alongside the formal Constitution another one appears which is made up of less formal but very real ground rules which define not only how the Constitution itself must be interpreted but also what is politically permissible and what is not. The triumph of the DC in the elections of 1948, the Cold War and the spread of anti-communism changed the political climate and created new 'real' ground rules different from those of the immediate post-war period. Although the end of the tripartite coalition of 1947 had the effect of making the constitutional debates much harsher, there was no drastic rupture.[34] Yet the effects were long-ranging: the exclusion of the Left from the government gave birth to a political principle which characterized the 'real' Constitution. This principle, described by the Catholic jurist Leopoldo Elia as a *conventio ad excludendum* (an agreement to exclude), sanctioned the non-legitimacy of the PCI as a government party and defined the arena of 'legitimate politics' in political and not in constitutional terms.[35] In the 1950s and 1960s the political parties which were supposed to administer and implement the Constitution corresponded to only a part of those who actually wrote it.

Soon after the promulgation of the Constitution the Corte di Cassazione (the highest court then, as there was as yet no Constitutional Court) made a distinction between 'prescriptive' and 'programmatic' constitutional norms, giving legal status only to the former. Prescriptive norms were those which established practical norms of political behaviour as well as organizational rules, for example that there are two chambers, that there must be elections, that everyone over a certain age has the right to vote, etc. Programmatic norms were all those which talked of the transformation of society, which pointed to a desirable future to be eventually achieved, for example the removal of inequalities. This distinction which had been made within a month of the promulgation of the Constitution, was overturned by the very first decision of the Constitutional Court, but not until it had finally been established in 1956.[36] Article 137 of the Constitution made Parliament responsible for passing the legislation essential for the creation of such a court. As a result many fascist laws were left on the statute books. The Constitutional Court itself did not repeal at once all unconstitutional laws. It was only in the few years following 1968 that much fascist legislation was repealed and labour rights were upheld.[37] By then, of course, the political climate had changed considerably. While the principle of excluding the communists from government office was maintained it was no longer possible to resort to the anti-communism of the 1950s, the Centre-Left governments had put back on the agenda the principles of social reforms and the trade-union organizations were stronger than they had ever been.

With the creation of the Supreme Council of the Magistrature, the self-governing organ of the judiciary, judges became more independent of the State. This formal independence, however, disguises the fact that the chief organizational principle of the Italian State, namely rule by political parties, applies also to this Supreme Council. Italian magistrates organize themselves into factions and pressure groups, each with its own electoral list and each faction is closely connected to one or more political parties. Even the Constitutional Court follows a practice which makes it at least partially dependent on political parties. This court is made up of fifteen members who serve nine years each. Five are chosen by the President of the Republic, five by Parliament in joint session and five by the highest ordinary and administrative courts. The five judges elected by Parliament require a three-fifths majority. Thus an agreement between the three main parties is needed to elect these judges.

The Constitutional Court has achieved a remarkable modernization of Italian legislation and has had a progressive role in Italian politics. What it has not been able to do is to remove the structural defects of the Italian legal system. This is a political task which must be undertaken by the governing parties. Our examination of the Constitution has highlighted some of the more progressive aspects. This should not disguise the fact for example that despite existing legislation the State can keep people in prison awaiting trial for a very long period of time. In 1983 there were 20,000 criminal cases still pending. The average delay between the opening of a case and its conclusion in front of a judge takes two years.[38] On 7 April 1979, the police arrested some leftist academics under charges of organizing terroristic activities. They were not tried until 1984. Blame, however, can only be attached to those who are politically responsible for this state of affairs. Constitutions can only provide the formal ground rules. The Italian one lays down the general conditions which make Italy a governable country. It can do no more.

REFERENCES AND NOTES

1. Terracini, U. (1978), p. 31.
2. Mortati, C. (1975), p. 11.
3. Ibid., p. 13.
4. Negri, A. (1977), pp. 38ff.
5. Mancini, G. F. (1975), p. 199.
6. Ibid., p. 203.
7. Baget-Bozzo, G. (1974), p. 208.
8. Ghezzi, G. (1980).
9. Ibid., pp. 119–125.
10. Romagnoli, U. (1975), p. 162.
11. This was the way the article was widely interpreted by practitioners, according to Romagnoli (1975), p. 166.
12. Quoted in ibid., p. 166.
13. Barbera, A. (1975), p. 51. See also Baget-Bozzo (1974), pp. 198–9.
14. Sullo, F. (1960), pp. 125–7.
15. Antonio Baldassare, 'Le trasformazioni dell'impresa di fronte alla Costituzione', in *Democrazia e diritto*, 1977, p. 27, quoted in Galgano, F. (1978), p. 24.
16. A referendum must also be held to decide on any amendments to the Constitution unless the same amendment has been passed by both chambers with a two-thirds majority.
17. See Galgano (1978), p. 44 and Mortati (1975), p. 8.
18. Galgano (1978), p. 55.
19. On Sturzo's position see Baget-Bozzo (1974), pp. 192–3.
20. The PCI had been so clearly against decentralization that its leading expert on the question, Renzo Laconi (Laconi, R., 1947, p. 184) justified the party's acceptance of the regional principle on the grounds that the decentralizing positions of the DC 'had been smashed to the ground'.
21. A new Concordat between the State and the Church would be arrived at only in 1984. This would no longer consider Roman catholicism as the sole religion of the State, no longer referred to the 'sacred' character of Rome, eliminated the jurisdiction of religious courts in divorce cases and

many educational and economic privileges hitherto enjoyed by the Church. This new Concordat, like the old one was achieved after negotations between the two parties; it was not a unilateral act.

22. Finocchiaro, F. (1975), p. 343.
23. Ibid., p. 347.
24. Terracini (1978), pp. 56–8.
25. Ibid., p. 89.
26. Rodotá, S. (1983), pp. 16–17.
27. Romagnoli (1975), p. 187.
28. Sullo, F. (1972), pp. 314–15.
29. Baget-Bozzo (1974), p. 197.
30. See the discussion in Mancini (1975), pp. 216–17.
31. Romagnoli, U. and Treu, T. (1977), p. 32.
32. Candeloro, G. (1982), p. 515.
33. Galgano (1978), p. 40.
34. See the recollections of Sullo (1960), pp. 125–7.
35. The expression was first used by Elia, L. (1970), p. 657.
36. Romagnoli (1975), p. 167.
37. Vercellone, P. (1972), pp. 127–8.
38. Angelo Maria Perrino and Chiara Sottocorona, 'Una giornata al palazzo', in *Panorama*, 28 Mar. 1983.

Chapter 12

THE REGIONAL SYSTEM

Local government in Italy is based on a hierarchy. At the bottom we have the *commune* (the municipality), then the *province* and finally the *region*. The communes are very different in size: they range from major cities such as Rome or Milan to small communities of a few thousand citizens. In Italy there are well over 8,000 communes. The province is constituted by the leading ninety-five towns and the surrounding communes. Thus Milan is a commune, but it is also a province and it includes all the smaller communes around it. The powers of the provinces and their functions are very limited. Thus the communal authorities of Milan have over 30,000 employees, but the province of Milan has only 4,000. Due to the delay in passing legislation, the elections of 1970 occurred before there was any definite legislative framework defining clearly the powers of the regions.

The Constitution had envisaged that the regions should have real powers and should become independent centres of decision-making. According to the Constitution the State should have established the main frame of reference within which the regions could regulate themselves and should have passed legislation to enable them to be financially autonomous.[1] However, the government has always been reluctant to give too much financial autonomy to local authorities. These have the right to raise revenue from local taxes which, however, provides only a fraction of what is required, so that they are forced to turn to the central government and to borrow from financial institutions. All this adds to their dependence on central government.[2]

From the very beginning there was extensive conflict between regional authorities (of whatever political persuasion) and the central government. Between 1970 and 1976 25 per cent of regional laws were delayed or vetoed by the central government. After 1976 the need to obtain Italian Communist Party (PCI) support in Parliament level forced the government to concede greater funding and greater powers to the regions and to extend the devolution of power through the creation of neighbourhood committees in the communes.[3]

Neighbourhood committees were also established because of two other distinct sets of pressures: in the first place it was getting increasingly difficult for large towns to govern themselves and there was an objective need for some form of decentralization at the micro level. In the second place, after 1968 there arose in Italy, as in many other Western countries, a plethora of issue-oriented movements asking, among other things, for more and better housing, child-care facilities, transport, etc. These movements were increasingly critical of political parties accused of being insensitive to local needs. The PCI had sought to pursue the aims of these movements in the cities they controlled, such as Bologna where they had established a highly effective system of neighbourhood committees.[4] Challenged by this the governing parties, and in particular the Christian Democrats (DC), moved towards meeting these demands so as to recoup some of the political support they seemed to be losing.

The 'explosion' of 1968 and 1969 had shown that the level of political tension in Italy was very high. The regions were, at least in part, a response to this in so far as it was an attempt to diffuse tension instead of concentrating it.[5] The bulk of the intelligentsia was at that time moving in favour of the maximum political decentralization possible. The governing parties, however, were not prepared to concede more than administrative decentralization. In particular, they wanted the regions to be a set of institutions which would be able to provide those social services which the governments of the Centre-Left coalition had not been able to provide. The State would still be able to control the regions through public spending and subsidies, but once it was no longer in direct charge of the services it would not have to assume any of the responsibilities.[6] Furthermore, the regions were also seen as an instrument which would enable the governing coalition, and in particular the DC, to involve the PCI in decision-making without granting any greater say at the centre. Besides, as the PCI's involvement at the local level increased it was likely that its own relations with the various social movements and pressure groups would become more tense.

The DC coalition was in favour of the regions as instruments of social control, but never gave them sufficient resources with which to satisfy local demands. The final word was left in the hands of central government.[7] It would be a mistake, however, to see the setting up of the regions purely in terms of an attempt to diffuse tension. Behind the regional system there was also a wide coalition which saw the regions as offering a way out of the crisis of the Italian political system. The regionalist movement was very diversified. We can isolate the following tendencies:

1. The 'planners'. These insisted that the regions should be seen essentially as planning mechanisms. The new regions should be given wide planning powers so that they could make the system of

public administration more efficient, ensure an adequate level of local participation in planning and allow a more diffuse and locally responsible system of state intervention. Not having been able to obtain an adequate planning system at the central level during the 1960s under successive Centre-Left administrations, the planners tried to respond by devising a regionally decentralized system of planning. This would go a long way towards responding in a positive manner to the new trade-union demands which had shifted away from being purely monetary and were increasingly directed towards social demands (e.g. social services, transport, etc.).[8]

2. The 'participationists'. These saw the local community as the principal basis for the political organization of the State. This position had captured some of the emerging anti-statist concerns and a good deal of the ideology of the late 1960s and 1970s: 'small is beautiful', ecology, control over one's environment, etc.

3. The 'state reformers'. These saw the regions as an instrument with which to increase the democratic basis of the State. The regions would provide the link between the smallest locally elected assembly and Parliament.[9]

None of these positions were identified with a single political party. Nevertheless, it is clear that the bulk of the planners were in the DC, the Socialist Party (PSI) and the Republican Party (PRI), in other words the political parties which had constituted the backbone of the Centre-Left coalition. The 'participationists' were in the more libertarian tendencies of the PSI and the PCI, but also in the new Radical Party which had become a vociferous exponent of the 'small is beautiful' movement and which was advocating a strategy they called 'the anti-institutional use of the institutions'. The second main component of this position was made up of Catholics who were the inheritors of the localism of the Italian tradition of political catholicism. These envisaged the local community as an instrument of families, local associations, charities, etc.

All parties were agreed that the central aims of the new regions would have to be:

1. Urban planning. This was felt to be vital because of the anarchic growth of cities which had occurred during the internal migration of the period of the 'economic miracle'.

2. Social services, particularly health, housing, eduation, child care, care of the elderly, leisure and transport, in order to balance the growth of the private sector in these fields.

3. Efficiency in public administration.

4. Meeting demands for more popular participation.

5. Breaking the power deadlock at the centre and opening up to new political forces such as the PCI.[10]

The regional experience was in part successful. In the first place it was able, albeit in a very limited way, to narrow the gap between the countryside and the town; to help small- and medium-sized firms; to begin a debate over the future of agriculture; to slow down the destruction of the environment; to enhance public health. Furthermore, the regions created a meeting-place where various interests could negotiate. In agriculture, for example, peasants, though they would still deal with the State mainly through their pressure groups, could now also turn to the regions.[11] There is now less secrecy in decision-making and functions which were fragmented are now better coordinated.

On balance, however, the regional reform has been a failure. In the first place the central administration has always refused to give the regions unimpeded control over any single function, in other words it has always tried, usually successfully, to retain some instruments which would give it overall control. The regions themselves have always been reluctant to stress their autonomy and have preferred the simpler way of trying to cooperate with the central government even when this 'cooperation' disguised the fact of ultimate central control. Often the regions have themselves been over-centralist and have preferred to control and direct rather than guide.[12]

The continuing strength of the clientele system has meant that the periphery–centre link runs not only from the town to the region to the central government but also from the local notable to the politicians in Rome. The relationships and the activities that enable the Italian mayor to gain some resources from the State are not dependent on institutional arrangements such as the regional system. Sidney Tarrow, who has examined this issue in depth, has established that the main network open to local politicians is a partisan network through their own political party. Tarrow quotes a mayor as saying: 'I prefer to go to the politicians first with something important, and then, possibly, I would turn to the prefect for minor questions.' Thus the use of partisan mechanisms for resource allocation, which in other countries may be the exception, in Italy is the rule.[13]

Had the reform been more radical it would have clarified the powers of both the centre and the periphery. Had that been done, however, then the clientele system would have been seriously challenged. A radical reform would not have necessarily destroyed it but, rather, modified its main features, for example by strengthening local ties and giving rise to various forms of separatism. What stopped the central government from promulgating a more radical reform, however, was not the fear of separatism, but the fear that this would weaken the clientele system. Thus the central government still directly funds projects which could be funded through the regions. Various state institutions, such as the *Cassa per il Mezzogiorno* (Fund for the Development of the South) coexist with the regions in such a way that there is considerable overlap. Because there is no clear demarcation between regions and central government there is a constant political bargaining, in the course of which the stronger and more efficient regions obtain more resources.[14]

Let us take, for instance, the question of southern development. Here

The fact that the regional framework has not achieved any significant redistributive effect except in favour of regions already well endowed with resources characterizes the main failure of regionalism. But it was not only the hopes of the pro-southern development forces which were dashed. None of the regionalist forces could feel satisfied with what had happened. Those who had thought that the regions would be able to plan had not foreseen that the inflationary spiral of the 1970s would have involved the government in anti-inflationary policies tending to centralize spending so that the regions became mere tools for the distribution of resources rather than instruments for their expansion. Those who had hoped that the regions would provide a closer arena for political participation were disappointed too because the 1970s witnessed an increased reluctance on the part of ordinary people to become involved in political activity; furthermore, when there was local participation this tended to be used more to increase support for ongoing politics rather than as a genuine form of control from below; finally, the new issues, such as ecology, feminism, consumer protection, etc. tended on the whole to transcend local politics. Those who had seen the regions as the stepping-stone towards a decentralization of the State and the creation of various levels of elected assemblies were never able to see their aims realized because the new structures had to coexist with the old ones: alongside the regional councils there was the state-appointed prefect, alongside the southern regions there was the *Cassa per il Mezzogiorno*, alongside the new school councils, democratically elected by parents and school staff, there was the old school superintendent appointed from Rome.[17]

What effects did regional reform have on Italian political parties? It had been assumed by some that the transformation of Italy into a regional state would have led to substantial changes in the Italian political system. The party system, in particular, would have had to adapt: at the very least political parties would have had to reorganize themselves at the regional level. On the whole this has not happened. Political parties did little more than strengthen their regional committees.[18] They have all remained centralist organizations and this has led to the politics of the centre being reproduced at the local level: the political conflict going on in Rome at the parliamentary and government levels was faithfully reproduced at the regional level and throughout all local elected assemblies down to the local neighbourhood committee. The regionalists had believed in the regions because they thought they would bring about a novel conception of political power. The party struggle, however, continued in the same old way.[19]

What the regions did do was to offer the existing political parties a further terrain of struggle, confrontation and cooperation. For the DC the very fact that the regional reform has not changed significantly the face of Italian politics constitutes a remarkable political success. In the regions they control, new powerful instruments of political patronage have been created; at the same time the PCI, as a pro-regionalist party, was forced to defend the regional experiment in spite of its bureaucratic distortion. In 1975 the PCI obtained a remarkable success in the regional elections. This not only confirmed its supremacy in the traditional 'red' regions of Tuscany, Emilia Romagna and Umbria but the PCI increased its vote and formed regional governments with the PSI in Piedmont, Liguria and the Marche. During the period of the government of national unity (1976–79) the PCI was also involved in one form or other in the government of other regions. In these – as a writer on regional affairs has stated - nothing could be done without PCI approval.[20]

The main party beneficiary of the new regional system, however, has been neither the DC nor the PCI but the PSI. The adoption of a system of proportional representation for local elections has meant that it is extremely difficult for a single party to form a regional or local government. Even when this is possible the leading party still tries to have other coalition partners because it may need their help elsewhere. Thus the PSI benefits from its unique position as the 'central' party between the PCI and the DC. It can choose with whom to ally and can dictate its own terms. With only 10 per cent of the vote (on average) the PSI can obtain considerable political control. In order to examine the disproportion between electoral success and political power, let us first look at the results for the three regional elections of 1970, 1975 and 1980 (Table 12.3) bearing in mind that we are only talking of the fifteen 'ordinary status' regions and that the results for the elections of the municipality (the commune) and the province do not differ significantly from the regional results. After each election and the subsequent formation of the regional governments the share of posts in all regional governments for each of the main parties is given in Table 12.4.

TABLE 12.3 Election Results. Regional elections; 1970–85. (fifteen ordinary status regions) (Percentage and numbers of seats won)

	1970	1975	1980	1985
PCI	27.9 (200)	33.4 (247)	31.5 (233)	30.2 (225)
PSIUP	3.2 (16)	—	—	—
Leftists	—	1.6 (8)	2.1 (10)	1.5 (9)
Green	—	—	—	1.7 (9)
PSI	10.4 (67)	11.9 (82)	12.7 (86)	13.3 (94)
PSDI	7.0 (41)	5.6 (36)	5.0 (31)	3.6 (23)
PRI	2.9 (18)	3.2 (19)	3.0 (18)	4.0 (25)
DC	37.9 (287)	35.1 (277)	36.8 (290)	35.0 (276)
PLI	4.7 (27)	2.5 (11)	2.7 (15)	2.2 (13)
MSI	5.2 (32)	6.3 (40)	5.9 (37)	6.5 (41)

Note: After 1970 the PSIUP (Partito Socialista Italiaňo di Unità Proletaria) decided to merge with the PCI

TABLE 12.4 Percentage of members of regional government per party

	% of posts in regional governments		
Party	1971	1976	1981
DC	57.8	45.4	44
PCI	11.5	17.4	16.4
PSI	14.2	20.2	23.6

Source: Cazzola, F. (1982), p. 62

Clearly the DC always obtains a greater percentage of posts than of votes and the PCI always a smaller percentage, but the outright winner is always the PSI who, in 1981, was able to obtain twice as many posts as it had votes. Further research shows that the PSI does better in obtaining more power when it is in coalition with the PCI than when it is in coalition with the DC. This is in part due to the fact that Left coalitions tend to be two-party coalitions between PCI and PSI while Centre-Left coalitions nearly always also include the smaller parties of the Centre and there is more competition for posts. The main reason, however, is that the PCI, being a more disciplined party, is not under the same kind of pressure as the DC: it does not need to satisfy powerful groups of local notables and therefore can grant more posts to its allies. The data demonstrating the political gains made by the PSI in Left and Centre-Left coalitions are given in Table 12.5. As can be seen, when the PSI is in coalition with the PCI it is able to obtain three times its share of seats, while when it is in coalition with the DC it obtains 'only' twice its 'proper' share.

The PSI's success rate in playing the PCI against the DC can be further demonstrated when we turn to examining the most important local government post in the ninety-two main municipalities (see Table 12.6). In 1971 the PSI and the PCI had the same number of mayors. The elections of 1975 signalled a significant advance of the PCI and a far smaller increment for the PSI, yet the PSI increased its share of mayors

TABLE 12.5 Percentage of PSI seats in regional councils and PSI posts in regional governments

	Coalitions with the PCI Govt.		Coalitions with the DC Govt.	
	posts (%)	Seats (%)	posts (%)	Seats (%)
1971	22	7.5	18.4	10.7
1976	31.5	10.9	21.2	11.9
1981	38.3	12.3	26.8	12.3

TABLE 12.6 Number of Mayors per party, 1971–81[21]

	DC	PCI	PSI	Others
1971	67	12	12	1
1976	50	21	16	5
1981	51	21	15	5

more or less in the same proportion as the PCI. In 1971 the PSI had 12 mayors of whom 8 were at the head of a left-wing coalition and 4 at the head of a Centre-Left coalition. In 1976 the PSI 16 mayors, 15 of whom were leading a left-wing coalition. In 1981 the PCI losses led to the PSI losing 4 mayors in left-run cities, but gaining 3 in Centre-Left cities[21].

Political bargaining has not been limited to the local level. Negotiations for the formation of a government have often spilled over to the periphery. When the first Centre-Left coalition was in the making, in the early 1960s, the DC had tried to obtain from the PSI the undertaking that whenever possible it would try to form a Centre-Left coalition at the local level. This was often difficult because local socialists tended to be reluctant to switch from the PCI to the DC in the knowledge that such deals were not acceptable to their electorate. As the PSI became more and more involved in the political system and as it acquired its own clienteles it became less reluctant to play the DC card, particularly as governing with the DC at the local level sharply increased their uninhibited use of political patronage. Furthermore, because the DC was in difficulty it was less reluctant to part with posts and power in order to consolidate its alliances. The PSI did gain from its local alliances with the PCI, but it had lost power at the centre in 1976–79 when it was being squeezed by the DC and the PCI in the government of national unity. The only real threat to the balancing act of the PSI was the historic compromise between the PCI and the DC. An agreement between the two not only limited the political resources left for the PSI, but the PSI would no longer be able to play one party against the other.

In 1983, following elections which signalled a massive loss for the DC, the PSI was able to obtain the most coveted prize: the post of Prime Minister. The price to pay was farly stiff: not only had the new socialist Prime Minister to grant the DC the most important portfolios in the Cabinet, give up the long-term project of a left-wing government with the PCI and adopt a programme of austerity, but he also gave an undertaking that he would endeavour to facilitate the formation of Centre-Left governments at the local level. In Florence the local socialists forced the resignation of the communist mayor and remained in power with their new DC allies. This trend was now going to continue in other areas. This political development illustrates clearly the failure of the regionalist dream: decentralization did not reform Italian politics.

On the contrary, coalition politics at the centre had a negative feedback at the regional and municipal level.

REFERENCES AND NOTES

1. Modica, E. (1983), p. 13.
2. Allum, P.A. (1973), pp. 217–20.
3. Putnam, R.D., Leonardi, R. and Nanetti, R.Y. (1980), p. 220.
4. For a journalistic account of the organization of the neighbourhood committees in Bologna see Jaggi, M., Muller, R. and Schmidt, S. (1977).
5. Farneti, P. (1976), pp. 99–100, cited in Rotelli (1979), vol. 2.
6. Rotelli (1979), vol. 2, pp. 424–5.
7. Ibid., pp. 425–7.
8. See Barbera, A. (1981).
9. Ibid.
10. See Barbera, A. (1979), p. 729. Barbera writes that party agreement existed only for the first three points. It seems to us that there was considerable agreement even on the last point as there were many in both the PSI and the DC who wanted to involve the PCI in government at the local level in order to unburden some responsibility on to the opposition.
11. Ibid., pp. 727–8.
12. Tarrow, S. (1974), pp. 18–29; see also his book on the same general topic, *Between Center and Periphery* (Tarrow, S., 1977).
13. Ibid.
14. Fichera, F. (1982), p. 98.
15. Cotturri, G. (1982). The same point is made by Compagna, F. and Muscara, C. (1980).
16. The research summarized here can be found in Putmann, R. *et al.* (1981).
17. See Barbera (1981), pp. 3–9.
18. Amato, G. (1980), p. 105.
19. Rotelli (1979), pp. 428–35.
20. Ibid., p. 429.
21. Cazzola, F. (1982), p. 62.

Chapter 13

THE POLITICAL PARTIES

It has become apparent from the preceding pages that the fundamental forces in Italian society are the political parties. There are a considerable number of factors behind this.[1]

In the first place the electoral system of proportional representation has facilitated the proliferation of political parties. This has made it difficult for any single party to achieve an absolute majority in Parliament and has forced the leading party to negotiate with others in order to form a government. This has given small parties considerable power: they are able to use political resources and to establish a relatively stable relationship with their particular electorate.

Secondly, the institutional system and in particular the Constitution has created a strong Parliament and a weak executive. Thus political parties in Parliament have been able to control the executive to a much greater extent than in France, West Germany, the USA or the UK.

Thirdly, the fact that economic institutions are directly or indirectly controlled by political parties has enabled them to strengthen themselves to a considerable extent.

But there are other considerations of a more historical nature. Some are connected to the formation of a unitary state in Italy, to the Risorgimento.[2] The dominant groups which led the process of Italian unification were not strong enough to eliminate or subjugate the various local interest groups tied to the agrarian system. They were forced to negotiate with them and to make alliances. One of the consequences was that the Italian dominant classes were always deeply divided. They could be united only by a constant process of bargaining and negotiating in Parliament. Excluded from this process were the peasant masses and the developing working class. The former had no vote and being deeply Catholic followed the papal decision not to take any part in the affairs of the new Italian State whose birth had been achieved against the wishes and at the expense of the Roman Catholic Church. The latter were in part disenfranchised and were, by and large, organized by the Italian

Socialist Party (PSI), a party which stood, at least ideologically, against most of the fundamental tenets of the Italian Liberal State.

Thus even before fascism the Italian ruling classes had not been able to produce a strong bourgeois party. Fascism, of course, destroyed all existing political parties and proceeded to organize society from above. It established centrally controlled organizations dealing with many aspects of social life, from the organization of leisure time to culture, trade unions, etc. Italian political parties revived during the Resistance and organized jointly its political leadership. After the end of the war, Italian political parties were the only organizations which had sufficient prestige to organize 'civil society' and to create or re-create its main institutions.

The multiplicity and importance of political parties are only one of the features of the Italian party system. It is not what constitutes the specificity of the Italian system. What distinguishes Italy from other Western European democratic countries is the fact that there has never been a turnover between government and opposition. The Italian Christian Democratic Party (DC) has always been the leading party of government and the Italian Communist Party (PCI) – apart from short periods in which it supported governments of 'national unity' – has always been in opposition.

As we have seen the domination of political parties in the Italian institutional system has constantly increased. The governing parties, in particular, have systematically 'colonized' most of the public sector. They have, however, lost ground in terms of public support. In other words: while they now control more than they did in 1945, they deliver less. Until the late 1960s the political parties were able to aggregate interests fairly successfully.[3] If a social group had a specific demand to make, the preferred instrument would always be a political party. Since the late 1960s, however, there has been the growth of new social movements and pressure groups. As we have seen in Chapter 6, the years after 1968 saw the rise of 'new political subjects' such as the students and the feminist movement.

Political parties are now faced with intermediary organizations which are better able than they are to channel popular demands. This is not their only difficulty. It has now become more difficult to perform another task which has been the preserve of political parties: the allocation of resources. It is not just a question of the difficulty in allocating resources in what is an increasingly complex society and with what is an increasingly inefficient machine of public administration: the fact is that resources have not been growing so as to match demands. The crisis of the Welfare State which has affected virtually all Western countries has had in Italy the effect of weakening those institutions which depend on control of the distribution of resources for political support: political parties and, in particular, the leading party, the DC.

Finally, political parties are no longer able to articulate an ideology or to initiate major political debates: they no longer monopolize the political agenda. As we shall see in the following pages the three main political parties, DC, PCI and PSI, have all had to modify their ideological image. The DC cannot use religous ideology as it could in the 1940s and 1950s and cannot resort to the crude anti-communism of that period. The PCI finds it increasingly difficult to use the traditional Marxist language of class solidarity: class is no longer the principal focus of loyalty or of self-identification. The PSI has attempted to become a centrist party committed to modernization.

The press, now more independent from political parties, plays a greater role in initiating debates; young magistrates have been in the vanguard of the ecology movement; small organizations (as well as the Radical Party) took the lead in the initial stages of the fight for civil liberties. Most of the debates on issues such as peace, women's rights and crime are increasingly dominated by the peace movement, feminist groups, religious organizations (including the Church which no longer takes the DC as its main political reference point), relatives of victims of criminal or terroristic acts, public personalities, etc.

It is, of course, difficult to measure the extent to which the political parties face a crisis of credibility. We can, however, offer an illustration. From the electoral point of view there is only one framework which allows popular feelings to be expressed outside of political parties: the referendum system. A referendum can only abolish or amend a law voted by Parliament, it cannot be used as a legislative tool. So far Italy has had eight referendums (not including the 1946 referendum on the monarchy). In all of these the people have decided to support the laws approved by Parliament. Thus, on the face of it, it would seem that parliamentary legislation has popular support. It does not follow from that, however, that the voters have always followed the advice of the parties for whom they usually vote.

Let us take the referendum on the legalization of divorce which took place on 12 May 1974. Only two parties told their supporters to vote in favour of abolishing the law on divorce: the DC and the (neo-fascist) Italian Social Movement (MSI). In the 1972 election these two parties obtained together 47.64 per cent of the vote. Yet only 40.74 per cent voted against the law on divorce.

On 11 June 1978 there were two other referendums. The first was supposed to sanction a new law establishing a system of public financing of political parties. The second dealt with anti-terrorist legislation. All the main parties advised their supporters to approve both laws. The referendum on public financing was seen as a test for political parties in general. Only 23.3 per cent voted against the anti-terrorism legislation (a high percentage when we consider that virtually all parties had recommended a vote in favour). When it came to the results on the funding of political parties, only 56.3 per cent voted in favour. Furthermore, there was a very high rate of abstention, 18.6 per cent. A majority of the population in the South had voted against state funding. A study of the electoral results area by area revealed that the communist electorate was relatively more disciplined than the DC electorate. Thus this referendum, like the one on divorce, suggests that the main victim of the crisis of political parties is the DC. This is confirmed by the results of the referendum of 17 May 1981 on abortion. Here the DC maintained a low profile throughout the campaign because it sensed that there would be a majority in favour of abortion. In the previous general election the anti-abortion parties (the DC and the neo-fascists) had had a total of 43.6 per cent, but the anti-abortion vote was only 32.1 per cent.

These examples do not prove there is a crisis of Italian political parties, but show that on certain important issues the electorate behaves independently of political parties. They also reveal an increased secularization among voters, a lessening of ideological commitments.[4]

We can now turn to a closer examination of the main parties.

THE CHRISTIAN DEMOCRATIC PARTY

It is impossible to give a simple and straightforward definition of this party. Like its main rival, the PCI, it is a unique party by European standards. The DC has been defined in a variety of ways: as the party of monopoly–capital, as the party of the 'state bourgeoisie', as the 'party of the Catholics', as a conservative party, as a social democratic party, as a conservative–democratic party with a popular mass base . . . .

The 'orthodox' Marxist position (never wholeheartedly adopted by the leadership of the PCI) had defined the DC as the party of monopoly-capital. According to this view the DC is a party which represents the interests of the Italian bourgeoisie or at least those of its dominant faction, that is, the large monopolies (e.g. Fiat and Pirelli). As evidence to sustain this thesis one could point to the growth and development of these monopolies during the period of DC rule and their connection with Italy's economic policies.

Even in the 1950s the Italian communists had not held this position. The PCI leader, Palmiro Togliatti, pointed out that after the war private capitalism was not able to develop its own mass party (something akin to the British Conservative Party) and was forced to give its support to the only mass party which could be an effective challenge to the PCI. Thus the relationship between the DC and private capitalism has always been more conflictual and less straightforward than it would appear to the exponents of the 'orthodox' view.

A second position sees the DC as the party which represents the interests of that social stratum which controls public spending and which benefits from it: the so-called state bourgeoisie. Evidence for this position can be found in the abnormal expansion of the state sector and the extent to which the Italian State has intervened in the economy. The DC had realized that in order to maintain and reproduce its power it was necessary to expand the state sector.[5]

Franco Cassano has argued against both these interpretations.[6] His starting-point is that, for historical reasons, the DC has emerged from the fascist period and from the Resistance as the leading party of the Italian political system. The peculiarity of this situation is that the only party alternative to it, the PCI, – like the DC – was an 'anti-system party' in the sense that it was anti-capitalist. Thus a 'normal' alternation between government and opposition (as in the UK) was not possible. The DC considered itself as being 'condemned' to be always the party of government.[7] In order to ensure the reproduction of the existing (capitalist) system the DC had to reconcile two positions: on the one hand it had to ensure the conditions for private capitalist accumulation, on the other it had to obtain and guarantee social peace and social legitimacy. Being the only party which could ensure the first condition (the bourgeoisie had no other party it could rely on) the DC always had great bargaining power *vis-à-vis* private capital. In order to contain the communist threat, the DC also had to adopt some of the communist demands for reform: the DC *had* to reform agriculture, *had* to intervene in the economy, *had* to accept the need for structural reforms, *had* to accept, even ideologically, the need to limit private capital accumulation. Thus the gradual extension of DC control over the state machine and the public sector is not a result of a particular DC ideology but rather the result of the chief peculiarity of the Italian political system: the presence of a strong opposition which could not be allowed to become government. This is why the DC cannot be classified purely as a conservative party.

The thesis advanced by Franco Cassano has the advantage of not reducing the DC to its social base or to the 'interests' it is supposed to 'represent'. It is clear that the DC is the party chosen by the most powerful economic groups in Italian society to be their 'party of government'. It is also clear that these groups had not, traditionally, had strong mass support. In 1945 Italy was still a relatively backward nation, the PCI was very strong. The DC could not establish its own rule without obtaining mass support: it had to organize the masses in competition with the PCI. Given the role of the Church in Italy the DC also had to have a special relationship with it. Given Italian backwardness, the DC also had to do something about economic development.

As the Catholic political scientist Gianni Baget Bozzo has written: 'The Christian Democrats know well that, if the PCI had not existed, they would have had to invent it.'[8] The existence of a party historically committed to international solidarity with the Soviet Union gave Italian voters from left of centre to the conservative Right a basic motivation to maintain the DC in power *irrespective of its actual policies or performance.* As the Italian communists distanced themselves from Moscow, it became increasingly difficult for DC leaders to describe the PCI as an anti-Western party. The present crisis of the DC is, at least in part, due to the difficulties it has in depicting the PCI as a pro-Soviet party.

Baget Bozzo illustrates another contradiction which affects the DC, stressing the fact that this is a dynamic party which has changed its role over the years. The DC, having emerged from the war as the Catholic party, saw its main task as one of mediation between the newly enfranchised Catholic masses and a capitalist state. [9] As it acquired control over this state it had to develop not only the economy, but also some of the values which 'fit' this economic system. The DC, writes Baget Bozzo, has become, increasingly a liberal–capitalist party committed to a 'Western' conception of individualism. It has become an 'American' party, not only in the sense that it is pro-American, but also in the sense that it supervises the evolution of Italy into an American-type society, a secularized, materialistic and consumeristic society.[10]

The DC has been able to be for so long the party of government in Italy because it had considerable and unique advantages.[11]

1. It had, thanks to the Church, an important social base, particularly in the Catholic regions of the North-east and in the South.
2. Its Catholic ideology could appeal to both middle classes and lower classes.
3. It had always given great importance to local associations and local movements as well as to a variety of forms of organizations. It was thus well implanted in Italian society.
4. Ideologically, it is not committed to any particular form of state or the dominance of private forms of ownership. It can thus attract support from different sources.
5. It could be anti-communist without being totally committed to a capitalist–liberal system.
6. During the fascist period the political personnel of the Liberal State had either been coopted by the regime or had been repressed by it. Left-wing political cadres had had to act clandestinely. The Church, however, had been allowed a relative degree of autonomy. Thus the only political organization which had emerged from fascism with competent political personnel was the DC.[12]

Thus from the very beginning of the Italian Republic the DC appeared as particularly suited to be *the* party of the institutions and of the State.

The DC obtained not only the support of the dominant classes but also the decisive support of the USA. In exchange the DC could guarantee the USA that Italy would be a loyal and devoted ally of the West and that it would never seek an independent role in foreign policy.

There were attempts on the part of DC leaders, such as Amintore Fanfani, to develop something like a Gaullist Italian foreign policy towards the late 1950s and early 1960s, but such attempts came to naught.

Any interpretation of the DC must also take into account the fact that this is a party which develops and changes position. After the war it faced several ideological and strategic options: the one which emerged victorious was that of its first leader, Alcide De Gasperi. De Gasperi had to defeat the attempt to transform the DC into a clerical party which would be subject to the dictates of the Church and at the same time prevent the success of the Dossetti group which sought to develop an original Catholic–populist line with unmistakable anti-capitalist traits.[13] At the same time De Gasperi had to ensure that no overtly pro-capitalist liberal party could gain popular support. The risk that this would happen was felt to be very real because of the relative prestige that some pre-fascist liberal figures, such as the philosopher Benedetto Croce and the economist Luigi Einaudi, had in Italy at the time.[14]

De Gasperi's strategy therefore had to operate at several levels. The task of the DC was to insert, for the first time in Italian history, the Catholic masses into the Liberal Democratic State. Excluded and self-excluded by the Risorgimento and the State which arose out of it, oppressed and dominated by the Fascist State, devout Italian Catholics never felt 'at home' in Italy. The DC would thus complete the task left unfinished by the Risorgimento.

The DC was also aware that it would have to tackle the problem of economic development by controlling politically the free-enterprise system. It was also necessary to promote social reforms, not only to preserve social peace but also in order to make sure that the creation of a larger working class which would result from economic growth would not strengthen the Left. At first the DC toyed with the Utopian idea of the 'non-proletarianization' of society, but it eventually aimed at creating a complex stratification in Italy by political–economic means so that the division of the labour force in a variety of strata would prevent the formation of a large politically united factory proletariat.[15]

Clearly, the strategy of the DC develops with a fixed point of reference which determines virtually everything: the PCI. The fundamental task of the DC is to prevent the PCI from dominating the Italian political system. It is able to achieve this thanks to its unique ability to combine what may appear to be a 'backward' ideology (traditional Catholicism) with a practical concern for the modernization of Italy. Thus the anti-communism of the DC is not simply the reflection of traditional Catholic values, it is also an instrument which is used to create a demarcation line between those who can participate and those who cannot participate in the DC system of political mediation.

When Amintore Fanfani became the leading strategist of the DC, after De Gasperi's death, he sought to develop the Italian economy by acquiring direct control over the public sector and expanding it. This was done by combining Catholic ideology and political realism: a 'Christian' view of the role of the State entails that the economy and private enterprise be subordinated to an ethical view.[16] At the same time it is necessary to control the activities of the dominant economic groups otherwise they will seek to obtain resources at the expense of less privileged groups, thus narrowing the consensus needed by the DC to maintain the existing social order. Furthermore, Italian capitalism is fundamentally weak, it is bound to have a subordinate role in the international economic system, devoid as it is of two necessary resources: energy and technological know-how.[17]

To achieve this strategy Fanfani attempted to multiply power centres (mainly public sector institutions and the banks) and to establish direct control over them, bypassing Parliament. To defend himself from the more traditionalist factions of the DC, he centralized power in his own hands. Thus in 1959 he managed the so far unique feat of being at the same time party leader, Prime Minister and Foreign Minister.[18] Fanfani was ousted (although his long-term project of alliance with the PSI was achieved soon after) partly because it became impossible to manage in a centralized manner a power bloc where power itself had been diffused in so many factions.

As power centres multiplied so did the factionalism of the DC.[19] The Centre-Left coalition was established only after Aldo Moro had managed to convince the other DC leaders that the 'opening to the left' was the best option for maintaining the centrality of the DC in the system. In the 1960s, with the Centre-Left well under way, ideology played a decreasing role in the DC, a process similar to that occurring in both the PCI and the PSI.

After the failure of the Centre-Left government the DC was even more ideologically fragmented and was no longer able to elaborate a general strategy. Its tasks become increasingly those of maintaining the existing system and, in particular, its dominant role in Italian society.

There is one aspect of the De Gasperi project which the DC would never abandon: the attempt to influence social stratification. Through the system of clientele and patronage the DC built a network of cleavages which cut across the social structure so as to form obstacles to the development of class solidarity.[20] The clientele system has often been considered a clear instance of the backwardness of Italy, both political and economic. This is a one-sided view which is based on the assumption that clienteles and modernization cannot go together. Yet the classical locus of a clientele system is that of American politics, a system which also exhibits the phenomenon, unique in advanced capitalist countries, of not having a strong working-class party. It is true that the clientele system originated in the system of local party notables, but soon, as Allum demonstrates in his study of Naples, this system gave way to a more modern one: on the basis of traditional local bosses a modern system of state intervention developed, modifying class relations in a massive way.[21] The agrarian reform and the creation of the *Cassa per il Mezzogiorno* restricted the numbers of absentee landlords, created a large class of small land-owning peasants and united them in a political bloc which stopped communist advance in the South.[22] Through the development of the state sector a large class of white-collar workers, of managers and entrepreneurs was created. This class owed its existence to the DC and did not – as in other countries – appear to be the 'natural' consequence of economic development.

The DC did not just contribute to the creation of various social strata. It also organized them. This was done at times by the DC as a political party, at times through its control of state institutions, but more often than not through the creation and development of a large number of organizations known as 'parallel organizations': the ACLI is an organization of Catholic workers, the CISL is the Catholic trade union, Azione Cattolica is a lay organization which appeals to all Catholics, the UCID is the Catholic organization of entrepreneurs and managers, the UCIIM is the Catholic organization of secondary-school teachers, the AIMIC that of primary-school teachers, the UGC that of Catholic lawyers; to these must be added youth groups, women's organizations, etc.[23]

Of course, the mere fact of creating social groups and associations does not ensure that they will continue to support the party which has generated them. Urban strata in particular, gradually deserted the DC who, after 1975 lost control of the major cities. Furthermore, the creation of a large state sector was not a mere act of will on the part of the DC. It was also a logical requirement of the economic system given the incapacity of Italian capitalism to look after itself. Finally, the creation and extension of public sector institutions generated interests which assumed, at times, a force of their own. Problems were 'resolved' by the DC by creating institutions to deal with them. These institutions, in turn, created 'problems' and developed their own autonomy.[24] This generated new 'solutions', greater spending and a more complex bargaining system. What kept the entire mechanism ticking over was the constant expansion of public spending made possible by the expansion of the national and international economy.

The extension of the state sector multiplied the numbers and size of social groups which owed something to the State: their jobs, their positions, their power, their status. This practice of government has been the subject of constant criticism in the Italian press by journalists and leading political scientists. One of the main critics has been Giuliano Amato, a socialist political scientist who eventually became an adviser to the PSI leader Bettino Craxi and who followed him in government in 1983. Amato, in his book, *Economia, politica e istituzioni in Italia* (1976) characterized the DC system as being based on a 'spoils' system (*governo spartitorio*).[25] This assumes that all divergent interests in society can somehow be reconciled. Whenever there are conflicts, be they due to old unresolved problems of economic and social development or due to novel contradictions, the State does not seek clear-cut solutions which might increase the numbers of its enemies. On the contrary it tries to distribute benefits to all and sundry.

In a spirited defence of the DC, Giovanni Bognetti pointed out[26]:

1. If Amato's analysis is correct, it does not follow that only the DC is responsible. It has always governed with allies which have quite explicitly accepted the rules of the game and have tried to use them to derive the same sort of political and electoral advantage.[27]

2. The opposition party, the PCI, has never sought to stop the distribution of benefits. On the contrary, it has set itself at the head of a large movement (workers, students, women, etc.) in order to wrest from the State even more benefits, concessions, etc. All political parties in Italy have been in favour of more public spending.

3. The line of compromise among competing interests is a reasonable and defensible line. Modern 'social-democratic' states do not seek the elimination of specific interests but their conciliation. The DC may have gone too far and may not have taken into account the limited resources of the country, but then it is no longer a question of principles at stake, rather of the extent to which they have been applied.[28]

4. There remains the chief accusation: the DC has nourished and developed the state sector to such an extent that it has created a middle class which serves no economic or productive purpose at all, it 'lives off' the State and drains precious resources which could have been better used in industry. Here too, writes Bognetti, the DC may be guilty, but it is not guilty on its own. It simply bought some social peace for itself by meeting without any resistance all the demands that the trade-union movement and the PCI were advancing.[29] This is why it accepted, after 1969, a constant increase in wages particularly in the state sector and never tried to fight against the ever-growing demands of public employees over pay, conditions, pensions, leave, etc.

I have quoted at length this 'defence' of the DC not only to redress the balance but because it makes an important point: the system which is being described is virtually the same as the 'social-democratic consensus' which prevailed in the UK and a number of European countries from the end of the 1940s to the mid 1970s. Here too we have a basic consensus, accepted by all political parties, regarding the construction of a Welfare State and the political use of public spending. Here too we have, among the motivations, the need to ensure a social consensus, to reconcile interests and constantly to increase the standard of living. The difference between the Italian experience and that of other European countries is that in Italy the distribution of benefits has not been undertaken by a State which appears to be above political parties which alternate at the helm of the State itself. The Italian State coincides largely with one specific political party: the DC. Thus the 'DC-State' has all the hallmarks of a *regime* and this is the specificity of the Italian political system.

With the recession of the 1970s there were fewer opportunities for brokerage and for an increase in public expenditure, and the DC began to face enormous difficulties. In the early 1980s, under the leadership of Ciriaco De Mita, the DC would attempt to present itself as a modernizing force ready to relaunch itself as a party with a neo-liberal ideology, and able to obtain the trust and support of the main entrepreneurial groups in order to restructure the Italian economy. In so doing it tried to challenge directly the PSI which was adopting a similar policy.[30] The results of the 1983 election showed that this new strategy was encountering massive difficulties: the DC lost six percentage points. In the 1984 election to the European Parliament the DC lost its position of leading Italian party by 125,000 votes: the PCI obtained 33.3 per cent while the DC had 33.0 per cent. One of the chief problems facing the DC is that it cannot adopt a credible policy of economic austerity because this would hit those interests and economic groups it had created over thirty years. Furthermore, De Mita's new strategy failed to unite the DC. Against it stood a group which included not only Fanfani, but also the traditional leaders of the central faction of the party, the Dorotei. This group, more moderate and conservative than De Mita's faction, accepted as given the crisis of the DC and its electoral losses and gave absolute priority to the strengthening of the ties with its coalition partners and particularly with the PSI. The purpose of this alliance was to enable the party to keep most of the positions of power which it had accumulated, to stabilize the system and to ensure the continuing emargination of the PCI. A third group, led by many of the followers of Aldo Moro, sought instead to build on Moro's strategy of mediation with the PCI and to maintain the popular roots and base of the DC. This group was by now in a minority. Their strategy stood little chance of survival after the PCI withdrew from the 1976–79 government of national unity and after the assassination of Aldo Moro by the terrorists of the Red Brigades group.

Moro had developed a distinctive strategy on the basis of the social strategy initiated by De Gasperi and Fanfani. As we explained in Chapters 2 and 3, in the late 1940s and 1950s the DC had tried to build up the strength of the middle classes in the South as the keystone of its power bloc. It was not the intention of this operation to establish a bulwark against the working class, but, on the contrary, to offer the southern working class a prospect of upward mobility. In making sure that the working class would not retreat into some sort of enclave dominated by the PCI, the DC, through public spending, ensured that the southern working class too would benefit from the rule of the DC as long as it adapted itself to the DC system.[31]

Moro was quick to recognize that the chief problem of the political system the DC had established was that it was still too narrow.[32] This had led to the Centre-Left governments of the 1960s.[33] Now the students' unrest of 1968 and the widespread strikes of 1969 had convinced him that the Centre-Left coalition could no longer provide the DC with the necessary political room for manoeuvre: a new strategic option had to be formulated: the so-called 'third phase' which would also involve the PCI, after the first phase of centrism in the 1950s and the second phase of the Centre-Left in the 1960s.[34]

The basis of this 'third phase' is the following[35]:

1. The possibility of ensuring the continuing economic development of the country with the support of the trade-union movement in exchange for including the trade unions themselves in a continuous bargaining process.
2. An attempt to reduce the rate of growth of public spending. This can be accepted by other political parties because a decrease in public spending entails a decrease in the political power of the DC.

The upshot of this strategy would be that while the DC would lose some of its political power, it would benefit from unloading on to others some of its own responsibilities. A policy of austerity can 'work' for the DC only if it is also accepted by the opposition, i.e. by the PCI. What this represents is a lucid attempt to make all other parties, including the PCI, into junior versions of the DC. In so doing Moro was delineating a clearly 'hegemonic' project where hegemony not only means dominance but the ability to shape a social system so that all political forces take it as given and do not challenge it. Moro's death and the PCI's decision to withdraw its support from the government of national unity put an end to the strategy of the 'third phase'.

THE ITALIAN COMMUNIST PARTY

This party emerged from the Resistance as a mass party. Before 1943 it was illegal and had only a few thousand cadres. By 1946 it had nearly 2 million members. This quantitative jump was so massive that it radically changed its central coordinates. The immediate priority established by its leader, Palmiro Togliatti, was to hold together this great mass of workers, peasants and intellectuals and to give it a purpose and a sense of direction. Many of the former partisans and old cadres had assumed that, having defeated fascism, the communists should once more take up the 'class struggle', stop cooperating with the other 'bourgeois' parties and prepare for a socialist revolution. The leadership argued strongly against this line. It offered two basic reasons:

1. The partisan movement was fundamentally weak. At its peak it had 300,000 men and women under arms, only half of whom were communists.[36] It was concentrated in the North and had been fighting a foreign force, the Germans, with the decisive help of a powerful international coalition. A struggle for socialism could not possibly count on this internal strength and would get no support from outside. The South, with its lack of a partisan tradition and socialist ideology, would be a strategic enclave for the regrouping of the counter-revolutionary forces.

2. The international situation was totally unfavourable to a communist take-over. There was no common boundary with the Soviet Union, American and British groups were still in Italy or could have easily returned. There would have been no support from the USSR: the international lines of division of the spheres of influence had been quite clearly drawn and Italy's position in the 'American sector' was unmistakable.

These considerations were sufficient to convince most of those who had been fighting in the Resistance assuming that it would lead to a socialist insurrection. The fundamental reason why this could not be the aim of the PCI was that Palmiro Togliatti was elaborating a strategy for socialism which owed little to the classical Leninist one and was much closer to the central features of the ideas formulated by his predecessor, Antonio Gramsci, from the depths of his fascist prison.[37] Togliatti was developing a conception of the revolution 'as a process' quite different from the Soviet model and remote from any insurrectionist temptation.[38] The Resistance had been a stage in the 'anti-fascist' revolution. The next stage was not to be socialism but the creation of 'a new type' of republic in whose organization the working class would have the 'leading' role. Instead of a momentous revolutionary rupture, there would be a 'progressive democracy'. Italy's road to socialism would be gradual and would not follow the pattern of the Russian Revolution. As Togliatti declared:

> International experience teaches us that in the actual conditions of the class struggle in the whole world, the working class and the advanced masses, in order to reach socialism – that is, in order to develop democracy to its extreme limit which is precisely that of socialism – must discover new paths different, for instance, from those which had been chosen by the working class and the labouring masses of the Soviet Union.[39]

The PCI consolidated its alliances with the other government parties and particularly with the DC, accepted the enshrinement of the Lateran Pacts in the Constitution and proposed a social truce between workers and entrepreneurs. Its freedom of action was guaranteed by the short period of international coexistence between the two superpowers.

The Cold War altered the situation remarkably. The PCI was expelled from the government, was excommunicated by the Church and criticized by the USSR for having been too keen on compromise politics. It continued to develop the ideas behind the Italian road to socialism, but in a muted form. In foreign policy it staunchly defended the USSR, opposed Marshall aid and Italy's membership of NATO and, later, of the EEC.

By the middle of the 1950s the PCI was in a most difficult situation. Italian capitalism was on the verge of a massive economic take-off. The trade-union movement was deeply divided along party lines. The PCI had lost its majority among the workers in the stronghold of Italian capitalism: the Fiat works in Turin. It was at this moment that the most important event in the post-war history of the international communist movement took place: the Twentieth Congress of the Communist Party of the Soviet Union of 1956. This is when the new Soviet leader, N. S. Khrushchev, revealed the extent of Stalin's purges, but the other novelty of this congress was the formal recognition on the part of the Soviet authorities of the possibilities of national roads to socialism. In Italy this was seen as the green light for the development of an 'Italian road to socialism'. In reality the light was never green. It was always conditioned by the state of play of the international context, that is, by the possibilities for peaceful coexistence. The invasion of Hungary polarized the situation once more and forced the PCI to choose the Soviet camp and to justify the intervention. Soon, however, the development of détente enabled the PCI to take a more independent role. Thus when the ideological conflict between the Russians and the Chinese erupted, the PCI refused to take part in any attempt to convene an international communist conference for the purpose of excommunicating the Chinese. This rejection was not motivated by any sympathies the PCI might have had with Peking's position but by objections to the very idea of international excommunications.[40] It was not merely a question of principles (Togliatti had admitted that the exclusion of the Yugoslav Communist Party in 1948 was a grave mistake), but was based on the view that the activity of individual communist parties should not be subject to the approval of the rest of the movement.

The principles around which the PCI was developing its international strategy were based on the Togliattian concept of 'polycentrism'. There were two dimensions to this expression. First, the international communist movement could no longer be directed from a single centre because there were different roads to socialism. Second, the international system itself was less and less bipolar and there could be, thanks to the process of *détente*, new possibilities for European countries to withdraw from the American sphere of influence. The Common Market expressed the potentialities for a movement towards European autonomy.[41] The PCI, by the early 1960s, had changed its hitherto hostile attitude towards the EEC. The split between China and the USSR meant that there was no longer a single unified and monolithic socialist camp, while the process of decolonization and non-alignment meant that a number of countries were rejecting the logic of bipolarism.

After Togliatti died in 1964 the PCI continued to develop an independent foreign policy. Under the leadership of Enrico Berlinguer who became leader in 1972, the PCI became ever more committed to the development of the EEC. It gradually ceased to ask for an Italian withdrawal from NATO and, at the Fourteenth Congress of the party (March 1975) Berlinguer announced that 'we too believe that the Italian government must not propose to undertake a unilateral action which would alter the military strategic equilibrium between the Atlantic Pact and the Warsaw Pact'; in other words there was no question of an Italian withdrawal from NATO.[42] A year later Berlinguer declared to a journalist that he felt 'safer' within NATO because this meant that the PCI could choose its own road to socialism without constraints from Moscow.[43]

This revision of the established position had come a few years after it had become clear what these 'Soviet constraints' could be: the PCI energetically condemned the 1968 Soviet invasion of Czechoslovakia and would renew its condemnation every year on the anniversary of the intervention. The PCI tried to achieve international backing for its position within the West European communist movement. The period 1974–78 saw the rise of 'Eurocommunism' sanctioned in 1975 by the joint declaration of the leading European communist parties, the French, the Spanish and the Italian, that they were committed to autonomy and independence from the USSR, that they recognized the value and importance of all democratic principles including all those of the liberal-democratic tradition: freedom of the press, of religious belief, civil liberties, political pluralism, elections, etc. Again, the development of this line was premised on the continuation of the process of détente because the growth of Eurocommunism depended on the degree of polycentrism existing in the world. Should the battle lines between East and West be drawn sharply again then the space for manoeuvre would be reduced. If the international situation was characterized by a clear 'either with us or against us' then there would be little room for the development of a third way or an intermediate position.

As it turned out the era of détente came to an abrupt end. The non-ratification of SALT II, the NATO decision to locate a new generation of nuclear weapons in Europe, the Soviet decision not to withdraw any of its new SS-20 missiles, the Soviet invasion of Afghanistan (1980), the US boycott of the Moscow Olympics and the USSR boycott of the Los Angeles Olympics (1984), and the unrelenting development of 'local wars' (often wars fought by proxy by the two superpowers) between China and Vietnam, between Vietnam and Cambodia, Somalia and Ethiopia, Iran and Iraq, the Israeli invasion of the Lebanon, the Turkish occupation of part of Cyprus – all these were so many obstacles to the continuation of the process of détente and the hopes of Eurocommunism. Soon the French Communist Party broke ranks and supported the Soviet intervention in Afghanistan while the Spanish Communist Party was reduced to a rump.

The weakness of Eurocommunism had been that it had never succeeded in going beyond the mere assertion of common principles. It was one thing to agree over pluralism and civil liberties, another to develop a joint programme of action over concrete questions such as energy, unemployment, the North–South dialogue, the EEC.

The PCI continued its relatively lonely path. The crushing of the Polish trade union Solidarity by the military in December 1981 caused it to break completely from Moscow. In a formal resolution it declared that the phase of socialist development which began with the Russian Revolution had exhausted its driving force, that the 'march of socialism depends, more and more on democratic and socialist ideas and achievements in the capitalist developed world and on the success of the most progressive experiences ... in the countries of the Third World'.[44] Thus the PCI defines the new situation: the October Revolution is finally over and the State which resulted from it has nothing to offer to the socialist movement.

The domestic equivalent of an international strategy based on disengagement from the two power blocs would have to be a more concrete formulation of the 'Italian road to socialism'. During the 1960s the PCI had to face the fact that it was the only real parliamentary opposition to the Centre-Left government (apart from the neo-fascists and the Liberal Party). It also had a monopoly of Marxist culture. In the years 1968–72 this monopoly was seriously challenged and eventually shattered by the student revolt. The PCI was accused of being revisionist and reformist and, at the same time, authoritarian and bureaucratic. The dual eruption of workers and students caused a massive crisis in the Italian political system. In 1969, as already mentioned, a bomb in a Milan bank killed sixteen people. It was the beginning of ten years of terrorism.

This situation induced the PCI leader, Enrico Berlinguer, to give the party's strategy a more concrete formulation. The immediate reason for this redefinition was the 1973 *coup d'état* in Chile. There a left-wing government had attempted to rule against a strong Christian Democratic party and was crushed by a military take-over. The essential problem was to provide the country with a radical reforming government without driving a large section of middle-class groups and other social forces into positions of overt hostility. Thus a mere electoral or mathematical majority was not sufficient:

> ... it would be illusory to think that, even if the left-wing parties and
> forces succeeded in gaining 51 per cent of the votes and seats in

Parliament ... this fact would guarantee the survival and work of a
government representing this 51 per cent.[45]

In order to achieve a political majority it was necessary to achieve an
alliance with the Catholic masses and enter into some form of
compromise with the DC. This was the political context which called for
'a great new historic compromise' among the political forces which
represented the overwhelming majority of the Italian people.

The PCI recognized that it faced a problem of national legitimation
and that it needed to offer some international guarantee that its presence
in government would not signify a shift in the balance of forces between
East and West to the disadvantage of the West.

The political events which followed the adoption of the strategy of the
historic compromise seemed favourable. The right wing of the DC, now
led by Amintore Fanfani, was defeated in the divorce referendum. The
local elections of 1975 were a stunning victory for the PCI: the 1970 gap
between DC and PCI of nearly 10 per cent was now reduced to 1.8 per
cent. Communist local government power, hitherto enclosed within the
three 'red' regions of central Italy, now spread to virtually all major
cities. The 1975 results were not a freak: they were confirmed in the 1976
general election. The DC, however, was able to make good its losses at
the expense of its potential junior partners in coalition: the Social
Democrats and the Liberals. A Centre-Left coalition was no longer
possible because socialists, republicans and social democrats refused to
enter into any coalition which rejected the PCI. In July 1976, for the first
time since the break-up of the tripartite coalition of 1947 (the first
'historic compromise') a DC Prime Minister, Giulio Andreotti, had to
appeal to the PCI to support his government in Parliament. At the local
level cooperation between communists and Christian Democrats was
becoming commonplace and by June 1977 a wide-ranging government
programme had been agreed between the DC, the PCI and the other
parties. Though not *in* government, the PCI seemed to have become a
party *of* government.

The Andreotti government of national unity was seen as a possible
stepping-stone towards fully fledged communist participation in
government.

This did not happen. In the space of three years the PCI lost some of
the support and goodwill it had accumulated in the preceding five years.
Communist leaders have accepted some of the blame, explaining that,
though they had a good programme, they were not able to implement it
and that, though aware of the complexity of the situation, they were not
really equipped to deal with it.[46] The PCI had not been able to defend
and protect all its own interest groups and had to be content with
modifying the initiatives taken by the government.[47] The policy of
compromise had turned into a policy of subordination.

The explosion of terrorism led the PCI to defend the State by refusing to negotiate with the Red Brigades over the Moro kidnapping and by accepting new anti-terrorist legislation. The intention was to uphold the democratic principles of the State and of the Constitution, but the PCI could not avoid appearing to many as the defender of the entire edifice of the Italian State with its corruption, degeneration and bigotry. It was accused by many on the Left of espousing an anti-libertarian cause purely in order to establish its long-sought-after 'historic compromise' with the DC. As these events unfolded, the DC played a subtle game: it allowed the PCI to emerge as the stoutest defender of law and order and of austerity and to antagonize many of its supporters.

Both parties played parallel strategies which turned out to be wrong: the PCI assumed that its alliance with the DC would enable this party to become a progressive force, while the DC gambled on the eventual transformation of the PCI into a mildly reforming machine which would bring its supporters and the masses it inspired under the political hegemony of a new governing coalition led again by the DC. Thus the DC's strategy was also a strategy of 'historic compromise'. The difference between the two parties was that each aimed at a different outcome.

At least on the surface, Moro's interpretation of the historic compromise seemed to prevail over Berlinguer's. But the DC was also in crisis because the economic crisis was restricting the political terrain for co-option. Furthermore, it proved impossible to co-opt the new terrorism, though it could be used to embarrass the PCI. The dramatic rupture of the 'historic compromise' occurred precisely when the Red Brigades terrorist group kidnapped Aldo Moro in a spectacular operation in the centre of Rome on 16 March 1978, killing his five bodyguards. They held Moro for fifty-five days before killing him too. Thus the Red Brigades destroyed the key man who could have paved the way for the entry of the PCI into the government. The target had been chosen with great accuracy. The victim was Moro but the target was the PCI and the policy of the historic compromise.

A new leadership emerged in the DC, taking over from the Zaccagnini group which had supported Moro. This successfully tried to re-establish its links with the PSI and its new leader, Bettino Craxi. Craxi, who had previously adopted a less intransigent line in dealing with the terrorists, sought now to use the crisis of the Italian political system to prepare the ground for an authentic refounding of his own party, breaking decisively with the socialist tradition and challenging the DC in the centre of the political spectrum.

By the end of 1978 the PCI had ceased supporting the government. By the end of 1980 it had changed line officially. Between these two events there was the 1979 general election in which, for the first time, the communists lost votes. The losses were heavy, and in the South they were extremely serious. The PCI thus paid for its failure during the period of 'national unity' to demarcate itself from the DC.

This was the nail in the coffin of the 'historic compromise'. Berlinguer announced that henceforth the PCI's policy would be to fight for a 'democratic alternative'. This meant, he explained, that the situation was ripe for a government without the DC.

This proposal had little immediate application. The PSI was by then pursuing single-mindedly its own course to power which brought Craxi to the office of Prime Minister in the summer of 1983 and had no intention of cooperating with the PCI.

The aim of the strategy of the PCI was to open up the Italian political system which had been stagnating under continuous DC rule. The 1976–79 experiment of 'national unity' had not achieved this, but had not been wholly negative. The DC had accepted the possibility of communist participation in government thereby 'legitimizing' the PCI.

The parallel between the 1976–79 period in Italy and the experiment of the 'social contract' in the UK in 1974–79 under a Labour administration is impressive. In both cases the Left tried to obtain moderate wage settlements, and in both cases any attempt to reflate the economy during an international recession failed.[48]

The defeat of the PCI must be seen in the context of the defeat of other left-wing forces in the rest of Europe in the 1970s. The prospects for the future are not very good. To be sure, electoral losses may be contained and there may even be some remarkable improvement, but the possibilities of a coalition with communist participation are fairly distant.

THE ITALIAN SOCIALIST PARTY

This party had played a relatively minor role in the fight against fascism during the 1930s. It re-emerged in 1943 as one of the fundamental forces in the Resistance. Although it did not have an organization able to match that of the PCI and it could not count on the general support enjoyed by the DC through the Church, the PSI had greater electoral influence than the PCI: at the 1946 election it emerged as the second party. It soon lost this position and, ever since the 1953 elections, it has become the largest of the small parties, well behind the DC and the PCI.

Even when it had more votes than the PCI it was subordinate to it: its internal organization was a replica of the PCI, but because it was not able to recruit widely it was a centralized party of cadres and militants without a mass base. It was subordinated to the PCI in other ways: first of all, most of its internal debates were directed not towards formulating a distinct political line but in establishing the degree of cooperation and of unity which it should have with the PCI. The most important feature of its National Council meeting of July 1945 was whether it should maintain its pact of unity with the PCI while keeping its own separate identity, or whether it should work for a fusion and the formation of a single large party of the working class.[49] The proponents of the first view (which obtained only 24% of the votes) formed the nucleus of the anti-communist Saragat faction which eventually left the PSI and formed the Social Democratic Party (PSDI). Secondly, the PSI was, from the very beginning connected to organizations already dominated by the PCI such as the cooperative movement, the leisure time and cultural organization ARCI and the trade union CGIL.[50] In foreign policy the PSI followed a relatively close pro-Soviet line until 1956 (its leader Nenni was awarded the Stalin prize).[51]

After the de-Stalinization process in the USSR and the invasion of Hungary the PSI began to become more independent from the PCI and tried to close the gap with Saragat's social democrats (who had been part of the DC centrist coalition since the late 1940s). This was the process which would eventually take the PSI to government in the 1960s. When it formed a Centre-Left government with the DC it suffered a split which led to the formation of the left-wing Socialist Party of Proletarian Unity (PSIUP). It was prepared to pay this price because it hoped that a formal merger with the PSDI would create a powerful 'lay pole' to counterbalance the power of the DC inside the coalition government. The new party, now called the Unified Socialist Party, was defeated at the 1968 elections. The disastrous results made it impossible to maintain the unity of the new party and socialists and social democrats went their separate ways once more.

All in all the experiment of the Centre-Left had been traumatic for the PSI. In the first place, it had to defend itself from the Left (the PCI and the left-socialists) while having to face the DC which was trying to sabotage the reform programme that was supposed to be the basis of the new coalition. In the second place, it began its transformation from a working-class party with a traditional base to a party of state and local government functionaries, of small entrepreneurs, of professional people and other urban groups.

When the workers' and students' movements emerged in 1968–69 the PSI tried to gain something from the PCI's obvious embarrassment at being outflanked from the left: it sought to become the institutional mediator between these social movements and the State, particularly as it had an advantage over the PCI: it actually was in government. In reality it gained nothing either politically or electorally while it resented the fact that the PCI could appear to have remained unsullied from the responsibilities of political power. When the PCI achieved its spectacular electoral success in 1976 the PSI was still stuck at around the 10 per cent mark. At that stage the socialist leadership felt it could no longer support a DC government on its own and let the PCI be the only opposition. In so doing the PSI increased the pressures on the DC to form a government of national unity with Giulio Andreotti as Prime Minister and with communist (and socialist) support.

The period of 'national unity' was a negative experience for the PSI. In the previous Centre-Left governments the PSI was essential to the stability of the government and was the second most important force, while the 'government of national unity' was based on a DC–PCI axis. To both the PCI and the DC the PSI seemed an irrelevancy. What the socialist deputies said in Parliament was hardly ever supported by the PCI who, in turn, had only one reference point: the DC. The communist attitude was further encouraged by the fact that the PSI played very little part in decision-making. Socialist deputies had a very high rate of absenteeism, and took very little interest in the policies being discussed. Out of 666 laws examined in those years the DC had expressed its official position in 94 per cent of the cases, the PCI in 90 per cent but the PSI in only 49 per cent.[52] The chief reason beyond this blatant socialist lack of interest in the policies of the government was that the PSI had an a priori negative view of the DC–PCI alliance, a view which, in the circumstances, was not entirely unjustified.

In this period the PSI was more concerned with the problem of reconstructing its own image and establishing what its long-term role would be in Italian society. Its official line was that it would work for a 'left-wing alternative' government, i.e. a PCI–PSI government which would exclude the DC. Considering that after 1979 the PSI tried to reconstitute the Centre-Left coalition and was in bitter polemic with the PCI it is difficult to establish how far this policy was taken seriously. However, in the period 1976–80 the main preoccupation of the PSI was to demarcate itself from both the DC and the PCI and the policy of 'left-wing alternative' – which was not then acceptable to the PCI – fulfilled this criterion and was sanctioned by two party congresses (the Fortieth in 1976 and the Forty-first in 1979) even though these also sanctioned the victory of the new leader, Bettino Craxi, whose distaste for the PCI had always been evident.[53]

The demoralization of the rank and file in those years can be illustrated by reference to the results of a survey conducted in 1978 among the delegates to the party's regional conferences: 72 per cent thought that the party had been too subordinated to the DC, 79 per cent thought that the party was too corrupt, 94 per cent that its chief weakness was that it was too badly organized. Only 45 per cent thought that the PSI ran the risk of being subordinated to the PCI in the case of a left-wing alliance (although among Craxi's own supporters this increases to 70%).[54]

The PSI was self-critically aware that it had a bad image and that it had failed to win votes in the 1976 elections when the rest of the Left had done so well. It realized that its members were increasingly concentrated in the tertiary sector and in the South while it was losing ground in the academic world, in the educational system and among the working class and the intellectuals. By 1979 it sought to present itself as the only party which could guarantee the 'governability' of the country: the DC was described as a traditional conservative party in decline while the PCI was a traditional working-class party condemned to be either a part of the 'support system' of the DC, as it had been in 1976–79, or a sectarian opposition. Thus the PSI could seek to occupy the 'central' position that the DC could no longer hold and the PCI could never hope to conquer.[55]

A battle on two fronts was necessary in order to obtain better representation at the central government level with the DC and at the local level with the PCI. The slogan of 'governability' meant essentially stable coalition governments and, as all stable coalitions need a central element, the PSI developed the image of the 'reformist party of the Centre'.

Not for the first time the PSI needed a new base on which to build its new image. After the hot autumn of 1969 it hoped to expand its working-class base: during the 1974 battle for the referendum on divorce it sought to become the party of modern secular Italy, and during the peak of terrorism and anti-terrorism legislation it tried to be the party of civil liberties against the 'repressive' tendencies of traditional catholicism and traditional communism.[56] The problem for the PSI is that the PCI had sufficient political resources and ability to manage, every time, to recuperate lost positions and to occupy or conquer these 'political spaces'. In Italy the PSI might have become the party of the progressive middle classes – an influential sector ill at ease in the DC and unwilling to support the PCI. Here, however, the PSI has had to compete not only with the DC but also with the other small parties of the Centre: social democrats, republicans and liberals.

In pursuing the 'Centre' the PSI cannot ignore the fact that the success of other European socialist parties has often coincided with their being identified not only with a new image of modernity and dynamism, but also with a radicalism of the Left: the electoral successes of the socialist parties of France, Spain and Greece has coincided with a diffuse desire for change. In the case of the Greeks and the Spaniards the success of the socialists has also been facilitated by the fact that they rose to power shortly after the defeat of authoritarian regimes and that they were able to build their support after the collapse of the previous regime.[57] The French Socialist Party was successful in the 1981 elections because it was able to be in alliance with the French Communist Party and yet clearly demarcated from them (this was made particularly easy by the sectarian behaviour of the French Communist Party). The PSI's problem is that it faces a communist party which is unlikely to repeat the mistakes of their French counterparts. Furthermore, the 1983 election showed that the Republican Party (PRI) was able to mobilize considerable support among those urban middle classes which had been the PSI's main target: thus the PRI became the third party after the PCI and the DC in Milan and Turin.

By 1984 the PSI had been successful in obtaining more power, but not more votes. It obtained the Prime Ministership, but with only 11 per cent of the votes it remained well below that 15 per cent which might enable it to reshuffle the cards of the political game.

REFERENCES AND NOTES

1. See Farneti, P. (1978), pp. 714–15.
2. The classic exposition of the thesis of the Risorgimento as an 'unfinished revolution' can be found in Gramsci, A. (1971), pp. 52–120.
3. The following discussion on the crisis of political parties is in part derived from Farneti (1978), pp. 717–19.
4. On the issue of secularization see Dalla Chiesa, N. (1983).
5. See the main proponents of this thesis: Eugenio Scalfari, E. and Turani, G. (1974); Galli, G. (1978); Galli, G. and Nannei, A. (1976).
6. Cassano, F. (1979).
7. See Orfei, R. (1976); Galli, G. (1966). Aldo Moro had written in 1974 that 'Realism forces us to accept those particularities which make less credible [in Italy] an alternance of political forces ... Italian democracy is a ... difficult democracy', in Moro, A. (1979), p. 298.
8. Baget-Bozzo, G. (1980), p. 69.
9. See Baget-Bozzo, G. (1974).
10. Baget-Bozzo (1980), pp. 37–50.
11. Cardia, C. (1979).
12. See Chiarante, G. (1980), p. 17; Giovagnoli, A. (1980); Moro, R. (1979).
13. See Chiarante, G. (1977), pp. 27–42; Scoppola, P. (1978), see also Chiarante's reply in the same issue; Ingrao, P. (1977), pp. 51–83.
14. Mastropaolo, A. (1973), pp. 316–17.
15. Cassano (1979), pp. 37–8.
16. Ibid., p. 65.
17. Ibid., p. 69.
18. Baget-Bozzo, G. (1977), p. 140.
19. Christian Democratic factionalism is a formalized affair and the relative strength of the various factions is calculated on a percentage basis. The following table gives an idea of the state of play in 1982.
20. Cassano (1979), p. 59.
21. Allum, P. A. (1973), has given the best account of the transition from traditional 'bossism' to a party-centred political machine, see in particular Chapter 9.
22. See Lanza, O. (1979), p. 181.
23. Menapace, L. (1974), pp. 45–9.
24. Cassano (1979), p. 76. See also Baget-Bozzo (1974) and (1977).
25. Amato, G. (1976), esp. pp. 157ff.
26. Bognetti, G. (1978).
27. Ibid., p. 88.
28. Ibid., p. 89.
29. Ibid., pp. 93–5.

Faction	Leaders	% strength	Regional strongholds
Zaccagnini 'Area Zac'	Zaccagnini Marcora Rognoni De Mita Andreatta Gullotti	27.76	Lombardy Emilia Romagna Tuscany Campania Sicily
Andreotti	Andreotti	15.36	Latium Sicily Apulia
Dorotei	Piccoli Bisaglia Gasperi Gava	23.62	Trentino Veneto Abruzzo Campania
Fanfani (Nuove Cronache)	Fanfani Forlani	13.59	Lombardy Tuscany Marche Umbria
Forze nuove	Donat Cattin V. Colombo	8.9	Piedmont Veneto
E. Colombo/ M. Rumor	E. Colombo M. Rumor	5.2	Basilicata Veneto
(others)		5.56	

30. See Chiarante, G. (1983), pp. 16–18.
31. Cassano (1979), pp. 53–4, 61–2. See also Donolo, C. (n.d.) pp. 121–4.
32. Asor Rosa, A. (1982), p. 6. In 1969 Aldo Moro was in a minority. The main centrist DC faction, the Dorotei, led by Mariano Rumor, though conscious of the need for reforms tried to continue the Centre-Left experiment while at the same time regularly consulting the PCI whose support they often needed in Parliament; see Mastropaolo (1973), p. 327.
33. See Chiarante (1980), pp. 84ff.
34. See Moro (1979), pp. 195–223.
35. Cassano (1979), pp. 108–10.
36. Valiani, L. (1973).
37. I have examined the development of the PCI's strategy in my *The Strategy of the Italian Communist Party. From the Resistance to the Historic Compromise* (Sassoon, 1981).
38. See Palmiro Togliatti's later comments in Togliatti, P. (1974), pp. 1073–4.
39. Togliatti, P. (1973), p. 56.
40. The objections to any return to centralization in the communist movement were reiterated in a confidential document written by Togliatti a few days before his death in Aug. 1964 and addressed to the Soviet

leadership. Known as the 'Yalta Memorandum' it was published in the PCI weekly *Rinascita* immediately afterwards (now in English in Togliatti, P., 1979).

41. A detailed analysis of the PCI's policy towards the EEC can be found in Sassoon (1976).

42. Berlinguer, E. (1975), p. 881.

43. Interview to the *Corriere della Sera*, 20 June 1976.

44. The resolution on Poland has been reprinted in Berlinguer, E. (1982), see in particular pp. 16 and 17.

45. Berlinguer's article on the Chilean events and the strategy of the historic compromise was published in three parts in successive issues of *Rinascita* (Sept. and Oct. 1973). An English translation appears in Berlinguer, E. (1974), the passage cited can be found on p. 41.

46. See Baldassare, A. and Di Giulio, F (1981), p. 6, and Napolitano, G. (1979), pp. xvii, xviii.

47. Cazzola, F. (1982), pp. 199–200.

48. For the PCI's role in moderating wages see Perulli, P. (1982).

49. See Pedone, F. (1968), pp. 53–5.

50. Carbone, G. (1982), pp. 339–40.

51. The PSI was the only Western socialist party to approve the merging of communist and socialist parties in Poland, Hungary and other East European countries. See Nenni, P. (1977), p. 90.

52. Cazzola (1982), pp. 188–9.

53. Pasquino, G. and Rossi, M. (1980), p. 83.

54. Ibid., p. 80.

55. Franchi, P. (1980), pp. 70–6.

56. Pasquino, G. (1982), pp. 325–9.

57. Pasquino, G. (1983), p. 37.

Chapter 14

A TENTATIVE CONCLUSION

Italy can be said to have been in continuous crisis since the war. In writing this I neither want to enlarge the concept so as to render it meaningless nor do I want to say that everything that has happened since 1945 has been negative. I simply want to underline the persistence of tensions which have characterized this whole period and their development.

Far from being 'immobile' Italy has changed enormously and rapidly, and many of these changes have been for the better. Compared to 1945 the average Italian is better fed, better housed, better educated, more literate and politically aware. The enormous gap which existed between Italians and Americans (and it is with the American model that all Italians compared their own country) has been considerably reduced. The average Italian may not be as well off as the Germans or the French, but is at least as rich as the English and has at least as many rights and civil liberties as other West European countries.

What has happened in these forty years is that Italy has become more similar to the rest of Europe. The same can probably be said of any other West European country. There is undoubtedly a process of continuous convergence. In terms of raw percentages Italy has a public expenditure roughly comparable to that of the other main West European countries and a similar level of welfare spending and public employment as Table 14.1 demonstrates.

In 1981 Italy spent a higher percentage of its GDP on education (6.4%) than the other top six Western industrial countries (USA, UK, Japan, West Germany, France and Canada), proportionately more on health (6.0%) than the UK, the USA, Canada and Japan and more on pensions (13.2%) than all of them except Japan.[1]

On the other hand, as we have repeatedly emphasized, Italy is the only country in Europe which has been ruled by the same political party since the war, even though this party has always needed coalition partners. We are thus faced by a paradox: no change in the political élites and massive changes in the social and economic fields. But, as has become

TABLE 14.1 Welfare and public expenditure and public sector employment in Europe

	Public expenditure Total outlay as a % of DP at current prices (1982)	Welfare expenditure as a % of total public expenditure (income maintenance, health and education, 1977)	Public sector employment as a % of total employment (1979)
Italy	47.4	56.5	20.6
W. Germany	48.6	54.8	22.5
France	51.6	65.3	23.3
UK	46.1	45.0	29.7
USA	45.4	52.3	18.0

Source: Therborn, G. (1984), pp. 27, 29, 34 (mainly based on OECD data)

evident, the paradox is only apparent: in order to survive and maintain its power bloc the Italian Christian Democratic Party (DC) has had to deal with the continuous crisis of the country by constantly changing strategies.

On the morrow of fascism the DC first took part in the Italian Resistance and then in postwar reconstruction in alliance with the socialist and communist forces of the Marxist Left. At the outset of the Cold War it linked its fate to that of the Western camp, to the USA and NATO, ousted the Left from the government, gave free rein to private accumulation while promulgating an agrarian reform, and established some form of economic control over those sections of the economy which private capital would not have been able to develop.

It was thus able to ride on the wave of the longest period of economic growth enjoyed by the West in this century. When this came to an end and when the underlying tensions which this kind of economic development (anarchic, uncoordinated, unplanned) were beginning to emerge, the DC resurfaced as a party of reform and of modernization. It split the Left separating the socialists from the communists in what was still the only country in Europe where this separation had not yet occurred. It systematically developed the State into the major economic force and subjected it to its own exclusive control. At the same time it loosened its ties with the Church and in its constant consensus-seeking trajectory colonized large segments of the private and public sectors.

It thus remained in control and in power, but had not provided the new republic with a wide and stable consensus: the student unrest of 1968 and the workers' explosion of 1969 testified to that. So the DC became the party of decentralization through the new regional legislation of 1970, it acceded to students' demands by expanding the university system and to workers' demands by promulgating the Workers' Statute in 1970. This did not resolve the crisis, though it changed it. More groups and social subjects emerged and demanded changes, and when the DC opposed these changes – as it did in 1974 when it tried via a referendum to abrogate the divorce law – it lost. Unable to cope with the economic consequences of the oil crisis of 1973, the DC was able, without any internal splits or major divisions, to turn to its only real opponent, the Italian Communist Party (PCI), and request its support in Parliament in 1976. It got this support for three years and was able to re-emerge and once more form Centre-Left governments with the Italian Socialist Party (PSI).

The DC may have ruled uninterruptedly and with no major change in personnel, except that which is imposed by the inexorable dance of time (no politician has ever been able to cope with death, particularly his or her own), but it has not stood still or immobile.

If the DC has changed, so has everybody else. The PCI, which had been forced by its past and by the circumstances to 'choose' the USSR when everyone else in Western Europe was turning to the USA, gradually and consistently abandoned the doctrine of 'Marxism-Leninism', opened its ranks to people of varying persuasions including Catholics, de-Stalinized thoroughly, accepted with increasing enthusiasm membership of the EEC and supported European federalism, accepted Italy's membership of NATO, disassociated itself from Soviet foreign policy, and supported a DC government for nearly three years.

The PSI, too, has had to change from being junior partner of the PCI in the 1940s and 1950s, to becoming a junior partner of the DC in the 1960s. Swinging repeatedly from Left to Right, perhaps unavoidably given its size and its position within the political spectrum, the PSI has increasingly espoused the cause of 'modernization', rejecting its traditions of a workers' party and becoming more and more a radical party of the Centre.

Everyone has changed then, but everyone has had to pay a price. The DC has maintained its power, but it has had to share it more and more with its coalition partners. Since 1975 it has lost control of many major Italian cities and by 1983 had the support of only one-third of the Italians (it had nearly 50% in 1948). It no longer knows what to do with its power except keep it. It has no perspective, no strategy, no long-term aim. Now it faces a Communist Party which topped the poll in the European elections of 1984. Perhaps the decline of the DC is inevitable, perhaps it will no longer be able to retain power. Yet it needs political power; first of all to maintain its links with its clientele system and the numerous interests it aggregates through the control it exercises on the public purse and, secondly, to avoid being broken apart by its constant internal factional struggle. This is a party which has built its entire political fortune on being the sole possible governing party of Italy, the foundation of the entire political system. No one knows what would happen to the DC if it found itself in opposition and whether it would know what to do.

As for the PSI, it has long ago discovered that it cannot influence the policies of the DC – this was the ambition it had in the 1960s when it participated in the Centre-Left governments. It remains in power with the DC in order to obtain a greater share of political and economic resources, seeking to establish its own clienteles and interests against those of the DC. In so doing it inevitably damages the DC but becomes, increasingly, another party of patronage and clienteles. Yet this has not paid off. Eight years after Bettino Craxi became leader of the PSI with the ambition of supplanting the PCI while weakening the DC, and one year after he became Prime Minister, the PSI was still stuck with less than 12 per cent of the votes.

It has been argued that these parties can no longer cope with the increasing complexities of the Italian political system and of Italian society. Such political complexity is well evidenced by the presence of ten political parties – all represented in Parliament through what is probably the most accurate system of proportional representation in Europe. Yet even these ten parties do not exhaust the options available: regional parties from the Val d'Aosta, the South Tyrol, Sardinia and Veneto are also represented in the Parliament elected in 1983 and, but for a few votes, even the party of old-age pensioners would have had a deputy in the Chamber of Deputies. Furthermore, there are not one, but three trade-union federations. Even these are not able to stop the development of new non-affiliated unions in the developing sectors of the economy which will be added to the old 'corporate unions' which existed among some sectors of the traditional skilled working class (nor must we forget that the neo-fascist party (MSI) has its own trade union: the Confederazione Italiana Sindacati Nazionali dei Lavoratori (CISNAL)). Every party has its own youth organization and its own women's organization, yet the bulk of organized women and youth are not in political parties and do not organize themselves in the way traditionally established by political parties.

Parties thus appear to be increasingly unable to cope with the complexities of modern Italy. But this is only partly true. Political parties can no longer represent everything, but the cause of this is not just 'more complexity' but also 'less resources'. Parties not only seek to 'represent interests' in a general way, but are also actively involved in a political market in which political resources are exchanged. Pressure groups and interest groups must seek the support of determinate political parties. These will give economic and political resources in exchange for political support. The model we are delineating is that of the modern Welfare State, i.e. a state which attempts to extend social protection to all groups or nearly all groups. In periods of severe economic depression the Welfare State is no longer able to expand, at times it has to contract and is therefore no longer able to extend social protection to all groups. Resources were distributed in an unequal manner even during periods of prosperity, but in sufficient quantity to ensure the legitimacy of all political parties who were protagonists of the market. In adverse economic conditions the choices are more difficult, some interests must be sacrificed. According to this view the crisis of all Italian political parties is due to the fact that most of them were competing on behalf of fairly similar groups, i.e. all tried to protect popular/working-class interests.

The third and most important aspect of the crisis of Italian political parties (but, obviously what I am writing about *Italian* parties can be applied to others) is the following: the principal point of reference of political parties is the nation-state and the institutions which are connected to it, and first of all the national Parliament. In the present era transnational corporations are able to escape national economic policies, international organizations tie nation-states in a thousand ways to complex international agreements, mass international communication systems penetrate deep into the national culture, transforming it into an aspect of a television-oriented world culture and, last but not least, a powerful military system backed by superpower technology reduces the hallowed limits of the traditional nation-state to cosmic insignificance.

In this situation it may not be surprising that national political parties are unable to offer solutions to pressing problems because the institutions they can use are all technically obsolete: they are all national in an era where there can be no national solution to crises.

I think there is something which is true in all these explanations: Italian society is too complex for the existing political parties, it is no longer possible to assume constant growth and thus resources are scarcer and, finally, the boundaries of the nation-state are too narrow.

Let us take as an example the oldest national question in Italy: the 'Agrarian Question' and the South. This is no longer a question of peasants and landlords. Now the 'Agrarian Question' must deal with an entire system of technical infrastructure, with a world market, with the advances of chemistry and biotechnology. It is now also the concern of technicians and experts of multinational firms. It is closely connected to the activities of the State and to the banking system. This means that the 'Agrarian Question' is no longer simply about the 'traditional' peasants but also about 'modern' social subjects: bankers and financiers, geologists and chemists, engineers and agronomists, etc. The 'Southern Question' in modern Italy is part and parcel of the mechanism of economic development and *hence* part of the political system because the central task of political decision-makers is to manage economic development. The concept of backwardness applied to the Italian South cannot deal with the complexities of the situation. There is, of course, 'backwardness', but it can only survive side by side with modernity by establishing some connections with it. If it were simply a question of backwardness then two solutions could be tried: one is to abandon the backward sector to its fate (the *laissez-faire* alternative) assuming it will gradually disappear unable to withstand the impact of modernity, the other is the technocratic solution: let us pour public funds into the South and modernize it directly, let us bring it up to the level of the North. Thanks to modern technology and the mixed economy, under-development will be transformed into development.

As we have seen in this book the South is not only an economic question, it is also a political one. In fact it is a textbook example of the impossibility of separating the two. Both the anti-interventionist liberal and the technocratic views assume that the kind of development which has occurred in the North is intrinsically valid. Yet this development has been financed by the systematic drainage of the South's sole resource: human labour. In exchange the South has received a constant stream of state funds which have underpinned the stability of the DC regime. This money is not directed towards 'modernization' but is channelled in a thousand directions under the supervision of all sorts of interest groups including the Mafia. When state funds cannot be used in this 'political' way, they remain unspent. In 1982 southern banks held public funds to the tune of 117,857 million lire (the rough equivalent of £50 million) which were supposed to be spent for child care as well as anti-natal and post-natal care. They remain idle; 1,679 publicly funded crèches were supposed to be developed; there are only 73 in the entire South.

Thus in the 1980s the Southern Question is not a matter of simple modernization, or of an increase in state funds. The role of the South cannot even be understood purely in terms of the Italian North, but must be thought of anew in terms of the relations between Italy and the rest of the EEC and the Mediterranean.

The key question then is the international role of the Italian South and therefore the international role of Italy. Here there is a considerable lack of ideas on the part of Italy's governing élite. Foreign policy has always taken a back seat and foreign economic policy has been virtually non-existent. The main reason why this book has not a separate chapter on foreign policy is that there is not much to say.[2] The twin pillars of Italian foreign policy have been NATO and the EEC. But membership of NATO has been interpreted as slavish adherence to whatever initiatives are undertaken by the United States. Membership of the EEC has been an opportunity for self-congratulation at the fact that the rest of Europe has recognized that Italy exists. As Gisele Podbielski has written in her report for the Association for the Development of Industry in the South (SVIMEZ):

> Successive governments did not have a clear and continuous view of the objectives they wanted to attain through European integration ... There was a certain passivity in the Italian participation in the Community decision mechanisms; this was also due to the fact that greater weight was

251

often given to the political importance of belonging to the Community than to defending the Italian point of view in negotiations on specific issues.[3]

The South, we have written, has had the fundamental task of transferring human resources to the North. It has also transferred human resources to the rest of Europe. Southern Italian labour can be found working in Belgian mines, in West German factories as well as in France and Switzerland. This drainage of labour came to an end at the beginning of the 1970s as the international recession ended the full-employment policies which had been a feature of most European countries. The sums sent back by workers abroad began to contract and public spending in the South now became the principal available resource.

In modern societies social conflicts tend to assume the form of conflicts over the distribution of economic resources. The South is no exception. The difference is that the conflict over dwindling resources has become increasingly violent and has led to the transformation of the Mafia into an independent economic and political force.[4]

Before 1945 the Mafia had been the servant of the landlords. Repressed by fascism it was reinstated in Sicily during the Second World War by the American Mafia in alliance with the US armed forces. Gradually it established political links with the local DC. Until the 1970s the Mafia was at the service of politicians. It delivered votes and financed political campaigns. In exchange it obtained local contracts, was allowed to develop protection rackets, was involved in tobacco smuggling, had a virtual monopoly over the water supply for agriculture and speculated in real estate.[5]

In the 1970s the explosion of new social conflicts could not avoid affecting the Mafia. The State was less and less able to control these conflicts because it tried to resolve the problem of economic development by simply sending more funds. These vast resources to be shared out provoked more violence. At the same time there was a wave of terrorism. Violence seemed to have become endemic. This highlighted the weakness of a political élite which seemed unable to fulfil its traditional 'law and order' obligations. It is at this stage that the Mafia became an independent economic force. Until then it had prospered within the DC system of power in the South. Now it became its own master: 'the entrepreneurial Mafia'. Old techniques were resurrected in order to finance modern economic activities. The shadow of state intervention was never very far from the aims of the new criminality: To cite just one example, in 1973 the kidnapping of Paul Getty Jr (whose ear had been sent back to his family to demonstrate – in time-honoured fashion – that he had really been kidnapped and that those who had done it were ready to kill) resulted in a 'profit' of 1,000 million lire (about £430,000). This was used to finance the purchase of a fleet of lorries which enabled the Mafia of Gioa Tauro in Calabria to obtain the monopoly of road haulage for the construction of a modern industrial harbour financed by the government to 'help' the development of the South.[6]

The real Mafia industry of the 1970s, however, has been heroin traffic. Until the late 1960s heroin had been essentially an American problem in the sense that most addicts were American. By the late 1970s there were proportionately more deaths caused by heroin in West Germany and more addicts in Italy than in the USA.[7] At the centre of this international racket is the Sicilian Mafia. This is an enterprise of authentic multinational dimensions: it involves importing opium from Pakistan, Afghanistan and Iran, its transformation into morphine in the Middle East and into heroin in Sicily. From there it is channelled to the USA and the other advanced industrial countries.

In most cases the initial capital outlay to finance the Sicilian operation came from the Italian State.[8] These are the vast funds which successive Italian governments have earmarked for the Sicilian region. Many of these sums have remained unspent in southern banks, thus providing liquid capital which could be injected into the circulation network of the Mafia economy. Furthermore, the Italian government has for many years used private firms (controlled by a handful of Mafia families) to collect local taxes, allowing them to keep 10 per cent of the moneys collected in payment. This has put enormous sums at the disposal of four leading Mafia families and has allowed them to enter the international heroin market. The revenues from this enterprise are in part ploughed back into the heroin business, in part invested in legal enterprises and in part sent to Swiss and Latin American banks. The Latin American connection is important because it links the Mafia to the activities of Italian financiers such as Umberto Ortolani and Licio Gelli (both currently wanted by the Italian police). Gelli had used his financial contacts and his numerous banks to recycle Mafia money in all directions. A favoured area of investment was the international traffic of arms. He was able to do so through his contacts with Latin American freemasonry and with the military in Argentina, Brazil, Peru, Paraguay, etc. His good offices were much appreciated to the extent that he hired the DC8 which former dictator Juan Perón used for his triumphant return to Argentina from exile in 1972. Gelli accompanied him on the flight.[9]

Licio Gelli was the head of the secret freemason lodge P2 whose members include leading Italian politicians. The connections between Licio Gelli and the Mafia have been clearly established. Gelli was also closely connected to Roberto Calvi, the Italian banker later found hanging from Blackfriars Bridge in London. The causes of his death have remained mysterious. Calvi's bank, the Banco Ambrosiano, had been acting for the Vatican to whom it had lent enormous sums. The Banco Ambrosiano had also acquired controlling interest in the *Corriere della Sera*, the leading Italian paper. Gelli's own connections with the USA are well established through the Italo-American circuit.

He was even invited to attend the inaugurations of Presidents Carter and Reagan (1981).[10]

Gelli's secret organization, the P2, was exposed in May 1981 when a membership list containing 962 names was found. What were the functions of the P2? In the first place it sought to acquire information through its extensive political contacts. The purpose of this information was political blackmail. Secondly, it sought to create a 'party' which remains in the shadows and connects people in key political and economic positions. The P2 can be everywhere precisely because it is hidden. Through its contacts in the secret services (and its network of informers) it acquired important files and contacts with terrorism. The people who – according to the documents found – are members of the P2 are important figures. We find Pietro Longo, leader of the Social Democratic Party and Budget Minister in the Craxi government of 1983–85. He was eventually forced to resign in July 1984 but remained at the head of his party. There were also leading socialists: Silvano Labriola and Enrico Manca, important Christian Democrats such as Gaetano Stammati and Massimo De Carolis, highly placed Civil Servants in the Ministries of Foreign Affairs, Trade and in the Treasury. Of the 195 members of the armed forces whose names were found on the P2 lists there were 12 generals of the Carabinieri, 22 generals of the Army, 8 admirals, 4 Air Force generals, the head of the Navy chiefs of staff and the heads of Italy's secret services as well as judges, journalists, and media tycoons.[11]

Most of those named have denied that they have ever been members. A Parliamentary Committee of Enquiry was set up in 1981 under the presidency of a Christian Democrat, Tina Anselmi, who reported in July 1984 to Parliament. The report declares that all members of the P2 lodge were responsible for belonging to an organization 'whose aim was to intervene secretly in the political life of the country', and maintains that virtually all those named in the list really were members of the P2.[12]

I could of course go on narrating a story which seems to come straight from a best-selling novel. I have wanted to bring these facts to the reader's attention to show some of the direct connections which link state intervention, the DC, the Southern Question, the Mafia, the P2, the USA, the banking system, etc. I have directed my attention to the Southern Question and the Mafia because these are two issues which – to many people – seem to be the hallmark of the backwardness of Italy. It is clearly not a question of backwardness: the present misery of the Italian South has extremely modern aspects, they are features not of underdevelopment but of a modern political system. As for the Mafia, it has obviously modernized itself remarkably by becoming a multinational organization. Modern *mafiosi* may use the murderous techniques they have inherited from the past, but they are at home in international financial circles.

We began this story with Italy entering the world market after the years of fascist autarky and the war. Inevitably, it did so from a position of weakness and yet was able to carve for itself a niche in the international division of labour.

Now its international position is weaker than ever. It has the highest inflation rate of the OECD countries, higher-than-average unemployment, the highest public debt. At the same time it no longer controls – if it ever did – its exchange rates or its interest rates. Furthermore, Italy must operate in an international economic system which is without rules.[13] Under the rules established by the Bretton Woods Conference of 1944 (fixed exchange rates, no exchange restrictions, currency convertibility and a multilateral system of international payments) Italy had a clearly defined subordinate position: a 'niche'. Now all this is over. The rule which prevails is that of unilateral action on the part of the USA through interest rates while international liquidity – which has grown spectacularly since the oil crisis – is in the hands of private banks able to influence the process of development of Third World countries. A country such as Italy cannot face this system on its own and cannot face it with the same kind of political regime it has had for the past forty years. The only existing alternative to it is a government which has the PCI as its fundamental force. The PCI is, of course, only too conscious of the fact that it cannot hope to escape the constraints of the international system any more than the DC. In fact the chances are that it would find it more difficult because it cannot expect any goodwill on the part of the superpower within whose sphere of influence it has had to operate. Nor can it expect much help from the USSR. The Soviet leaders are unlikely to be favourably disposed towards a party which owes a large measure of its political success to its independence from Moscow and whose entire foreign policy is aimed at reversing the process of division of Europe which began during the Second World War. Furthermore, the PCI is the only main left-wing European political party which is in the special position of being the country's leading reformist party and yet never having been able to control directly the implementation of those social reforms it has advocated and fought for.[14]

The PCI has always tried to live up to its slogan of being both 'a party of government and a party of struggle', but so far it has never been put to the actual test of government, though it can perhaps claim to be the best opposition party in Europe.

Thus with a governing party which no longer knows how to rule and an opposition which has never governed (and perhaps never will) Italy faces the future.

BIBLIOGRAPHY OF WORKS CITED

Note: The abbreviation AA.VV. denotes various authors.

Accornero, Aris (1978) 'Il rapporto dei giovani con la società: il lavoro', in Istituto Gramsci, *La crisi della società italiana e le nuove generazioni,* Ed. Riuniti, Rome.

Accornero, Aris and Carmignani, F. (1978a) 'La "giungla" delle retribuzioni', in G. Pinnaró (Ed.) *L'Italia socio-economica 1976-77,* Ed. Riuniti, Rome.

Accornero, Aris and Carmignani, F. (1978b) 'Classe sociale e modificazioni nella struttura sociale' in G. Pinnaró (Ed.) *L'Italia socio-economica 1976-77,* Ed. Riuniti, Rome.

Addario, Nicoló (1982) *Una crisi di sistema,* De Donato, Bari.

Ajello, Nello (1980) 'Il settimanale d'attualità', in V. Castronovo and N. Tranfaglia (Eds) *Storia della stampa italiana,* Laterza, Rome-Bari.

Alberoni, Francesco (1970) *Classi e generazioni,* Il Mulino, Bologna.

Alberoni, Francesco (1979) 'Movimenti e istituzioni nell'Italia tra il 1960 e il 1971', in Luigi Graziano and Sidney Tarrow (Eds) *La crisi italiana,* 2 vols, Einaudi, Turin.

Aldcroft, Derek H. (1978) *The European Economy 1914-1980,* Croom Helm, London.

Allum, P. A., *Politics and Society in Post-War Naples,* CUP, 1973.

Allum, P. A. (1973) *Italy – Republic without Government?,* Weidenfeld and Nicolson, London.

Allum, P. A. (1972) 'The South and national politics, 1945-1950', in S. J. Wolf (Ed.) *The Rebirth of Italy, 1943-50,* Longman, London.

Amato, Giuliano (1976) *Economia, politica e istituzioni in Italia,* Il Mulino, Bologna.

Amato Giuliano (1980) *Una Repubblica da riformare,* Il Mulino, Bologna.

Amendola, Giorgio (1968) 'I comunisti e il movimento studentesco, necessità della lotta su due fronti', *Rinascita,* 7 June.

Amendola, Giorgio (1979) 'Interrogativi sul "caso" Fiat', *Rinascita,* 9 Nov.

Ammassari Paolo (1977) *Classi e ceti nella società italiana,* Edizioni della Fondazione Giovanni Agnelli, Turin.

Amoroso, B. and Olsen, O. J. (1978) *Lo Stato imprenditore,* Laterza, Rome-Bari.

Andreotti, Giulio (1977) *Intervista su De Gasperi,* Laterza, Rome-Bari.

Anselmi, Tina (1984) *Relazione della commissione parlamentare d'inchiesta sulla loggia massonica P2*, Camera dei Deputati e Senato della Repubblica, Doc. XXIII, no. 2, 12 July, Rome (Anselmi Commission Report).

Apter, D. and Eckstein, H. (Eds) (1963) *Comparative Politics* The Free Press, New York.

Ardigò, A. (1966) 'La condizione giovanile nella societa industriale' in AA.VV. *Questioni di sociologia II*, La scuola, Brescia.

Arlacchi, Pino (1983) *La mafia imprenditrice. L'etica mafiosa e lo spirito del capitalismo*, Il Mulino, Bologna.

Asor Rosa, Alberto (1982) 'La cultura politica del compromesso storico', *Laboratorio Politico*, nos. 2–3.

Asor Rosa, Alberto (1981) 'Il giornalista: appunti sulla fisiologia di un mestiere difficile', in Corrado Vivanti (Ed.) *Storia d'Italia. Annali 4. Intellettuali e potere*, Einaudi, Turin.

Baget-Bozzo, Gianni (1974) *Il Partito Cristiano al potere. La DC di De Gasperi e di Dossetti 1945–1954*, Vallecchi, Florence.

Baget-Bozzo, Gianni (1977) *Il Partito Cristiano e l'apertura a sinistra. La DC di Fanfani e di Moro 1954–1962*, Vallecchi, Florence.

Baget-Bozzo, Gianni (1979) *Questi cattolici*, Ed. Riuniti, Rome.

Baget-Bozzo, Gianni (1980) *Tesi sulla DC. Rinasce la questione nazionale*, Cappelli, Bologna.

Bagnasco, A. (1977) *Le tre Italie*, Il Mulino, Bologna.

Balbo, Laura (1976) *Stato di Famiglia*, Etas Libri, Milan.

Balbo, Laura (1978) 'La doppia presenza', *Inchiesta*, vol. 8, no. 32.

Baldassare, A. and Di Giulio, F. (1981) 'Lotta politica e riforme istituzionali', *Democrazia e Diritto*, no. 5.

Baratta, P., Izzo, L., Pedone, A., Roncaglia, A. and Sylos Labini, Paolo (1978) *Prospettive dell'economia italiana*, Laterza, Rome–Bari.

Barbano, F. (1979) 'Mutamenti nella struttura sociale delle classi e crisi (1950–1975)', in Luigi Graziano and Sidney Tarrow (Eds), *La Crisi italiana*, 2 vols, Einaudi, Turin.

Barbera, Augusto (1975) 'Articolo 2', in Branca G. (Ed.) *Commentario della Costituzione. Principi Fondamentali*, Zanichelli and Il Foro Italiano, Bologna and Rome.

Barbera, Augusto (1979) 'Le Regioni dieci anni dopo', *Democrazia e Diritto*, no. 6.

Barbera, Augusto (1981) 'Le componenti politico-culturali del movimento autonomistico negli anni '70 (appunti da sviluppare)', mimeo.

Barclays Bank (1984) *InternationalEconomic Survey*, Dec.

Bassi, P. and Pilati, A. (1978) *I giovani e la crisi degli anni settanta*, Ed. Riuniti.

Battaglia Filippo (1980) *L'allergia al lavoro*, Ed. Riuniti, Rome.

Berlinguer, Enrico (1974) 'Reflections after the Events in Chile', *Marxism Today*, Feb.

Berlinguer, Enrico (1975) *La Questione comunista*, 2 vols, (Ed.) Riuniti, Rome.

Berlinguer, Enrico (1982) *After Poland*, Spokesman Books, Nottingham.

Bianchi, Marina (1979) 'La condizione femminile nella crisi del "Welfare State"', *Critica Marxista*, vol. 17, no. 5.

Birindelli, Anna Maria (1976) 'The postwar Italian emigration to Europe in particular to the EEC member countries', *Census*, vol. 32, nos. 1–2.

Boccia, Maria Luisa (1980) 'I tempi lunghi del rapporto donne-politica', *Rinascita*, 22, 30 May.

Bognetti, Giovanni (1978) 'Stato e economia in Italia: "Governo spartitorio" o crisi del "modello democratico-sociale" ', *Il Politico*, vol. 43, no. 1.

Braghin, P., Mingione, E. and Trivellaro, P. (1974) 'Per un'analisi della struttura di classe dell'Italia contemporanea', *La Critica Sociologica*, no. 30.

Branca, G. (Ed.) (1975) *Commentario della Costituzione, Principi Fondamentali*, Zanichelli and Il Foro Italiano, Bologna and Rome.

Caldwell, Lesley (1978) 'Church, State and family: the women's movement in Italy', in Annette Kuhn and AnnMarie Wolpe (Eds) *Feminism and Materialism*, Routledge and Kegan Paul, London.

Calise, Mauro and Mannheimer, Renato (1979) 'I governi "misurati". Il trentennio democristiano', *Critica Marxista*, no. 6.

Calise, Mauro and Mannheimer, Renato (1982) *Governanti in Italia*, Il Mulino, Bologna.

Calvaruso, Claudio (1980) 'Rientro dei migranti e condizione delle collettività italiane in Europa', *Civitas*, vol. 31, no. 1.

Calza Bini, P. (1973) 'Problemi per un'analisi delle classi in Italia', *Inchiesta*, July.

Candeloro, Giorgio (1982) *Il movimento cattolico in Italia*, Ed. Riuniti, Rome (4th edn).

Cantelli, Paolo (1980) *L'economia sommersa*, Ed. Riuniti, Rome.

Carbone, Giuseppe (1982) 'Il difficile modello di un partito secondo', *Il Mulino*, vol. 31, no. 281, May–June.

Cardia, Carlo (1979) 'L'area cattolica dopo il 20 giugno 1976', *Critica Marxista*, vol. 17, no. 1.

Cardia, Carlo (1979) 'La Democrazia Cristiana: dalle origini cattoliche alla gestione dello Stato', *Democrazia e Diritto*, no. 2.

Carli, Guido (1946) 'La disciplina degli scambi con l'estero e dei cambi nell'esperienza recente', *Critica economica*, no. 3.

Carli, Guido (1977) *Intervista sul capitalismo italiano*, Laterza, Rome–Bari.

Carmignani, Fabrizio (1980) 'Mercato del lavoro e identità giovanile', *Rinascita*, no. 45, 14 Nov.

Casmiri, Silvana (1980) 'Mondo cattolico, questione agraria e questione contadina', in AA.VV. *Campagne e movimento contadino nel Mezzogiorno d'Italia*, De Donato, Bari.

Cassano, Franco (1979) *Il teorema democristiano*, De Donato, Bari.

Castellino, O. (1976) *Il labirinto delle pensioni*, Il Mulino, Bologna.

Castles, Stephen and Kosack, Godula (1973) *Immigrant Workers and Class Structure in Western Europe*, OUP.

Castronovo, Valerio (1975) *La Storia Economica Storia d'Italia*, vol. IV, part I, Einaudi, Turin.

Castronovo, Valerio (1980) *L'Industria italiana dall'Ottocento a oggi*, Mondadori, Milan.

Castronovo, Valerio (1981) 'Cultura e sviluppo industriale', in Corrado Vivanti (Ed.) *Storia d'Italia. Annali 4. Intellettuali e potere*, Einaudi, Turin.

Cazzola, Franco (1972) 'Consenso e opposizione nel parlamento italiano. Il ruolo del PCI dalla I alla IV Legislature', *Rivista Italiana di Scienza politica*.

Cazzola, Franco (Ed.) (1979) *Anatomia del potere DC. Enti pubblici e 'centralità democristiana'*, De Donato, Bari.

Cazzola, Franco (1982) 'La solidarietà nazionale dalla parte del Parlamento', *Laboratorio Politico*, nos. 2/3.

Cazzola, Franco (1982) 'Partiti e coalizioni nei governi locali. Primi risultati di una ricerca', *Democrazia e Diritto*, no. 5, Sept–Oct.

Cecchi, Amos (1975) 'Le nuove generazioni nella società italiana', *Critica Marxista*, vol. 13, no. 1.

Centro Riforma dello Stato (1983) 'I termini attuali della questione istituzionale', *Democrazia e Diritto*, no. 1.

Cesareo, Giovanni (1981) 'Il "politico" nell'alba del quaternario', *Problemi del Socialismo*, vol. 22, no. 22.

Chiarante, Giuseppe (1977) 'A proposito della questione democristiana', *Critica Marxista*, no. 3.

Chiarante, Giuseppe (1979) 'Il papato di Wojtyla: la Chiesa del dopo-Concilio', *Critica Marxista*, vol. 17, no. 4.

Chiarante, Giuseppe (1979) 'Ragioni e declino della "centralità" democristiana', *Critica Marxista*, no. 5.

Chiarante, Giuseppe (1980) *La Democrazia cristiana*, (Ed.) Riuniti, Rome.

Chiarante, Giuseppe (1983) 'Tre ipotesi sulla DC di De Mita', *Critica Marxista*, vol. 21, no. 1.

Chiesi, Antonio (1975) 'Alcune note sulla distribuzione dei redditi e la struttura di classe in Italia nel periodo postbellico', *Quaderni di Sociologia*, vol. 24, no. 3.

Chinnici, Rocco (1982) 'Magistratura e mafia', *Democrazia e Diritto*, vol. 22, no. 4, July–Aug.

Coda-Nunziante, G. and De Nigris, M. (1970) 'Projections for food and agricultural products to 1972 and 1975', in A. M. M. McFarquhar (Ed.) *Europe's Future Food and Agriculture*, Amsterdam.

Colajanni, Napoleone (1976) *Riconversione grande impresa partecipazioni statali*, Feltrinelli, Milan.

Comito, Vincenzo (1982) *La FIAT tra crisi e ristrutturazione*, (Ed.) Riuniti, Rome.

Compagna, Francesco and Muscara, Calogero (1980) 'Regionalism and social change in Italy', in Gottman Jean (Ed.) *Centre and Periphery. Spatial Variation in Politics*, Sage, London.

Cotta, Maurizio (1976) 'Classe politica e istituzionalizzazione del Parlamento: 1946–1972', *Rivista Italiana di Scienza Politica*, no. 1.

Cotturri, Giuseppe, (1982) 'Abolire il bicameralismo?', *Rinascita*, no. 21, 4 June.

Cotturri, Giuseppe (1982) 'Quale potere per il Sud?' *Rinascita*, no. 29, 30 July.

Cotturri Giuseppe (1983) 'Il sistema politico italiano dopo il voto del 26 giugno', *Democrazia e Diritto*, no. 5.

Cutrufelli, Maria Rosa (1980) 'Il circolo del lavoro e degli affetti', *Rinascita*, no. 29, 18 July.

D'Alemma, Giuseppe (1983) 'La P2 e le connessioni economiche, finanziarie e politiche internazionali', in Marco Ramat *et al. La Resistibile ascesa della P2*, De Donato, Bari.

D'Antonio, Mariano (1973) *Sviluppo e crisi del capitalismo italiano 1951–1972*, De Donato, Bari.

D'Antonio, Mariano (1977) 'Questioni di politica economica: l'esperienza italiana', in AA.VV. *Lezioni di economia. Aspetti e problemi dello sviluppo economico italiano e dell'attuale crisi internazionale*, Feltrinelli, Milan.

Dalla Chiesa, Nando (1983) 'Dai bisogni alla politica. Una riflessione sui referendum del 1981', *Democrazia e Diritto*, no. 2.

Daneo, Camillo (1975) *La politica economica della Ricostruzione 1945–1949*, Einaudi, Turin.

De Cecco, Marcello (1971) 'Lo sviluppo dell'economia italiana e la sua collocazione internazionale', *Rivista Internazionale di Scienze Economiche e Commerciali*, Oct.

De Cecco, Marcello (1972) 'Economic policy in the reconstruction period, 1945–1951', in S. J. Woolf (Ed.) *The Rebirth of Italy*, Longman, London.

De Grand, Alexander (1976) 'Women under Italian fascism', *The Historical Journal*, vol. 19, no. 4.

Department of Health and Social Security (1975) *Social Security Statistics*, HMSO.

Di Palma, Giuseppe (1979) 'Risposte parlamentari alla crisi del regime: un problema di istituzionalizzazione', in Luigi Graziano and Sidney Tarrow (Eds) *La crisi italiana*, 2 vols, Einaudi, Turin.

Doglio, Daniele (1981) 'Crisi e prospettive dei servizi pubblici radiotelevisivi, in Giuseppe Richeri (ed.) *Il video negli anni 80*, De Donato, Bari.

Donolo, Carlo (n.d.) 'Sviluppo ineguale e disgregazione sociale. Note per l'analisi delle classi nel Meridione', *Quaderni Piacentini*, no. 47.

Elia, Leopoldo (1970) 'Forme di governo', in *Enciclopedia del diritto*, vol. 19, Giuffrè, Milan.

Fabiani, Guido (1977) 'Agricoltura e mezzogiorno', in AA.VV. *Lezioni di economia. Aspetti e problemi dello sviluppo economico italiano e dell'attuale crisi internazionale*, Feltrinelli, Milan.

Fabiani, Guido (1980) 'Per quale agricoltura: un nodo della trasformazone', *Problemi della Transizione*, no. 3.

Falzone, V., Palermo, F. and Cosentino, F. (Eds) (1976) *La Costituzione della Repubblica italiana*, Mondadori, Milan.

Farneti, Paolo (Ed.) (1973) *Il sistema politico italiano*, Il Mulino, Bologna.

Farneti, Paolo (1976) 'I partiti politici e il sistema di potere', in AA.VV. *L'Italia Contemporanea*, Einaudi, Turin.

Farneti, Paolo (1978a) 'The troubled partnership: trade unions and working class parties in Italy, 1948–1978', *Government and Opposition*, vol. 13, no. 4,.

Farneti, Paolo (1978b) 'Elementi per un'analisi della crisi del partito di massa', *Democrazia e diritto*, vol. 18, nos. 5/6.

Federmeccanica (1984) 'Imprese e lavoro', mimeo, 30 Nov.

Fedele Marcello (1975) 'Il loro rapporto con la società', in *Rinascita*, no. 22, 30 May.

Fichera, Franco (1982) 'Le regioni: dalla programmazione ai "governi parziali" ' *Democrazia e Diritto*, no. 1.

Filippini, Giovanna (1978) 'Movimenti femminili, femminismo', in Istituto Gramsci, *La crisi della società italiana e gli orientamenti delle nuove generazioni*, Ed. Riuniti, Rome.

Filosa, Renato and Visco, Ignazio (1980) 'Costo del lavoro, indicizzazione e perequazione delle rettribuzioni negli anni '70', in Giangiacomo Nardozzi (Ed.) *I difficili anni 70. I problemi della politica economica italiana 1973/1979*, Etas Libri, Milan.

Finocchiaro, Francesco (1975) 'Articoli 7–8' in Branca G. (Ed.) *Commentario della Costituzione. Principi Fondamentali*, Zanichelli and Il Foro Italiano, Bologna and Rome.

Fisichella, D. (1975) 'The Italian experience', in S. E. Finer (Ed.) *Adversary Politics and Electoral Reform*, Anthony Wignam, London.

Forcellini, Paolo (1978) *Rapporto sull'industria italiana*, Ed. Riuniti, Rome.

Forte, Francesco (1966) *La congiuntura in Italia*, 1961–1965, Einaudi, Turin.

Forte Francesco (1974) 'L'impresa: grande piccola, pubblica privata' in F. L. Cavazza and S. R. Graubard (Eds) *Il caso italiano*, vol. 2, Garzanti, Milan.

Fracassi, Claudio (1982) 'Poltrona per poltrona tutto il potere lottizato alla Rai-TV' *Paese Sera*, 6 Mar.

Franchi, Paolo (1980) 'Il PSI e la sinistra', *Critica Marxista*, vol. 18, no. 6.

Frey, Luigi (1981) *Tendenze dell'occupazione*, Bulletin of CERES, Jan.

Fuà, Giorgio and Sylos Labini, Paolo (1963) *Idee per la programmazione economica*, Laterza, Bari.

Galgano, Francesco (1978) *Le istituzioni dell'economia di transizione*, Ed. Riuniti, Rome.

Galli, Giorgio (1966) *Il bipartitismo imperfetto*, Il Mulino, Bologna.

Galli, Giorgio and Nannei, A. (1976) *Il capitalismo assistenziale. Ascesa e declino del sistema economico italiano 1960–1975*, Sugarco, Milan.

Galli, Giorgio (1978) *Storia della DC*, Laterza, Rome–Bari.

Gambino, Antonio (1975) *Storia del Dopoguerra. Dalla Liberazione al potere DC*, Laterza, Rome–Bari.

Garavini, Sergio (1974) *Crisi economica e ristrutturazione industriale*, Ed. Riuniti, Rome.

Garavini, Sergio (1977) 'La struttura industriale italiana e la crisi dell'impresa', *Critica Marxista*, vol. 15, no. 1.

Garelli, Franco (1977) 'Istituzione ecclesiale e mutamento sociale', *Quaderni di Sociologia*, vol. 26, no. 2.

Gasbarrone, Mara (1984) 'Le donne e il terziario', *Quaderni di Azione Sociale*, vol. 33, no. 33.

Gentiloni, Stefano (1980) 'L'informazione dopo la riforma', in G. Vacca (Ed.), Comunicazioni di massa e democrazia, Ed. Riuniti, Roma.

Ghezzi, Giorgio (1980) 'Il sistema negoziale delle informazioni e della consultazione del sindacato nell'attuale contesto politico sociale', in Carlo Smuraglia *et al.* (Eds) *La democrazia industriale*, Ed. Riuniti, Rome.

Ghezzi, Giorgio (1981) *Processo al sindacato*, De Donato, Bari.

Ghini, Celso (1975) *Il voto degli italiani*, Ed. Riuniti, Rome.

Giovagnoli, Agostino (1980) 'Sulla formazione della classe dirigente democristiana' Il Mulino, vol. 29, no. 267, Jan.–Feb.

Gottman, Jean (Ed.) (1980) *Centre and Periphery. Spatial Variation in Politics*, Sage, London.

Gramsci, Antonio (1971) *Selections from the Prison Notebooks*, Quintin Hoare and Geoffrey Nowell-Smith (Eds and trans.) Lawrence and Wishart, London.

Graziani, Augusto *et al.* (1969) *Lo sviluppo di una economia aperta*, ESI, Naples.

Graziani, Augusto (1969) *Lo sviluppo dell'economia italiana come sviluppo di un'economia aperta*, Fondazione Agnelli, Turin.

Graziani, Augusto (Ed.) (1971) *L'economia italiana: 1945–1970*, Il Mulino, Bologna.

Graziani, Augusto and Meloni, Franca (1980) 'Inflazione e fluttuazione della lira' in Giangiacomo Nardozzi (ed.) *I difficili anni '70. I problemi della politica economica italiana 1973/1979*, Etas Libri, Milan.

Graziano, Luigi and Tarrow, Sidney (Eds) (1979) *La crisi italiana*, 2 vols, Einaudi, Turin.

Grussu, Silvino (1984) 'Ascesa e declino dell'operaio massa', *Rinascita*, no. 22, 2 June.

ILO (1965) *Bulletin of Labour Statistics* (first quarter).

Ingrao, Pietro (1977) *Masse e potere*, Ed. Riuniti, Rome.

Ingrao, Pietro (1982) *Tradizione e progetto*, De Donato, Bari.

Isenburg, Teresa (1980) 'La popolazione', in *Storia della Società Italiana* vol. 14: *Il Blocco di potere nell'Italia unita*, Teti Editore, Milan.

Isnenghi, M. (1979) *Intellettuali militanti e intellettuali funzionari. Appunti sulla cultura fascista*, Einaudi, Turin.

Istituto Gramsci (1978) *La crisi della società italiana e le nuove generazioni*, (Ed.) Riuniti, Rome.

Jaggi, Max., Muller, Roger and Schmidt, Sil (1977) *Red Bologna*, Writers and Readers, London.

Jerkov, Antonio (1966) 'Alcune considerazioni sul concilio', *Problemi del Socialismo*, vol. 8, no. 6, Jan.–Feb.

John Paul II (1979) *Redemptor Hominis* (4 Mar. 1979), Ed. Paoline.

Kindleberger, Charles (1964) *Economic Development*, McGraw-Hill, New York.

Laconi Renzo (1947) 'La regione nella nuova Costituzione italiana', *Rinascita*, no. 7, July.

Lama, Luciano (1976) *Intervista sul sindacato*, Laterza, Rome-Bari.

Lanchester, Fulco (1981) *Sistemi elettorali e forma di governo*, Il Mulino, Bologna.

Lanza, Orazio (1979) 'Gli enti del settore agricolo', in Franco Cazzola (Ed.), *Anatomia del potere DC. Enti pubblici e 'centralitá democristiana'*, De Donato, Bari.

Leonardi, Robert, Nanetto, Raffaella and Pasquino, Gianfranco (1978) 'Institutionalization of Parliament and parliamentarization of parties in Italy', *Legislative Studies Quarterly*, no. 1, Feb.

Libertini, Lucio (1976) 'Fascismo e antifascismo nella politica delle forze economiche', in Guido Quazza (Ed.) *Fascismo e antifascismo nell'Italia repubblicana*, Stampatori, Turin.

Livolsi, M. (1976) 'Il fenomeno giovanile come sottosistema culturale', *Studi di Sociologia*, no. 3.

Lombardo Radice, Lucio (1967) 'Intervento sulla Populorum Progressio', *Problemi del Socialismo*, vol. 9, no. 18, May.

Longo, Luigi (1968) 'Il movimento studentesco nella lotta anti-capitalista', *Rinascita*, 3 May.

Maddison, Angus (1982) *Phases of Capitaist Development*, OUP.

Mafai, Miriam (1979) *L'apprendistato della politica. Le donne italiane nel dopoguerra*, (Ed.) Riuniti, Rome.

Magister, Sandro (1979) *La politica Vaticana e l'Italia 1943–1978*, (Ed.) Riuniti, Rome.

Maitan, Livio (1975) *Dinamica delle classi sociali in Italia*, Savelli, Rome.

Mancina, Claudia (1981) *La Famiglia*, (Ed.) Riuniti, Rome.

Mancini, G. F. (1975) 'Articolo 4' in Branca G. (Ed.) *Commentario della Costituzione. Principi Fondamentali,* Zanichelli and Il Foro Italiano, Bologna and Rome.

Mangoni, Luisa (1974) *L'interventismo della cultura. Intellettuali e riviste del fascismo,* Laterza, Bari.

Mannheimer, Renato and Sebastiani, Chiara (1978) 'Lavoro e condizione sociale', in Pinnaró Gabriella (Ed.) *L'Italia Socio-economica 1976–77,* Riuniti, Rome.

Mannheimer, Renato (1979) 'Un'analisi territoriale del calo comunista', *Il Mulino,* no. 265, Sept.–Oct.

Mannheimer, Renato and Biorcio, Roberto (1985) 'Autoritratto dell'elettore communista', *Rinascita,* no. 10, 23 Mar.

Maranini, G. (1967) *Storia del potere in Italia 1848–1947,* Vallecchi, Florence.

Mastropaolo, Alfio (1973) 'I partiti e la societa civile', in P. Farneti (Ed.) *Il sistema politico italiano,* Il Mulino, Bologna.

Mattelard, A. (1979) *Multinational Corporations and the Control of Culture,* Harvester, Brighton.

Melucci, Alberto, 'Dieci ipotesi per l'analisi dei nuovi movimenti' in *Quaderni Piacentini,* vol. 17, nos. 65–66, Feb.

Menapace, Lidia (1974) *La Democrazia cristiana. Natura struttura e organizzazione,* Mazzotta, Milan.

Milanesi, G. (1976) 'Religious identity and political commitment in the Christian for Socialism Movement in Italy', *Social Compass,* vol. 23, no. 2–3.

Modica, Enzo (1983) 'Come non è stata applicata la Costituzione' in *Regione Aperta,* vol. 13, no. 2, Mar.

Moro, Aldo (1979) *L'intelligenza e gli avvenimenti. Testi 1959–1978,* Garzanti, Milan.

Moro, Renato (1979) *La formazione della classe dirigente cattolica (1929–1937),* Il Mulino, Bologna.

Mortati, C. (1975) 'Articolo 1', in Branca G. (Ed.) *Commentario della Costituzione. Principi Fondamentali,* Zanichelli and Il Foro Italiano, Bologna and Rome.

Napolitano, Giorgio (1979) *In mezzo al guado,* Ed. Riuniti, Rome.

Nardozzi, Giangiacomo (Ed.) (1980) *I difficili anni '70. I problemi della politica economica italiana 1973/1979,* Estas Libri, Milan.

Negri, Antonio (1977) *La forma-stato,* Feltrinelli, Milan.

Negri, Antonio (1976) *Proletari e stato,* Feltrinelli, Milan.

Nenni, Pietro (1977) *Intervista sul socialismo italiano,* Laterza, Rome-Bari.

Occhetto, Achille (1978) *A dieci anni dal '68,* Ed. Riuniti, Rome.

Occhionero, Marisa Ferrari (1976) 'La posizione della donna nella burocrazia ministeriale italiana', *Sociologia,* vol. 10, no. 2.

Onida, Fabrizio (1977) 'Il ruolo dell'Italia nella divisione internazionale del lavoro', in AA.VV. *Lezioni di economia. Aspetti e problemi dello sviluppo economico italiano e dell'attuale crisi internazionale',* Feltrinelli, Milan.

Orfei, Ruggero (1976) *L'occupazione del potere. I democristiani 1945–1975,* Longanesi, Milan.

Paci, Massimo (1973) *Mercato di lavoro e classi sociali in Italia,* Il Mulino, Bologna.

Parboni, Riccardo (1981) *The Dollar and Its Rivals,* Verso Paperback, London.

Pasquino, Gianfranco (1980) *Crisi dei partiti e governabilità*, Il Mulino, Bologna.

Pasquino, Gianfranco (1982) 'Centralità non significa governabilità', *Il Mulino*, vol. 31, no. 281, May–June.

Pasquino, Gianfranco (1983) 'La strategia del Psi: tra vecchie e nuove forme di rappresentanza politica', *Critica Marxista*, vol. 21, no. 1.

Pasquino, Gianfranco and Rossi, Maurizio (1980) 'Quali compagni, quale partito, quale formula politica' in *Il Mulino*, vol. 29, no. 267, Jan.–Feb.

Pedone, F. (Ed.) (1968) *Il Partito socialista italiano nei suoi congressi*, vol. V: 1942–55, (Ed.) del Gallo, Milan.

Peggio, Eugenio (1976) *La crisi economica italiana*, Rizzoli, Milan.

Pennacchi, Laura (1982) 'Il sindacato non sta tutto nello "scambio politico" ', *Rinascita*, no. 24, 25 June.

Perulli, Paolo (1982) 'Il conflitto del compromesso', *Laboratorio Politico*, nos. 2/3.

Pestalozza, Luigi (1967) 'Intervento sulla *Populorum progressio*', *Problemi del Socialismo*, vol. 9, no. 18, May.

Picchieri, Angelo (n.d.) 'Classi sociali', in *Il Mondo Contemporaneo*, vol. I, *La Storia d'Italia*, La Nuova Italia, Florence.

Pierini, Maria Novella (1965) 'La Chiesa cattolica e la politica italiana' in *Problemi del socialismo*, vol. 7, no. 2, May–June.

Pinnarò, Gabriella (Ed.) (1978) *L'Italia Socio-economica 1976–77*, (Ed.) Riuniti, Rome.

Pinto, Francesco (1977) *Intellettuali e Tv negli anni '50*, Savelli, Rome.

Pizzorno, Alessandro (1974) 'I ceti medi nei meccanismi del consenso,' in F. L. Cavazza and S. R. Graubard (Eds) *Il caso italiano*, Garzanti, Milan.

Pizzorno, Alessandro (1980) *I soggetti del pluralismo*, Il Mulino, Bologna.

Podbielski, Gisele (1974) *Italy. Development and Crisis in the Postwar Economy*, Clarendon Press, Oxford.

Podbielski, Gisele (1978) *Twenty-five Years of Special Action for the Development of Southern Italy*, Giuffre Editore, Milan.

Poggi, Gianfranco (1972) 'The Church in Italian politics, 1945–50', in S. J. Woolf (Ed.), *The Rebirth of Italy 1943–50*, Longman, London.

Porter, William (1977) 'The mass media in the Italian elections of 1976', in Howard R. Penniman (Ed.) *Italy at the Polls*, American Enterprise Institute, Washington, D.C.

Protocollo d'intesa tra IRI e sindacato', *Rassegna Sindacale*, vol. 31, nos. 1–2, 4–11 Jan. 1985.

Putnam, Robert D., Leonardi, Roberto and Nanetti, Raffaella (1980) 'Le regioni "misurate" ', *Il Mulino*, no. 286, Mar.–Apr.

Putnam, Robert D., Leonardi, Roberto, Nanetti, Raffaella and Pavoncello, Franco (1981) 'Sul rendimento delle istituzioni: il caso dei governi regionali italiani', *Rivista Trimestrale di Diritto Pubblico*, no. 2.

Revelli, Marco (1982) 'Defeat at Fiat', in *Capital and Class*, no. 16, Spring.

Reviglio, Franco (1977) *Spesa pubblica e stagnazione dell'economia italiana '*, Il Mulino, Bologna.

Richeri, Giuseppe (Ed.) (1980) *Il video negli anni 80*, De Donato, Bari.

Ridolfi, Luca (1975) 'A proposito del "saggio" di Sylos Labini. La base statistica', *Quaderni Piacentini*, no. 57, Nov.

Rieser, Vittorio (1981) 'Sindacato e compozizione del lavoro, *Laboratorio Politico*, no. 4, July–Aug.

Rodano, Giulia (1978) 'La riaggregazione delle forze giovanili cattoliche' in Istituto Gramsci, *La crisi della società italiana e le nuove generazioni*, Ed. Riuniti, Rome.

Rodotà, Stefano (1983) 'I diritti di libertà: valori emergenti e nuove tutele', in Centro Riforma dello Stato, *Violenza sessuale: come cambiare i processi per stupro*, Rome.

Romagnoli, Umberto (1975) 'Articolo 3, coma 2', in Branca G. (Ed.) *Commentario della Costituzione. Principi Fondamentali*, Zanichelli and Il Foro Italiano, Bologna and Rome.

Romagnoli, Umberto and Treu, Tiziano (1977) *I sindacati in Italia: storia di una strategia (1945–1976)*, Il Mulino, Bologna.

Rositi, Franco (1981) 'Sistema politico soggetti politici e sistema delle comunicazioni di massa', *Problemi del Socialismo*, vol. 22, no. 22.

Rossanda, Rossana (1968) *L'anno degli studenti*, De Donato, Bari.

Rossi, Rosa (1978) *Le parole delle donne*, Ed. Riuniti, Rome.

Rotelli, Ettore (1979) 'Le regioni dalla partecipazione al partito' in Luigi Graziano and Sidney Tarrow (Eds) *La crisi italiana*, 2 vols, Einaudi, Turin.

Salvati, Bianca (1972) 'The rebirth of Italian trade unionism 1943–54', in S. J. Woolf (Ed.) *The Rebirth of Italy 1943–50*, Longman, London.

Salvati, Michele (1973) 'L'inflazione italiana nel contesto internazionale', *Quaderni Piacentini*, no. 50, July.

Salvati, Michele (1975) *Il sistema economico italiano: analisi di una crisi*, il Mulino, Bologna.

Salvati, Michele (1977) 'Il mercato del lavoro in Italia', in AA.VV. *Lezioni di economia. Aspetti e problemi dello sviluppo economico italiano e dell'attuale crisi internazionale*, Feltrinelli, Milan.

Sani, Giacomo (1976) 'Le elezioni degli anni '70: terremoto o evoluzione?', *Rivista Italiana di Scienza Politica*, no. 2, Aug.

Sani, Giacomo (1979) 'Ricambio elettorale, mutamento sociale e preferenze politiche', in Luigi Graziano and Sidney Tarrow (Eds), *La crisi italiana*, 2 vols, Einaudi, Turin.

Saraceno, Chiara (1979) 'Trent'anni di storia della famiglia italiana', *Studi Storici*, vol. 20, no. 4.

Saraceno, Pasquale (1972) 'La politica di sviluppo di un'area sottosviluppata nell'esperienza italiana', in Augusto Graziani (Ed.), *L'economia italiana: 1945–1970*, Il Mulino, Bologna.

Saraceno, Pasquale (1977) *Intervista sulla Ricostruzione 1943–1953*, Laterza, Rome-Bari.

Sartori, G. (1973) 'Proporzionalismo, frazionismo e crisi dei partiti' in *Correnti, frazioni e fazioni nei partiti politici italiani*, *Quaderni della Rivista Italiana di Scienza Politica*, Il Mulino, Bologna.

Sassoon, Donald (1976) 'The Italian Communist Party's European strategy', *The Political Quarterly*, vol. 47, no. 3, July–Sept.

Sassoon, Donald (1978) 'The making of Italian foreign policy', in William Wallace and W. E. Paterson (Eds) *Foreign Policy Making in Western Europe*, Saxon House, Farnborough.

Sassoon, Donald (1981) *The Strategy of the Italian Communist Party. From the Resistance to the Historic Compromise*, Frances Pinter, London.

Sassoon, Donald (1985) 'Italy: the advent of private broadcasting', in R. Kuhn (Ed.) *The Politics of Broadcasting*, Croom Helm, London.

Scalfari, Eugenio and Turani, Stefano (1974) *Razza padrona. Storia delle borghesia di Stato*, Feltrinelli, Milan.

Scoppola, Pietro (1977) *La proposta politica di De Gasperi*, Il Mulino, Bologna.

Scoppola, Pietro (1978) 'Sulla questione democristiana (e sulla questione comunista)', *Critica Marxista*, no. 2.

Sereni, Emilio (1948) *Il mezzogiorno all'opposizione*, Turin.

Silva, Francesco and Targetti, Ferdinando (1972) 'La politica economica e sviluppo economico in Italia: 1945–1971', *Monthly Review* (Italian edn), Jan. 1972 (Part I); Feb. 1972 (Part II); Mar. 1972 (Part III).

Smith, Anthony (1978) *The Politics of Information*, Macmillan, London.

Somaini, Eugenio (1979) 'Crisi della sinistra e ripresa neo-conservatrice in Europa. Dinamiche distributive e mediazioni politiche', *Critica Marxista*, no. 5.

Stern, R. M. (1967) *Foreign Trade and Economic Growth in Italy*, Praeger, New York.

Sullo, Fiorentino (1960) 'Il dibattito sulla programmazione economica in Italia dal 1945 al 1960', in *I piani di sviluppo in Italia dal 1945 al 1960*, Giuffrè, Milan.

Sullo, Fiorentino (1972) *La repubblica probabile*, Garzanti, Milan.

Sylos Labini, Paolo (1974) *Saggio sulle classi sociali*, Laterza, Rome–Bari.

Sylos Labini, Paolo (1975) *Oligopolio e progresso tecnico*, Einaudi, Turin.

Tarrow, Sidney (1974) 'Local constraints on regional reform', *Comparative Politics*, no. 1, Oct.

Tarrow, Sidney (1977) *Between Center and Periphery*, Yale UP, New Haven.

Telò, Mario (1983) 'Mutamento sociale e blocco politico istituzionale: un'ipotesi sul "caso italiano" (1974–1984)', *Problemi del Socialismo*, nos. 27/2, May–Dec.

Terracini, Umberto (1978) *Come nacque la Costituzione*, (Ed.) Riuniti, Rome.

Therborn, Goran (1984) 'The prospect of Labour and the transformation of advanced capitalism', *New Left Review*, no. 145, May–June.

Togliatti, Palmiro (1974) *Opere scelte*, Ed. Riuniti, Rome.

Togliatti, Palmiro (1973) 'La nostra lotta per la democrazia e il socialismo', in *Il Partito*, Rome.

Togliatti, Palmiro (1979) *On Gramsci and Other Writings*, Lawrence and Wishart, London.

Trentin, Bruno (1977) *Da sfruttati a produttori*, De Donato, Bari.

Trentin, Bruno (1980) *Il sindacato dei consigli*, (Ed.) Riuniti, Rome.

Trentin, Bruno (1982) 'Dal sindacato dei consigli alla cultura del cambiamento', *Rinascita*, no. 24, 25 June.

Trigilia, Carlo (1976) 'Sviluppo, sottosviluppo e classi sociali in italia', *Rassegna Italiana di Sociologia*, vol. 17, no. 2.

Triola, A. (1971) 'Contributo allo studio dei conflitti di lavoro in Italia', *Economia e Lavoro*, no. 5.

Tunstall, Jeremy (1977) *The Media are American*, Constable, London.

Turi, Gabriele (1980) *Il fascismo e il consenso degli intellettuali*, Il Mulino, Bologna.

Turone, Sergio (1974) *Storia del sindacato in Italia 1943–1969*, Laterza, Rome–Bari.

Turone, Sergio (1976) *Sindacato e classi sociali*, Laterza, Rome–Bari.

Unesco (1980) International Commission for the Study of Communication Problems (the McBride Commission), *Many Voices One World*, Kogan Page, London.

Vacca, Giuseppe (Ed.) (1973) *PCI mezzogiorno e intellettuali*, De Donato, Bari.

Vacca, Giuseppe (1977) *Quale Democrazia?* De Donato, Bari.

Vacca, Giuseppe (Ed.) (1980) *Communicazioni di massa e democrazia*, Riuniti, Rome.

Vacca, Giuseppe (1982) 'I contenuti informativi e culturali dell'emittenza televisiva', mimeo, 24 May.

Vacca, Giuseppe (1983) 'Vecchio e nuovo dal mezzogiorno', in AA.VV. *La cultura: una nuova risorsa per il mezzogiorno*, Bari.

Vacca, Giuseppe (1984) *L'Informazione negli anni ottanta*, (Ed.) Riuniti, Rome.

Vainicher, Marco Eller (1977) 'La questione del terziario e la crisi italiana', *Critica Marxista*, vol. 15, no. 1.

Valiani, Leo (1973) 'La resistenza italiana', *Rivista Storica Italiana*, vol. 85, no. 1.

Valli, Vittorio (1979) *L'economia e la politica economica italiana (1945–1979)*, Etas Libri, Milan.

Valli, Vittorio (1980) 'La politica economica: una cronaca ragionata del periodo 1973–1979', in Giangiacomo Nardozzi (Ed.) *I difficili anni '70. I problemi della politica economica italiana 1973/1979*, Etas Libri, Milan.

Venditti, Renato (1981) *Il manuale Cencelli*, (Ed.) Riuniti, Rome.

Vercellone, P. (1972) 'The Italian Constitution of 1947-48', in S.J. Woolf (Ed.), *The Rebirth of Italy 1943–50*, Longman, London.

Villari, Lucio (Ed.) (1975) *Il Capitalismo italiano del novecento*, 2 vols, Laterza, Rome–Bari.

Visco Vincenzo (1985) 'E' inutile vantarsi se migliora l'economia', *La Repubblica*, 5 Jan.

Weber, Maria (1981) 'Italy', in Joni Lovenduski and Jill Hills (Eds) *The Politics of the Second Electorate. Women and Public Participation*, Routledge and Kegan Paul, London.

Wertman, Douglas (1977) 'The Italian electoral process: the elections of June 1976', in Howard R. Penniman (Ed.), Washington, D.C.

Williamson, J. G. (1968) 'Regional inequality and the process of national development: a description of the patterns', in Needleman L. (Ed.) *Regional Analysis*, Penguin, Harmondsworth.

Woolf, S. J. (Ed.) (1972) *The Rebirth of Italy 1943–50*, Longman, London.

INDEX

Index

Index

free trade, x, 15, 29, 53
French, 39, 56, 67, 70, 174, 174, 200, 246
   Communist Party, 235–6, 242
   Socialist Party, 242
Friuli–Venezia–Giulia, 201, 214
Frosinone, 57
Fua, G., 48

Galileo, G., ix
Gedda, L., 143
Gelli, L., 253–4
Genoa, 2, 41, 99
Germany, German(s), 10, 70, 98, 174,
   189, 233, 246, 252
   Nazi Germany, 3
   West Germany, 30–1, 37, 42, 49, 51,
      55–6, 70–3, 75, 79, 82–3, 99, 112,
      130, 140, 154, 182, 184, 221, 246–7,
      253
Getty Jr., P., 252
Giannini Massimo Severo, 196
Gioia Tauro, 252
Giolitti, Antonio, 53
   Giolitti Plan, 53
Giolitti, Giovanni, 1
government(s), x, xi, 1, 4, 7–11, 15–16,
   19–25, 28–9, 35–6, 41–2, 45, 47–8,
   52–3, 61–3, 70, 77, 83, 94, 96, 117,
   123, 125, 127, 129, 131–4, 136, 138,
   142, 145, 153, 172, 174–5, 178–81,
   184, 186, 190–2, 195, 201–2, 204, 206,
   210, 216, 219, 222, 225, 234, 237,
   239, 241, 253
Gramsci, A., 5–6, 102, 233
Graziani, A., 31–3
Greece, 112, 124, 242
Green Plan, 55, 57
Grilli, 203
Gross Domestic Product (GDP), 57, 75,
   82, 246–7
Gross National Product (GNP), 51, 70–1
   rate of growth, 30–1, 37, 39–40, 73, 75,
   83

Heath, E., 184
'hidden' economy, *see* economy
historic compromise, 9, 219, 237–9
Hoffman, P., 21
Hollywood, 154
Hong Kong, 72, 74
hot autumn, 62, 66–7, 78, 99, 140, 242
Hungary, 5, 47, 234, 240

Il Giornale nuovo, 154
Il Giorno, 154
Il Sole-24 ore, 154
IMF (International Monetary Fund), 26,
   72
immigration, 99
Imperiali system, 170
imports, 16, 33, 69, 71, 73, 76
incomes policy, 34, 62, 69, 72, 126, 184
   wage restraint, 52
India, 17
industrialists *see* entrepreneurs
inflation, 2, 11, 24–6, 30, 42, 49, 51–2, 64,
   66, 68–9, 72–3, 80, 82–3, 124–5, 184,
   216, 255
INPS, 9
interest groups, 8–9, 132, 190, 191, 237,
   249, 251
interest rates, 42, 68–9, 72, 82, 255
investments, 26, 29, 32–3, 37–8, 42, 44,
   51–2, 54, 56–9, 61, 63, 67, 69, 71, 73,
   75–7, 97, 142
Iran, 235, 253
Iraq, 235
Ireland, 17, 56
IRI (Istituto per La Ricostruzione
   Industriale), 3, 21–3, 39–41, 56, 58,
   61, 127–8, 140, 142, 156
Israeli, 235
ISTAT, 75, 92, 214
Italcementi, 61
Italsider, 56
Ivrea, 108
Izvestia, 147

Japan, 29–31, 51, 71–2, 75, 83, 98, 140,
   153, 246
Japanese, 30, 44, 76, 152
Jews, 148
John XXIII, 116, 145, 147
John Paul II, 151
Jotti, N., 107, 203

Keynes, J. M., 18, 20
keynesian, 18, 21, 39, 53, 135, 184, 205
Khrushchev, N. S., 147, 234
Korean War, 26, 28

L'Unita, 154
L'Occhio, 154–5
La Malfa, U., 21, 52–3, 136
La Repubblica, 154–5
La Stampa, 137, 154

272

Index

Index